Secrets of Musical Confidence

About the Author

Psychologist and musician Andrew Evans is uniquely qualified to understand what makes a musician 'tick'. Trained at the Royal Academy of Music in London, his musical career as a bass and keyboard player has encompassed classical orchestral work, free-lance jazz, and latterly rock music as a bandleader and songwriter. His work as a psychologist has taken him through careers work and student counselling in a music college to founding, in 1988, Arts Psychology Consultants, a psychology practice dealing exclusively with the lifestyle of the performing and creative artist.

The Secrets of Musical Confidence

How to Maximise Your Performance Potential

ANDREW EVANS

Thorsons
An Imprint of HarperCollins*Publishers*

This book is for my son, Adam.

Thorsons
An Imprint of HarperCollinsPublishers
77–85 Fulham Palace Road,
Hammersmith, London W6 8JB
1160 Battery Street,
San Francisco, California 94111–1213

Published by Thorsons 1994

1 3 5 7 9 10 8 6 4 2

Illustrations by Rachel Busch

A catalogue record for this book is available from the British Library

ISBN 0 7225 2972 4

Printed in Great Britain by
Mackays of Chatham, Kent

Contents

Acknowledgements

My foremost debt of thanks is to Martin Lloyd-Elliott. Together we founded Arts Psychology Consultants, which started our whole concept of offering specialised counselling help to those in the arts and media. He has constantly shown the way forward by personal example, unfailing support and his own unique contribution to the theory. I would also like to thank all those who have been part of our work in Arts Psychology Consultants: Angelica MacArthur, Jacob Zelinger, Pixie Holland, Mary Priestley, Sharon Tyler, Viv Young, Geoffrey Elkan, Dr Liz Valentine, Dr Gloria Litman, Dr Brian Tully and Lady Caroline Conran.

The work done by Carola Grindea of ISSTIP, Dr Ian James, Dr Garfield Davies, Dr Ann Fingret and Dr Wynn Parry of the British Performing Arts Medicine Trust, and Dr Anthony Storr – the guru in this field – has been totally invaluable in taking forward the theory and practice of health care in the performing arts. I thank them all for their unique contributions.

I would like to thank the whole of my family: my mother, Dr Olwyn Evans, and my father, Dr Bill Evans, in ways far too profound to adequately describe in words; my brother, Dr Mike Evans, for his humour and support; and my uncle, Professor J. Lyn Evans, who taught me at an early age what the differences between intuition, deduction and induction were (I still remember having a sneaking preference for intuition). I was fortunate to come from a happy and musical home where ideas and feelings were freely expressed and there was a tradition of caring for the feelings and wishes of other people.

I would particularly like to thank a number of special and original people who were an inspiration to me: Luis Gambolini and Dr

Hernan Rincon Gallardo who introduced me to the riches of Latin American culture and thought; American guitarist Paul Weeden who was the best all-round musician and human being I ever worked for; violinist Di Hourston, guitarists Paul Hirsh, Lakki Patey and Bill Mulholland, pianists Jeff Young, Melissa Vardey, Anders Klette and Lionel Grigson, drummers Martin Ditcham, Pete Pipkin and Chris Fletcher, and bassists John Taylor, Pete Matthews and Kent Hambrick – all unique musicians and people; and lastly Helene Giorgi, Ida Rypdal and Brit Stensholt, who inspired my songs. All of these people – my closest friends – have known just when to be supportive and when to give me a sharp prod in the right direction. They have constantly enriched my life with their humour and vitality.

This book would have been hard to write without the practical help of my wife Lilly and our friends Jelena Matkovic, Helen Cross and Ann Sutton, who took care of our three-year-old son Adam while I toiled for hours a day. I fully appreciate Adam's sacrifices in doing without a number of stories, computer graphics of fast red cars and walks by the river, all of which he seems to have accepted philosophically.

I would finally like to thank those who helped and encouraged me to produce this book: Jessica Kingsley who gave me invaluable confidence in my work; my agent Ann Dewe of Andrew Mann Ltd, who takes care of business and more; and Jane Graham-Maw and Michele Turney of HarperCollins for their editorial skills.

There are a number of other important names I cannot mention – those musicians who have been my clients in therapy and who have given me the personal insights on which this work is based. They will know who they are and why I dedicate this book uniquely to them. I have learned so much from their experiences that they have been – more than anything else – the direct inspiration for my understanding of all the deeper implications of what it means to be a musician.

Introduction

Confidence is regarded by musicians as the cornerstone of professional success and inner wellbeing. The goal of this book is to help you to increase your confidence as a musician. This process tips the balance of success much more firmly in your favour, and gives you a real chance of living up to your own expectations.

Foremost in the idea of confidence are two main things – consistency and reality. When our living environment is stable and predictable it is easier to meet life with confidence and power. This book helps you identify the 'unstable' factors in the inner and outer life of the musician and replace them as far as possible with the 'stable' qualities and talents that give you confidence in your music-making. A reliable source of personal effectiveness makes you feel equal to or stronger than obstacles and threats that lie in your path. This confidence in yourself helps you confront your challenges, rather than avoiding them.

We need the feedback of doing well because 'nothing succeeds like success'. Setting realistic career aims, and achieving them step by step, proves to yourself that you can reach targets. This important middle way – neither perfectionism nor low self-worth – ensures you do what you do well, and are well regarded by your fellow musicians.

This book has been written with an ideal in mind – that of the confident musician. This is an ideal that we can all go some way towards achieving, and key insights and skills we need to do so are included in the following chapters. Every effort has been made to cover all aspects of the musician's life and work. The 'ideal musician' is therefore one who:

- Has successfully dealt with problems of indifference, rejection or demands for over-achievment which have resulted from family environment, school or early music tuition.
- Has successfully reduced anxieties such as stage fright to coping levels.
- Has developed a distinct musical personality, including musical likes and dislikes, correct choice of instrument, correct musical function (composing, performing, teaching), and a clearly focused idea of how to express himself naturally through improvisation, composing or interpretation.
- Is able to be assertive with fellow musicians and teachers, and express clearly what he does and does not want.
- Is able to negotiate and make contracts with people in the business side of music (agents, managers, record companies, banks etc.) in order to get a fair deal without being exploited.
- Has adequate ability to manage his own publicity, time, finances and other commitments.
- Has a real love of music which is rewarded by the pleasure to be had through performing it.
- Has a mature, responsible and friendly attitude to fellow musicians and the profession in general. This includes loyalty to his art and a nurturing attitude to younger musicians who are learning the business.

The 'secrets' within this book are not, for the most part, new knowledge – what is new is the way they have been put together and presented to the musician. Parts of the book are based on an accurate personal knowledge of the profession, which has supplied the background familiarity with the life of the musician. Other parts are based on psychological theory and therapy methods which have previously been largely unavailable to the music profession, and which have needed careful selection and adaptation to make them relevant and understandable to musicians. Still other parts contain new material which has come from several years of counselling sessions with musicians.

At the time of writing, arts psychology is still catching up with sports psychology as a 'new' way of enhancing perfomance, and much work still needs to be done to further this. *The Secrets of Musical Confidence* is intended as a step in that direction.

Musicians are inquisitive, challenging, intelligent and well equipped to understand what lies behind such psychological theories, provided they are presented in plain language, not jargon. Because clear language is a priority, the text contains no detailed references to books and articles, though the main bibliographical references have been carefully listed.

It is hoped that readers will go on to study some of the main theories referred to in the book. For this reason the psychological terms are the accepted standard ones. There is no attempt to confuse readers by claiming a 'new method' which simply changes the old methods round a bit and replaces the original terms with wacky new ones. At times, however, it has become necessary to create new expressions like 'musical map' or 'constant self' where there was nothing in existence that accurately fitted the context. Where this has been done the terms have been made as accessible and common-sense as possible.

A particular difficulty with using the English language is that of gender. It is a perpetual problem for authors that there is no alternative term for 'he or she'. Since there is no natural way out of this problem, the solution used – with great regret – is to use the masculine 'he'. This has the only virtue of being more traditional, but it is obviously only half of the truth. Music-making could not exist without the part played in it by the huge numbers of female musicians who uniquely contribute to its success. If you are a female reader, please ignore the 'masculine' identifier and apply all the contents equally to yourself.

The whole purpose of the book is straightforward: to enable musicians as easily as possible to acquire confidence in the one thing that matters most – achieving pleasure, satisfaction and reward through making music. It is written for the profesional, the semi-professional and the amateur alike – all who share in the enjoyment of music-making.

As humans we are all fallible, and not all of us will reach the top of the profession. This does not stop us living life with confidence, and setting out to achieve as much as we can. At all levels of success, music can be richly rewarding, and a life in music can offer us good friends, the excitement of performing, creative satisfaction and the feeling that we are contributing something meaningful to our own lives and the lives of others.

1 The Musician's Personality

We can get a good idea of the 'typical' personalities of popular and classical musicians by putting together data from personality tests. Although individual musicians will vary considerably, such data helps us identify common personality types, traits, work preferences and values, providing further insight into their motivations.

Personality Types

The idea of personality 'types' comes from psychoanalyst Carl Jung. A later version of his basic theories, the Myers–Briggs Type Indicator® (MBTI)®, is widely used. It proposes that there are 16 different types of personality in our population. None of these types is 'good or bad' – they are simply all different, and a successful musician can be any one.

The MBTI personality type is built up of four different personality dimensions or 'indices': Extraversion–Introversion, Sensing–Intuitive, Thinking–Feeling, Judging–Perceptive. Within each index we all tend to have a natural preference for one trait or 'function' rather than its opposite, such as for 'Feeling' rather than 'Thinking'. We make use of the stronger or more typical function more often – by relying on feelings to make a decision, for example. We do not, however, use the preferred function exclusively, in much the same way as a right-handed person will continue to use the left hand for certain tasks, such as holding a fork.

The following brief descriptions of the features of each function will help you interpret the graph of musicians' results which follows.

E–I (EXTRAVERT–INTROVERT)

The first index describes how we orient ourselves towards life: extraverts tend to focus outwards into the world, introverts inwards into thoughts and feelings.

Extravert (E)

Extraverts like variety and action, and are sometimes impatient with long, slow jobs. They tend to act quickly, and sometimes without thinking. They are good at greeting people and take an interest in who they are and how they do their jobs. They like having people around them in the working environment, and like talking on the telephone rather than writing. When they learn a new task, they enjoy talking it through with someone as a good way of picking it up.

Introvert (I)

Introverts are interested in the ideas behind things. They like a quiet atmosphere for concentration. They are quite happy working alone for long periods, sometimes on a single project. They would just as soon communicate in writing, and like reading through the instructions for a new task, rather than talking it over with someone. They like to think before acting, and sometimes consider things rather than actually doing them. They can find themselves lost in their thoughts, and sometimes fail to notice others or have difficulty in remembering names and faces.

S–N (SENSING–INTUITIVE)

The second index describes how we gather information about the world: sensing types trust actual information gathered through the five senses, while intuitive types speculate on hidden meanings behind what is immediately apparent.

Sensing (S)

Sensing types focus on reality, enjoying the uniqueness of each event. They like applying what they have learned to a problem and think established ways of doing things are often the right ways. They tend to work steadily, with a realistic idea of how long things will take. They like it when things are simple, concise and easy to follow. They believe facts are important, and can be good at precise work. They may not put much faith in 'inspiration', thinking that 'imaginative' people tend to exaggerate rather than see the obvious.

Intuitive (N)

Intuitive types like to focus on how things could be improved, and enjoy challenges, possibilities and learning new things. They tend to follow inspirations and hunches, and to leap to conclusions quickly even if this means getting the facts a bit wrong. They do not like doing the same thing repeatedly or having to take time for precision when they want to get at the larger picture. They often work in bursts of energy with slack periods in between, and can be quite enthusiastic about new tasks. They constantly question things, and tend to make things more complex than some think necessary.

T–F (THINKING–FEELING)

The third index reflects how we make decisions. Thinking types decide 'with the head' by using objective reasoning, while feeling types decide 'with the heart', weighing up feelings and hunches.

Thinking (T)

Thinking types believe they are logical, can put things in their right order, have a talent for analysing people and situations, and can speculate on the outcomes of various choices. They are attracted to principles and often respond to people's ideas rather than their feelings. They hate injustice, and like to be treated fairly. Where the situation warrants, they can be firm or tough-minded, even to the point of hurting people's feelings without realising it.

Feeling (F)

Feeling types believe in people: their values, their feelings and what makes them happy. They like harmony and will work to make it happen. They dislike having to tell people unpleasant things and so try to get around it or make it less hurtful. They tend to be sympathetic to people and try to please them. In return, they feel good when others praise them. They put people before principles, and think of choices in terms of the effects they will have on people.

J–P (JUDGING–PERCEPTIVE)

The fourth index shows how we tend to deal with the meanings and events of our lives. The judging type has a preference for decision making, and will do this through either thinking or feeling, as indicated above. The perceptive type has a stronger response to the actual information-gathering process, and will do this through either sensing or intuition, as indicated above. It is as if judging types are happier with 'answers', while perceptive types remain curious about the actual questions life continually poses.

Judging (J)

Judging types work best when they can plan things from the outset and then follow that plan. They enjoy getting things settled and finished so they can move on to other matters. They need only the basic essentials to start work, and then schedule projects so that each step gets done on time, using lists as agendas for action. They dislike having plans interrupted or rescheduled by others once they have been made. They tend to be satisfied once they have made up their mind over something, and tend to decide things more quickly than others who seem to labour over various choices.

Perceptive (P)

Perceptive types believe in keeping an open mind, adapting well to changing situations and leaving things open for last-minute changes. They like to know all about a new job, and find it difficult to make correct choices if they feel they need more information. They tend to postpone unpleasant jobs, and while periodically making lists of things to do, they tend not to finish things on the list. They can make a start on a lot of projects and find it hard to finish them all, but get a lot done when under pressure from a deadline.

Typical Results for Musicians

The MBTI questionnaire not only gives accurate results for each function, it also gives scores indicating strength of preference. The graph in Figure 1.1 shows the scores for samples of 67 popular and 40 classical musicians (data courtesy of Andrew Evans).

EXTRAVERT OR INTROVERT

Popular musicians appear to be borderline introverts on the MBTI, but more extraverted on Raymond Cattell's 16 Personality Factor Questionnaire (16PF) (see page 7). Classical musicians, however, appear as extraverted on both. Musicians are more extraverted as a whole than people involved in other creative professions, such as artists. These tendencies may reflect lifestyles and typical working habits: painters lead a largely solitary existence; popular musicians often work alone on creative ideas; whereas classical musicians

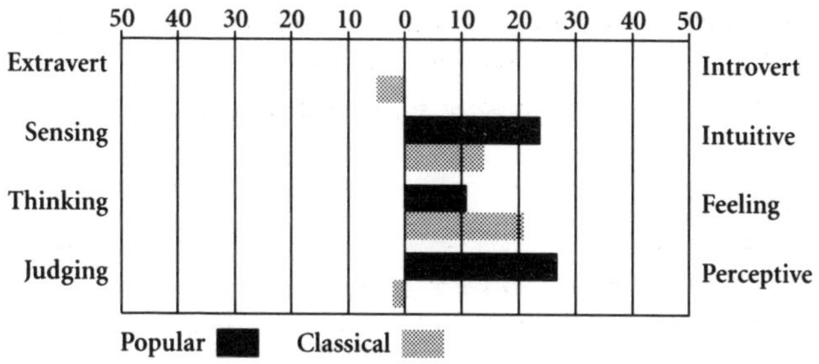

Figure 1.1. **The typical personality types of classical and popular musicians.**

rehearse, play and tour in larger groups. There may well be two distinct parts of the musician's psyche – the sociable one that responds to audiences, fellow musicians and new acquaintances, and the introverted one that creates alone and has an inner focus of concentration while playing or improvising.

SENSING OR INTUITIVE

The artistic personality as a whole is heavily biased towards the imaginative, which Jung calls 'intuitive'. Both types of musician are considerably more imaginative than the average person, and this proneness to fantasy may account for the difficulty some musicians have in establishing realistic and objective goals for their careers.

THINKING OR FEELING

Both types of musician have a distinct preference for feeling. This may come from their familiarity with music as a non-analytic, non-verbal form of communication. This preference shows in their strong bias towards helping and caring activities, such as counselling, charity work and indeed self-help.

Musicians tend as a whole to be warm personalities and to value the fellowship that is found in the profession. One drawback with a feeling preference is that musicians are dependent on praise and sensitive to being criticised, ignored or misunderstood – even by people who are not really capable of understanding them. They may continually look for acceptance from those who show a consistent inability to provide it.

JUDGING OR PERCEPTIVE

As one would suspect from their practice, rehearsal and concert routines, classical musicians tend to have a preference for judging and planning functions. Planning has obvious uses in preparing scores, and musicians tend to think ahead while reading their part. A concentration on planning alone can, however, leave the musician more nervous if music has to be played spontaneously or things unexpectedly go wrong. Popular musicians tend to be more perceptive and improvisatory, and set standards internally rather than through sight-read parts. For jazz musicians this is particularly important since music is being created 'on the fly'.

The quality of openness and willingness to follow the flow of inspiration may be important in contributing to 'peak experiences' where musicians feel they play unusually well 'as if by some sort of magic'. Among classical musicians this is more likely to occur for soloists who play from memory rather than diverting their attention from the flow of the music to the notes on the score.

The drawback of spontaneity, however, may be inadequate organisation when this is needed. Unemployed musicians are often guilty not of lack of talent but of lack of planning, the highest single factor indicating why they make less of their careers than the middle range of professionals. At the very top level of talent there is a swing back to the spontaneous attitude, but here talent may be unstoppable, or recognised and exploited by others. Planning may favour careers while openness may favour performance – both are part of success.

• Personality Traits of the Average Musician

When we start to go beyond basic preferences, such as extroversion or introversion, we enter the world of personality traits. Nobody has yet established how many traits are either 'fundamental' or mutually exclusive: some favour five or seven, some sixteen, others many more. And while there is broad agreement on many of the traits, no theory is exactly the same as another.

16 Personality Factor Questionnaire

One of the widely accepted definitions of personality traits is that of Raymond Cattell, which is used in his 16 Personality Factor Questionnaire (16PF)©. In order to work out scores for each trait, a sophisticated questionnaire is required. It is beyond the scope of this book to provide such detail, but the following descriptions of each trait should give you an idea of how your personality fits into the picture.

COOL–WARM

- Cool – Detached and emotionally reserved. Critical and at times uncompromising. Attracted to ideas or things rather than people, and able to work alone happily.
- Warm – Good-natured, warm-hearted and easy-going with people. Ready to participate, co-operate and adapt to others. Generous, and able to compromise and take criticism.

CONCRETE–ABSTRACT

Unlike the other traits, this is based on a short reasoning test, the results of which give a broad measure of intelligence. Higher scores correspond to a more abstract ability to reason.

MOODY–STABLE

- Moody – Affected by feelings and mood swings and prone to frustration, anxiety, sleeplessness or hypochondria. May get upset easily.

- Stable – Calm, mature and able to cope with reality. Able to keep inner conflicts and emotions under control.

PASSIVE–COMPETITIVE

- Passive – Mild-natured and able to accommodate or conform to the wishes of others. May bottle-up inner aggressions or show them as correctness or fussiness.
- Competitive – Self-assertive, preferring to put ideas into practice and have things one's own way. Outer forcefulness may disguise some inner insecurities.

PRUDENT–IMPULSIVE

- Prudent – Restrained and cautious. Perceived as serious and dependable.
- Impulsive – Enthusiastic, responsive and happy-go-lucky. Needs variety.

EXPEDIENT–CONSCIENTIOUS

- Expedient – Disregardful of social standards or obligations, particularly where they conflict with one's own norms or inner beliefs.
- Conscientious – Persevering, responsible, aware of social duties and respectful of ethical norms. At times may take a strict or moralistic view of other people's actions.

SHY–BOLD

- Shy – Timid, reticent and sensitive to threats. Cautious of revealing one's real self to larger groups, preferring the comfort of small groups or personal contact.

- Bold – Venturesome, uninhibited and responsive to challenge, seeing the occasional risk as part of living life to the full.

TOUGH–SENSITIVE

- Tough – Effective, practical and down-to-earth, with a logical and no-nonsense approach to reality. May undervalue experimental aspects of art and culture as fanciful or pretentious.

- Sensitive – Tender-minded, refined and sensitive to culture and inner feelings. Perceived by more practical people as self-indulgent, dependent or over-protected.

TRUSTING–SUSPICIOUS

- Trusting – Adaptable, tolerant, easy to get on with and ready to forget difficulties and ill-feelings.
- Suspicious – Prone to anxious insecurity and feelings of mistrust or resentment. Tending to control this insecurity in stubborn, demanding or opinionated behaviour.

MATERIAL–IMAGINATIVE

- Material – Careful, conventional and concerned with the details of practical reality. May undervalue imagination and inner fantasies in oneself and others.
- Imaginative – Self-motivated, wrapped up in inner urgencies and speculations, and drawn to the larger picture. Careless or Bohemian over practical constraints and details.

NAIVE–SHREWD

- Naive – Forthright, natural and unpretentious, approaching people and events with an open warmth. Tending to see the best in people, but not always to perceive their negative qualities.
- Shrewd – Diplomatic and calculating, with a penetrating and unsentimental approach to people and problems. Perceived as streetwise and hard to fool.

CALM–WORRYING

- Calm – Self-assured about one's capacity to deal with people and events. May sometimes be over-confident, overlooking feedback from others.
- Worrying – Prone to high expectations of oneself and to worrying over difficulties. May be self-reproaching and harbour exaggerated feelings of inadequacy.

TRADITIONAL–RADICAL

- Traditional – Conservative, preferring established ideas and

approaches to experimental innovations. Tolerant of traditional difficulties.
- Radical – Liberal, free-thinking and able to devise creative new approaches to traditional problems. Distrustful of tradition for its own sake.

TEAM-ORIENTED–SELF-ORIENTED

- Team-oriented – A 'joiner', valuing the spirit of group activity and the support of others in following a course of action.
- Self-oriented – Resourceful, able to work alone, preferring to rely on own decisions rather than those of others.

FLEXIBLE–CONTROLLED

- Flexible – Careless of conventional social protocol, preferring to follow inner urges and impulsive feelings. Tolerant of ambiguity and disorder, but may suffer from too little self-control.
- Controlled – In control of feelings and actions. Precise, and aware of self-image. Favouring planning over spontaneity.

RELAXED–STRESSED

- Relaxed – Leisurely, unfrustrated and unwilling to sacrifice personal wellbeing for stress and tension. Tending to calm down easily and ~~not~~ let things dwell on the nerves.
- Stressed – Easily irritated and frustrated by things large and small, taking time to calm down when upset. Prone to constant 'workaholic' activity, and may need to relax more.

OVERVIEW

Figure 1.2 gives an indication of how musicians have responded to this questionnaire. As in the MBTI, each trait has two opposite poles, such as 'cool–warm'. Scores closer to either pole (small or large scores) show distinct characteristics of the trait in question. Middle scores (around 5.5) show a balance of both tendencies, neither being very marked. The averaged-out scores shown here are less extreme on each trait than those of actual individuals, but show a similar diversity in direction and strength of tendency.

One of the most obvious characteristics of the musician is creativity, shown in high intelligence, sensitivity, imagination, com-

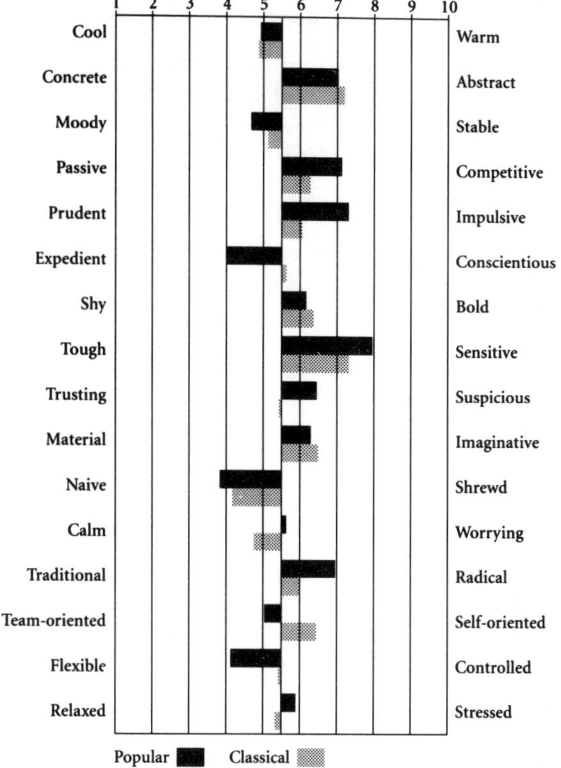

Figure 1.2. **Typical personality traits.**

petitiveness and radicalism. (For more on creativity, *see Chapter Ten*). All musicians are somewhat detached and critical towards their work and fellow musicians, but they also have a more impulsive social side. While musicians all show independence of judgement, popular musicians are temperamentally more team-spirited than classical musicians. They are also more expedient and nonconformist and less conscientious than their classical counterparts.

Musicians do not suffer grossly from stress, guilt or worry. Where anxiety shows up is in terms of mood swings and feelings of insecurity towards others and the profession itself. The particular combination of self-criticism and insecurity about being criticised by others is one of the most typical and damaging sources of anxiety. Musicians, for this reason, do not appear to be fundamentally 'neurotic' – it is more true to say that they are naturally sensitive, respond with their feelings, and become particularly affected by the insecurities typical of the music profession.

One reason for musicians' vulnerability is their naive and trusting nature, which tends to see the good in people and lacks the cynical penetration to deal shrewdly with business matters. One useful coping mechanism they have is a sharp sense of humour. Aside from its capacity to create good social bonds and relax the atmosphere, this also shows a good underlying tolerance for ambiguity and even a relish for experiencing it. Musicians are thereby less prone to the frustrations felt by more inflexible people when their wishes do not fall into the frameworks they set for them.

The 16 traits shown above can be used to derive further 'major traits', as shown in Figure 1.3. As in the above, very high or low scores show strong tendencies, while middle scores around 5.5 show a balance.

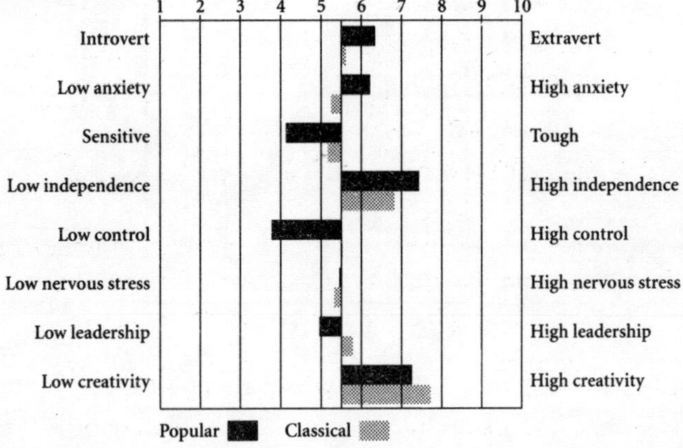

Figure 1.3. Typical major traits of the average musician.

• Organisational Roles and Skills of the Musician

A large number of organisations were analysed by R. Meredith Belbin to determine the commonest roles people played in them. The following eight typical roles were obtained (*see Figure 1.4*). The scores that musicians obtain have been calculated from their 16PF scores (*see Figure 1.2*). In a larger context, these can be related to the roles musicians play within their own kind of organisational groups.

The first five roles are production-oriented, from the plant

(Creative) who originates ideas, through the researcher (Resourcer) and project leader/negotiator (Shaper) who develops the ideas, to the production evaluator (Monitor) who tests them against reality and the finisher (Completer) who ensures the product is complete and ready on time. The other three roles are more hierarchical – the team leader (Chairperson), the team person (Team worker) and the worker under instruction (Company worker).

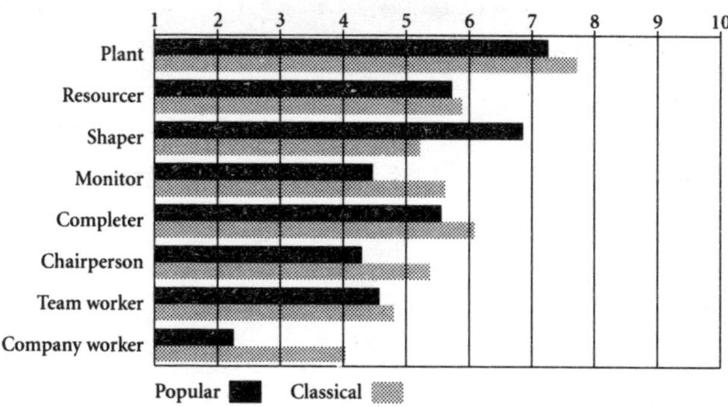

Figure 1.4. **Organisational skills of the average musician.**

When we see the creative process as a 'production line', with the idea at one end and the product at the other, then musicians – like all creatives – are best in the first stages. They are above average at creative ideas, research and problem-solving. What is less good is the ability to monitor and control the creative process shrewdly and conscientiously. Classical musicians are better than popular ones in this respect, but both have a tendency towards naivety and impulsiveness, and their decision-making may be questionable. When it comes to completing work, however, all musicians can be critical and painstaking – even perfectionists.

In terms of hierarchical structure, musicians are generally loners who prefer 'projects' to regular routine. None have very marked leadership qualities, though they are around average in this respect. Popular musicians are reasonably good at team work but well below average in their tolerance of taking orders from others. Classical musicians are less team-spirited but more tolerant of taking orders. All musicians, however, are below average in these respects.

Occupational Interests

The world of work has been divided into different occupational categories in many ways. The method used by John Holland is widely used and respected. The responses of musicians to different occupational interests are shown in Figure 1.5.

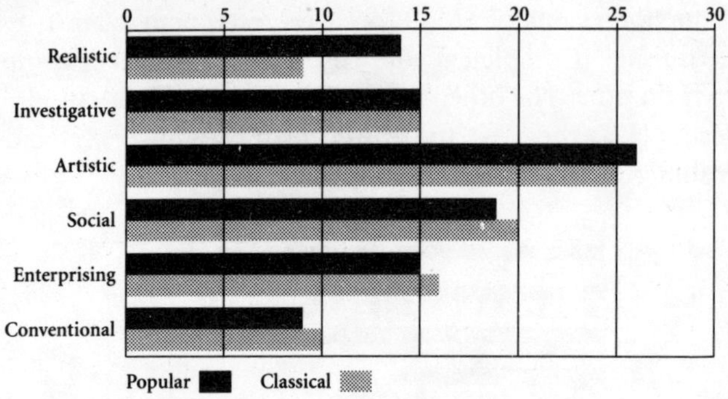

Figure 1.5. **Typical occupational interests.**

Within these various occupational categories, musicians tend to be employed as follows:

- Realistic careers – typically involve manual and trade skills, tools, machines or working with animals. Within music they involve looking after and transporting equipment, such as the job of the 'roadie' during rock tours and concerts.
- Investigative careers – tend to be found within the fields of science and technology. Applications within music include studio work, computing and electronics.
- Artistic careers – span the arts and media, within which music is a leading element.
- Social careers – include teaching, counselling, and the health and helping professions. Musicians are naturally drawn to them because they frequently teach, and take a lively interest in people and the 'meaning of life'.
- Enterprising careers – typically deal with business, sales and management. Musicians need certain business and promotional qualities to do well in the profession, and a number go into sales or management within the music business.
- Conventional careers – tend to be administrative, and are generally avoided by musicians, though some do work administratively in agencies, broadcasting or record companies.

The graph in Figure 1.5 shows that musicians have a marked interest in the arts and in many aspects of working with people, such as teaching, counselling and the helping professions. This double interest is very consistent from one musician to another, and reflects their feeling preference. It is even possible to say that the musician and the teacher/counsellor/psychologist are fundamentally the same person, and this is borne out by strong tendencies to combine social and helping activities with musical ones.

Besides these two dominating interests there is a lesser but still appreciable interest in technology and scientific ideas. This is particularly the case with popular musicians who come into more regular contact with technology. There is also an interest in enterprising, business or project skills, which correspond to musicians' creative potential and their generally self-employed status. Many musicians have difficulties with invasive sales techniques, which go against their genuineness and social ethics, but they can be very effective persuaders if they develop the requisite skills and attitudes. Where musicians are generally poor is in repetitive administrative tasks. Popular musicians can be much better in practical handskills than classical musicians, and have much more practice in maintaining or putting together their equipment.

Job values

In any career our job values indicate what we need to feel fulfilled and happy. If our work includes a large measure of preferred values it should be naturally interesting or congenial. Figure 1.6 lists 34 typical job values (see page 16). You can rate yourself by ticking how important each is to you, then noting the three most and least preferred. Make sure that you do not miss any.

Figure 1.7 lists the 10 most liked and disliked job values for musicians.

Creativity, artistic work, communication and variety predictably come top of the list, and closely reflect the musician's typical lifestyle. Social/feeling values such as friendship at work and contact with others are also high. Independence and time freedom are valued (and largely enjoyed) by musicians, and so are challenge and learning new things. Among popular musicians there is more emphasis on expertise, recognition and money, and also on good working conditions – an area where they suffer more than their classical counterparts.

Low values are largely the opposite of these but are not always easy to eliminate from the musician's life. A predictable routine is universally disliked, and musicians get round this by freelancing

	Very	Quite	Medium	Fairly	Not very
A predictable routine					
Artistic work					
A well-known organisation					
Challenge					
Chance of promotion					
Communication					
Community work					
Competition					
Contact with others					
Creativity					
Excitement					
Expertise					
Fast pace					
Friendship at work					
Helping others					
Ideal Workplace					
Independence					
Learning new things					
Making decisions					
Money					
Peace					
Persuading people					
Physical challenge					
Precision work					
Pressure					
Recognition					
Responsibility					
Security					
Status and respect					
Taking risks					
Teamwork					
Time freedom					
Variety					
Working alone					

My three most preferred values are:

1 2 3

My three least preferred values are:

1 2 3

Figure 1.6. **Your most and least important job values.**

Most liked job values:

	ALL MUSICIANS	POPULAR	CLASSICAL
1	Creativity	Creativity	Artistic work
2	Artistic work	Artistic work	Creativity
			Variety
3	Variety		Communication
	Friendship at work		
4			
		Friendship at work	Friendship at work
			Time freedom
5	Communication	Variety	
		Money	
6	Time freedom		Learning new things
7	Learning new things	Learning new things	Communication
		Time freedom	
8	Money		Contact with others
			Being an expert
			Peace
			Independence
			Challenge
9	Ideal place of work	Ideal placeof work	
	Excitement		
10		Being an expert	
		Recognition	

Least liked job values:

	ALL MUSICIANS	POPULAR	CLASSICAL
1	Predictable routine	Predictable routine	Predictable routine
2	Physical effort	Competition	Physical effort
3	Competition Persuading people	Physical effort	Persuading people
4		A well-known organisation	Competition
5	A well-known organisation	Persuading people Pressure	Working alone
6	Working alone		Fast pace
7	Pressure	Working alone	A well-known organisation
8	Fast pace	Responsibility for others	Helping the community Pressure
9	Responsibility for others	Fast pace	
10	Helping the community	Security Taking risks	Peace Responsibility for others Working in a team

Figure 1.7. **Musicians' most liked and disliked job values.**

alongside regular orchestral work, and by 'depping out' (putting other musicians into their residencies for enough nights to allow them to do a variety of other work).'Pressure' situations are also disliked (physical effort, competition, persuading people, fast pace). It is paradoxical that musicians – who are so competitive – dislike competitiveness in others or suffering its effects, just as they do with criticism. It is also interesting that while they have social values, musicians dislike large organisations and are reluctant to take responsibility for helping in the community. Again, their independent spirit makes them better loners than leaders.

• How Knowing Yourself Can Help You

1) Your natural character type is typically your most relaxed way of doing things, so using it to build up a positive self image can help identify your key talents. If you've got it, flaunt it.
2) At times we all talk and act on the assumption that it would be nice if others were like ourselves, as when Professor Higgins says in *My Fair Lady* – 'Why can't a woman be more like a man?'. Since others are doing this to us constantly, we need to interpret their comments in the light of who they are. Professor Higgins is a typical example – the logical man who thinks the feeling-centred woman is stupid or unable to make 'proper' decisions. This is a total fallacy – intelligence is not the same as logic, and instinctive decisions that come from the emotions may not only be right, they may sometimes be the only ones possible in a non-verbal medium such as music. Conversations and transactions between opposite types may effectively be parallel monologues, like the hospital manager who says 'We have to lose 10 beds,' and the nurse who replies 'That's impossible; there are people in them.' Both are true to type, and compromise may require a conceptual leap into another view of the world. If you are able to make such 'leaps' into the inner world of other people, you can gain valuable insights.
3) Personalities come in all shapes and sizes – some are more prone to working in certain roles or professions, but all types will be found in any job, including the music business. You are not handicapped because you do not have certain 'key' traits – all traits have positive uses, and people with one type of trait may complement those with others.

4) You only have *tendencies* towards preferred traits – you actually use all of them at some time.
5) Different personalities cope with life in different ways, and knowing your own range of 'coping' strategies gives you an idea of how you deal with life events. Humour and generosity have been shown in surveys to be top of the list of effective coping mechanisms, and the typical musician who has these qualities is already using some very effective personal skills.

Acknowledgements

Sixteen Personality Factor Questionnaire (16PF) copyright © Institute for Personality and Ability Testing, Inc., 1956, 1970, 1973, 1982, 1986, 1988. International copyright in all countries under the Berne Union, Buenos Aries, Bilateral and Universal Copyright Conventions. All property rights reserved by the Institute for Personality and Ability Testing, Inc., PO Box 1188, Champaign, Illinois 61824, USA. All rights reserved.

Reproduced with permission of the exclusive English-language publisher of the 16PF in the European Community, a division of NFER-NELSON Publishing Company Limited, Darville House, 2 Oxford Road East, Windsor, Berkshire SL4 1DF.

®Myers Briggs Type Indicator and MBTI are registered trademarks of Consulting Psychologists Press, Inc.

The tests in this chapter can be done by those interested in finding out their own scores through contacting Arts Psychology Consultants (*see page 253*).

2 Early Talent and Becoming a Musician

• Questionnaire

Note your answers to the following questions about early influences on your musical life; this will help you to get more out of the rest of the chapter.

Family Role Models

Think back to when you were a child. Who lived at home with you, and how did they affect you? Who were your role models? What did you admire and imitate? What did you rebel against? How did these family role models affect your desire to be a musician?

Encouragement or Discouragement

Out of the same list of role models, think of the people whom you felt were for or against your music-making activities as a child. Then think of the same people and how they reacted when you later wanted to make a career out of music. Did they react the same way, or did they change their attitudes?

What Others Said

What was said to you about music as you were growing up? Who said it, and what did they say? Examples could be something like:

Father: Let's hope he never turns out to be a penniless musician like his grandfather.
Mother: I always wanted to be a singer. Why don't you do something like that.
Teacher: Go into a proper profession; that way you'll never be out of work.

How did these things affect your impression of music as a good or bad thing to do?

Where Does Musical Talent Come From?

A large amount of research shows that musical ability runs in families, and is more prevalent when both parents* and all grandparents are musical. Not all the members of such families need to be musicians themselves, but several are likely to have potential musical ability in the sense of being able to sing in tune, remember melodies easily, hear musical intervals and rhythms and understand the notes in harmonies.

But despite the favourable influence of family background, studies show that several highly talented musicians have come from humble homes where there was little musical activity, and that there is up to a 25-per-cent chance that a child will be musical even if neither parent is apparently so. It is equally true that a number of children of musical parents have shown little musical motivation or talent.

It is also difficult to determine whether musical ability is determined by genes or a musical upbringing because the home environment will already have played a role by the time musical ability is apparent. So it may be partly an innate talent, but is likewise a skill that is enhanced by a favourable milieu.

*The term parent as used throughout this book can also refer to step-parents or guardians.

• Early Rewards and Setbacks

One of the most important factors in the making of future musicians is the amount of reward given for signs of musical promise. In homes where there are musical instruments a child may be encouraged to play them from an early age, and early efforts – banging on a piano or strumming a guitar – are met with applause. Even a two-year-old child, when asked 'What is clever?' is capable of answering 'Clever is when people clap their hands.' So a very early association is made between performing and receiving love and attention from family members. Other associations with love and closeness come from listening to music, as when a child sits on a parent's knee while he or she plays the piano, or when parents sing nursery rhymes to a child.

These early associations may be intensely pleasurable, physical and exciting, and are like magic in the child's imagination. Music is an enchanted world of sound, rhythm and feeling. Creating it makes good things happen, just like magic spells make good things happen in stories. Music brings love, closeness, excitement, rewards, applause and all sorts of other things. So music is firmly fixed in the emotions as a 'good thing'. Later, the child's recognisable attempts to imitate tunes are further rewarded, and when he makes up little tunes of his own, composing may be added to the list of 'good things'. In the jargon of therapy, all these good things represent 'permission' to make music.

But as in myths and fairy tales, there is good and there is bad. So in the same enchanted world, bad things can happen to you when you do certain things. When creating music is met with indifference, anger at the noise being made or irritation at mistakes or off-notes, bad feelings become mixed into the child's concept of music. It can be 'bad' to make a noise or make mistakes, and people get angry and make you feel unhappy. In the jargon of therapy, all these bad things represent 'injunctions' not to make music.

We all have a mixture of permissions and injunctions. Some are weak, some are strong. Permissions guide us on and give us a following wind. Injunctions hold us back and make us feel naughty, criticised or unloved.

Spells and Curses

As the child starts to understand language, good and bad feelings become words and phrases. The child hears parents say 'Nice piano', or 'Don't make a noise'; he remembers these sayings and repeats them back to others. Such sayings and commands are colloquially known in the therapy world as 'spells' and 'curses', just as the child experiences them. These are internalised and later become self-directed, since these early events are characterised by the simultaneous development of our belief systems about good and bad.

Some of these early phrases are forgotten, but they stay in the memory as primitive commands, and may lie undiscovered at the bottom of the mind while the belief systems they create carry on acting throughout adult life. We may never remember what was actually said, but we act on the consequences.

To those that make them, spells and curses are simply careless comments. What is not realised is the power of such comments in the primitive mind of the child, and even less the ability of the child to take the words literally. 'I'll murder you if you carry on making that noise' may be literally terrifying to a child, whereas the parent may have simply remembered saying something like 'Stop making a noise'. In the random lottery of childhood experiences there is little way of controlling all the words and events the child witnesses, but a number make their mark.

If the same words are repeated frequently throughout the child's verbal development, they may then get stored verbally as internal sayings, such as 'Don't make too much noise'. To these early spells and curses get added a whole host of later ones from teachers, fellow musicians, and even overheard conversations between others. All these make up the repertoire of 'ground rules' about music-making which may never even be questioned as to their value or appropriateness.

Actions not only have internal spells and curses, they also have consequences. A 'good action' gets repeated when it consistently gets rewards. A 'bad action' leaves the child feeling rejected and miserable, and when repeated later in life may recall the same feelings of rejection and misery. Without the immediate association of the original action, such misery and rejection may be experienced as a diffuse and inexplicable feeling of unhappiness, melancholy or loneliness.

All these belief systems are magnified by the importance of the person who initiates the spells and curses. A stranger may not carry much weight, but a parent, grandparent or sibling has a much greater significance. If a curse comes from a person of lesser importance its power may be neutralised by good spells. But if it comes from a 'good' person, such as a mother, it can be a much stronger message. This message is internalised and interpreted as 'Mummy won't love me if I do that'.

In the world of the child, people – like fairy-tale kings and demons – have enormous power. Just as the child 'projects' on to parents the power to manipulate happiness and misery, it may then 'project' the same degree of power to manipulate good and bad feelings on to parent-like figures who seem to react in the same way. Teachers, critics, audiences, audition panels and fellow musicians may later be associated, through their criticism, with the same primitive and magical powers.

But in the child's world, the child himself often has equal or even more fantastical power. In his imagination he can fly, see through walls, know what others are thinking and possess superhuman abilities. When he is rewarded for creating music he may see music as a magic power capable of almost anything. It can make strangers smile and laugh, it can make people clap, it can make daddy and mummy love him forever, and it can create magic sounds out of nothing.

This superhuman power of the child can be loosely summed up in the feeling that 'I'm the greatest'. Put in this way it is an important part of our self-evaluation equation. It provides the inner conviction that 'I'm really special, have special powers, can do anything, can be as good as I want to be....' As we will see later, this is the part that gets set up alongside the later reality of a musical career, where we soon find out that we are not, in fact, the greatest, and will have a long and hard path ahead of us to achieve real results.

Dealing with Spells and Curses

We cannot remember many of the actual words and situations of early childhood, so we often cannot remember how our belief systems actually originated. To deal with this, we need to examine our beliefs in the light of present reality, and 'rewrite' our internal commands accordingly.

Beliefs that seem objectively illogical to others may well be illogical, and with help these can be changed. The purpose of help is not only to give objective views, but also to give moral support throughout the process of changing behaviour habits and to deal with the emotions unleashed by such change. A new belief system that 'it is all right to play loudly and make a noise' may have to be accompanied by the reassurance that 'when you were a child mummy didn't like noise, but that doesn't matter now, and mummy would still love you just as much'.

Actual sayings that can be remembered can be written down on a piece of paper and examined in the cool light of adult reality. Some will be clearly seen to be inappropriate, and others may be found to be so after further examination. Many will be seen to be clearly a product of the person who said them – if an uncle who didn't like opera said 'opera is a horrible cacophony', then this can be reinterpreted as 'he didn't like it, but I've discovered that I do'. This example shows clearly how we can change a meaningless global stereotype – 'all opera is horrible' into a meaningful particular instance – 'my uncle didn't like opera'. Such generalisations, containing words like 'always', 'all', and 'never', need to be carefully looked at for this very reason.

Another important aspect of re-evaluating spells and curses is accentuating the positive. We can take out all the good and encouraging things said to us, and the love of people who wished us well and liked our music-making, and make these things sacred and valuable. We can make a point of carrying their permissions with us as perpetual reminders, and we can call them up in moments of crisis or before important concerts.

• The 'Internal Critic'

Our internal critic is the voice we use to comment on all the various aspects of our behaviour. It tells us what to do and what not to do, sometimes arguing both ways, and criticises the results of actions. It can carry on a running commentary during performance, and can be both positive and negative.

As we have seen, it is closely allied to spells and curses, but also includes new material we have created ourselves. It synthesises new belief systems based on life experiences with old belief systems based on imitating or taking in what others have said. Sometimes the difference between these is indicated by the first person, second person or third person doing the 'talking' inside our head:

'I should...' is probably an adult response based on life experience.
'You should...' is often a repetition of what somebody said to you at some point.
'He/she should...' is probably either a projection of 'you should' onto another person, or what you have heard someone say to others.

The most useful of these three is the first, because it contains a personal intent which is more likely to be acted on. Voices saying 'you should' are all too easily rebelled against by alternative voices saying 'But I'm not going to...'. Sometimes the voice is negative and the response positive ('You should get a proper job' – 'I think music *is* a proper job'). Sometimes 'you should' is desirable and the response is a cop-out ('You should stop smoking' – 'I will, one of these days').

Such 'talking' inside one's head is quite natural. This internal dialogue goes on constantly in the background of what we do, and consists of silent phrases which are heard as if they were spoken. Arts psychologist Martin Lloyd-Elliott compares such talking to a 'psychic tape recorder' which repeats and repeats, or a more interactive 'psychic mixing desk' where some voices are turned up and some turned down. The mixing-desk image is a useful one, since it gives you control of such voices and enables you to turn down unhelpful 'curses' yourself, turn up helpful 'spells', or turn the whole thing off for maximum concentration during performance.

Another aspect of words which the musician absorbs from these early years is their 'feel'. Words which some musicians consider to have an unpleasant 'feel' include: grip, pull, push, concentrate, practise, should, don't, shouldn't, speeding, dragging, stop, start, try, force, louder, harder, need, shake. Most of these are 'effort' or 'trying' words, used negatively by teachers ('stop dragging', 'concentrate harder', 'play louder' etc.).

Words which usually 'feel' better and more encouraging include: flow, touch, move, rest, swing, feel, open, style, dance, give, love, listen. They are directed at helping the musician cure problems rather than aggressively criticising shortcomings, and their very sound quality is at times softer and more harmonious.

A highly effective system of analysing such verbal 'transactions' and where they come from, as well as the whole theory of permissions/injunctions and spells/curses, is known as Transactional Analysis, or 'TA' for short. TA, the brainchild of Eric Berne, is an excellent way for a relative beginner to understand some quite advanced aspects of human behaviour, and is heartily recommended to musicians. Further reading into the basic principles of Transactional Analysis will clarify the ideas presented here and in Chapter Three, and do so in easily accessible self-help form. *Born to Win* is a good beginner's book, while the Eric Berne texts are classics from the founder of the movement. Martin Lloyd-Elliott's contribution is particularly written for performing artists from a leader in this field (*see Further Reading, page 251*).

• The Transition from Child to Musician

What is a period of transition? We are in transition all of our lives, so how can we identify a period of transition from making music as a child to making music as an adult? Freud describes the time between childhood and teens as a 'latent period'. During this time few real decisions are made about careers. Schools understand this and offer a general education before later choices have to be made.

The period of transition is therefore one which marks the movement from a general interest in music to the beginnings of a desire to chose music as a career. The actual period of choice then becomes one where adults – teachers, parents etc. – expect to get an 'adult' response to the idea of a career in music. New factors are brought into play:

How realistic is such a career?
How much money is in it?
How insecure is it?
Should I get a university education first or go straight to music college?
Should I simply join a band?

During this period, negotiation can be a big issue. Music teachers may say one thing; the school in general may say another. Parents may indicate a clear preference for or against music as a career; or they may be split. They may make a bargain of some kind, like going to university and doing music afterwards; or they may be so keen on encouraging music as an option that they overlook other desires.

In such negotiation, the musical child is usually in a weaker position than the adults offering advice. There are practical concerns, such as a need for financial support from parents, or help in getting a grant. Psychologically, the child may find it exceptionally difficult to resist the arguments of parents or teachers who are loved and respected. This is particularly trying when they suggest a path of action that the child cannot willingly accept, such as not going straight to music school or not joining a band with his friends.

By and large, children are subjective about their decisions, but this is important in deciding their futures. Teachers and career counsellors are reasonably objective but prone to fads. Parents, on the other hand can be objective, subjective, manipulative or any mixture. They are likely to be protective, through love of the child as much as anything else, and so start with vested interests.

With the benefit of hindsight, the motivations of the people involved in career decisions may become clearer. Unfortunately, this does not help at the time. During this vital period of transition, emotional reactions in the child can easily turn to rebellion if the desire to do music as a career or not is treated unsympathetically and subjectively.

Dealing with the Transition into Music

A successful transition into a musical career involves getting the decision-making process right. What is required of parents, teachers or career counsellors is above all to listen to the child very carefully before introducing arguments for or against. This means 'hearing' in an unbiased way, not simply picking up the elements you want to hear. All sides to the question should be put on the table and looked at. If it helps, write things down.

SUBJECTIVE AND OBJECTIVE ARGUMENTS

One way of identifying and trying to eliminate bias and ulterior motives is to divide statements into subjective and objective.

Subjective statements include:

- 'I want to do it' – child.
- 'Music is a hobby' – parent who sees it that way.
- 'It would be so nice if you were a musician' – parent who wants the child to be a musician.
- 'Musicians are insecure and poor' – parent who is disturbed by insecurity and poverty.
- 'Get one of those synthesisers and we might get in the charts' – friend who fancies being in your band.

Subjective reasoning usually follows inner desires and beliefs. In the case of the child this can be helpful in revealing true motives. It can also be partly or wholly unrealistic, or just a passing phase. On the other hand, subjective statements by others are likely to say more about the people concerned than about the child, and their motivation should be cautiously assessed.

Objective statements include:

- 'I really want to do music and I think I have both motivation and talent' – child.
- 'Music can be a good career if you treat it like a career and really try' – parent.
- 'Music makes some people well-off and others insecure' – career counsellor.
- 'You have the talent to do quite well but I'm not sure if you'll be world class' – teacher.
- 'You'll get a good training at a top music school if music is your decision' – teacher.

The difference is clear: objective reasoning tends to show that a realistic or thinking judgement has been made. This can be the case for three main reasons:

1) The person involved has no apparent vested interest in the child. A career counsellor can be a good person to give the child an objective opinion, although some may have areas of ignorance and prejudice.
2) The person involved has a realistic or thinking personality. This is not infallible, because while such people tend to be more shrewd or analytical, they are not necessarily the most imaginative or the most concerned with the effects of choices on people. They may also base their opinions on a different set of principles from that of the child.
3) The person involved is forthright and not a manipulative sort of personality. Some people can be very clever at manipulation, disguising a biased judgement as an 'I'm only doing this in your best interests...' sort of approach, which may seem quite plausible on the face of it, but which feels wrong and hides underlying subjective interests.

OPEN AND CLOSED QUESTIONS

As we have seen, there are subjective and objective, or even manipulative, ways of asking questions. Consider the difference between 'open' and 'closed' questions.

Open questions seek information without controlling or filtering the answer:

'How much do you want to be a musician?'
'How important is music compared with your other interests?'
'How would you envisage studying?'

Closed questions, on the other hand, seek to manipulate the answer:

'How would you expect to earn a living in such an insecure profession?'
'What sort of life would you have if you didn't get a degree and wanted to change career?'

Such closed questions start with one premise or more. These may be true of some instances but not all, so they are not facts but assumptions, for instance:

- All musicians are insecure.
- People get degrees only immediately after school.
- Musicians generally change careers at some point.

All the likely points for or against should be broken down into their essential elements:

'How would you expect to earn a living?'
'How would you deal with insecurity?'
'What sort of career do you envisage?'
'Can you imagine changing career if another strong interest became important?'
'Would that other interest need a university degree or another type of training?'*
'Is the job market such that you would need a degree whatever happened?'
'Do only degree-holders have secure, well-paid jobs?'
'Does a degree make you a more knowledgeable and effective human being?'

Only when both child and parent (or other advisor) agree on these points should they be brought together into decisions and plans of action.

Fear of Losing Parental Love

The child begins life by associating all its needs with the mother: feeding, warmth and cuddling. Only later does it progressively detach the qualities of the mother, like love, from the 'physical' mother. Fear of losing the love of the parent, as in when the child is naughty and mummy says 'I won't love you if you are naughty', may seem to the child the same as 'losing the parent'. The subjective feeling may be 'mummy will leave me if I'm naughty and I'll be all alone'.

The freedom for the child to be himself may therefore have to be

*Music colleges now often award B.Mus. degrees instead of diplomas.

bought at the cost of a 'sacrifice of love' for not doing what the parent desires. The issue of a child following a musical (or other artistic) career often brings about such a situation. There are two main reasons for this:

1) Some parents see a life in the arts as insecure, and want something more 'professional' for their children, with the promise of money to support a family.

2) Other parents see life in the arts as glamorous or creative and wish they could do it themselves, and the next best thing is to live it through their children.

Whatever the reasons behind the mutual opposition, the subjective reaction in the artist may be considerable loneliness. Some artists, like Salvador Dali, were actually disinherited at the point when they decided not to follow the career offered by parents – often a last-ditch bargaining tool. The threat of loss of money, however, may not go so deep as the emotional feeling of being disinherited.

Logically, the musician at this stage could argue that:

- People differ in their career aims.
- Children do not have to be clones of their parents.
- Your parents really only want to see you secure and happy.
- You cannot please people who do not understand or agree with your goals.
- Other people will like and support you.

However one does this, there may still be an emotional transition to be made before feeling right about following an action that is not supported by the ones you love and who have loved and probably still do love you. A further anxiety that can result from disapproval is the fear that 'if they told me not to be a musician it must be dangerous, because they loved me and wanted the best for me'. Consequently there may be a timid rather than wholehearted embracing of a musical career, or an undertow of foreboding below consciousness.

The models given above are largely examples of what can go wrong. Many parents show consistent love and understanding throughout the growing-up period of the child, and have an open mind in terms of what the child wants to do.

Dealing with 'Loss of Love'

Where there is a feeling that parents or others have 'deserted' you by showing disapproval and criticism for your musical aims, or by consistently confronting you with different or grossly enlarged expectations, it may be necessary to remind yourself deliberately of the following statements:

- You do not lose your parents, just their approval.
- You may only lose their approval at one point in their lives – at other times they may have shown a lot of love and attention, especially when you were a child.
- Disapproval may be only temporary – people change during their lives.
- Disapproval may only be expressed on the surface – secretly they may be proud of you, and express as much to others in your absence.
- It may be of no real use seeking approval from those who do not really understand or sympathise with your goals.

The early years of the musician are imbued with all the strong emotions of childhood – enthusiasms, fears, joy, angry rebellion and, above all, love. It is this love that must be safeguarded, since it is the basis of all pleasure in music.

The Generation Gap

Another important factor in the period of transition is the generation gap. This is quite familiar in its usual sense of a difference in attitudes between people brought up at different points in the world's cultural history. Such differences affect a variety of different factors, including musical preferences, dance styles, hair and clothing, attitudes to money, and preferred types of employment.

The generation gap has, however, another important aspect which is easily overlooked. The musical child may have based his love of music-making on the identification he had with one or other parent when he was 2–5 years old. This would commonly mean that the parent was about 30. This is often a fresh and creative time for an adult, and parents of this age will probably read stories or sing or play musical instruments for the child.

When the child is on the brink of adulthood, however, it will be 15 years later. The child may expect the same 'permission' from his parents to be a musician as before, but the reaction may be quite different. Parents may say, for instance, 'go into business', or 'train for a worthwhile profession'. This is not at all baffling, although it may feel so emotionally – the parents are simply 15 years older and may have become worldly-wise, disillusioned or materialistic.

There may be a still further aspect to this. Those same parents have gone through a substantial change in attitude during the process of getting older. Their own starting point may, in fact, have been startlingly similar. As children they may themselves have gone through the same struggle. Just as they (in the words of Oscar Wilde) 'killed the thing they loved', so out of badly understood inner motives and 'good advice' they instruct the child to do the same. Generation upon generation of professional people have inner creative desires which are lived out in amateur music-making and conveyed with much positive emotion to their young children.

The irony of the generation gap is that the rebels of yesterday become the establishment figures of today. The works that were hissed and booed (like Stravinsky's *Rite of Spring*) are now applauded. So inviting the child to 'be like the establishment' of today has a very different sense to inviting the child to 'become the establishment' of tomorrow.

This model of the generation gap is all too familiar to teenagers who want to follow their inner convictions and enthusiasms in the face of opposition. While it is the most dramatic model – and is reproduced in all the Hollywood misfit movies – it is far from the only one, since many enlightened parents give children full support and understanding over their choice of careers.

Dealing with the Generation Gap

Make an age chart (*see Figure 2.1*) by drawing horizontal lines on a piece of paper for each of your parents on top, and for yourself at the bottom. Start your own line with your birth, and on the lines above it write the ages of parents at your birth. Consider what they were like at that age, what they did socially, what their career aspirations were, what their personalities were like, what their musical activities and tastes were, how happy or disillusioned they were, how idealistic or materialistic their values were. Then extend the chart, marking each year of your development to the age of about 20, with the corresponding ages of your parents.

Think about how your parents were when you were in your first years, say up to six, then continue the chart until you are now in your mid and late teens. How had your parents changed by that time? Go through the same questions as above. What does this tell you about their attitudes to music and to your becoming a musician? Did their support stay the same? Were they over-ambitious? Did they reward your music-making when you were little and they were younger, but reflect different or more sober values as they grew older and their lives changed?

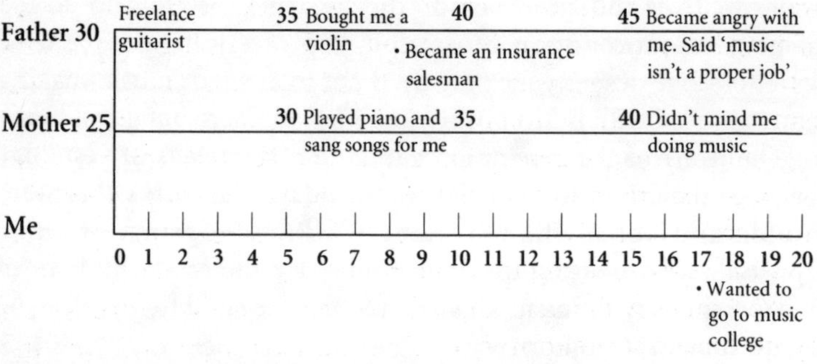

Figure 2.1. **An example of an 'age chart'.**

Choosing Your Instrument and Style

A conflict of motivation can occur where there is a stated or understood expectation that a child will play a certain instrument, often bought by the parent involved, or play a certain type of music. What happens to the child who wants to play the saxophone but is given a clarinet? Or the child that wants to play soul music but is sent to a classical teacher with no knowledge of or sympathy for popular music?

Such a child may continue to live out such expectations for a certain time, and then simply stop. After a period of reflection – often not without its painful arguments – a better way of proceeding may be decided on which is much closer to aspirations.

The real confusion comes where there are feelings of both love and alienation for an instrument. Playing the piano may be the most natural thing to do, but also the most 'expected' thing to do. Father or mother may already be well-known pianists, and may be a difficult act to follow. It may be easier to take up another instrument, or sing, and this alternative route into music may proceed for some time. But what if, after all, it is the piano that remains the first love? Do you go back to it and risk not being as good as expectations, or carry on with something else and feel yourself in 'free territory' where there are no expectations and no precedents? And when would you go back to the piano? As soon as possible, later or never? Would the love of the instrument be adequate compensation for the reduced career prospects?

Later confusion in this case may be on quite a fundamental emotional level: 'did I give up simply out of rebellion or because I wanted to?'. What is the right action and what is the wrong one? Solving this problem may be difficult. One way of knowing is honestly to admit to yourself what feels most natural and gives most pleasure. Another is simply noting what tends to be the natural urge and where the most time is spent. Some flip a coin and find out how they react to the result – with pleasure or misgiving. The problem is identifying the wishes that are being blocked out because we are reluctant to admit them.

Workshops with musicians indicate that choice of instrument is by no means straightforward. One musician may say, 'My first instrument was the guitar. I've always liked it best and been successful playing it. If I had to start again I'd still be a guitarist, and my ambition is just to get better and better at playing it.' Another may say, 'I started out playing recorder, I think. After that I wanted to play the saxophone but ended up playing the double-bass because they had one left over in the school orchestra. I stuck with the bass because everyone gave me work on it and I became quite successful. Although I wouldn't stop playing the bass, I wish I had really worked at my piano playing and been a pianist: the piano is the closest thing to how I really think.'

The same is true of musical styles: there are classical musicians who wish they could have more fun playing popular music, and jazz musicians who return to their classical roots as their careers progress. To work out your own choices, fill in the following questionnaire:

YOUR MUSICAL INSTRUMENT*

What was your first musical instrument?
What has been your most successful?
What is your favourite?
What is your 'fantasy' musical instrument in an ideal world, or if you were to start again from the beginning?

YOUR MUSICAL MEDIUM**

What was your first musical medium?
What has been your most successful?
What is your favourite?
What is your 'fantasy' musical medium in an ideal world, or if you were to start again from the beginning?

When you have done this, take a look at it. You may be a little surprised at the results if they are not straightforward. Ask yourself how you can come closer to your favourite forms of music-making. Do you need some more tuition to take up a better option? Are you happy with real-life choices because they give you better career opportunities? Can you explore some of your hidden desires in another way, as in amateur music-making?

Children and students in the process of making important career decisions about instrument and style may be guided on the one hand by 'logical' arguments such as: 'study classical technique first, then play jazz' or 'start with the flute, then play sax if you want to', and on the other by heartfelt desires. Making a long commitment to an instrument requires you to love it, so make sure that you get tuition on the instrument you really want to play. If you want to make a transition later, do it because you want to, as many violinists have done with the viola. As you get progressively more successful at playing an instrument, it gets increasingly difficult to turn back. Going from violin to viola, or between clarinet, sax and flute is rela-

*Instrument also refers to voice and composition.

**This refers to the type of music you play, such as classical, pop, rock, jazz, folk and ethnic.

tively easy. Going from French horn to cello is a totally different affair.

Once you have made the right choice of instrument, you should then consider the instrument itself. Is it properly set up? Does it sound good? Do you really identify with it and love it, or do you have distant or negative feelings towards it? Are negative feelings caused by the person that bought it for you? Would you prefer to have a different instrument, or one you have chosen or bought yourself? Would your instrument be good enough if properly set up, or will it always hold you back? Answering these questions properly ensures that your motivation and playing comfort is as good as it can be.

Getting the Best out of Music College

Music college is often the last transitional stage in a musician's life. It may be the final period during which a full range of teaching and support services is available. After this, musicians are left to sink or swim in the profession. Without adequate preparation they will learn about the profession through trial and error, and may take steps which are later regretted. The 'reference' and superstructure of the college will also have to be replaced by another personal and professional set of values.

As a 'half-way house' between the safety of being musically nurtured and the realities of earning a living, the music college should take responsibility for facilitating the journey into self-reliance. It can do this by giving the musician a viable career and business plan which can be put into operation instantly on leaving college. Like art colleges, music colleges have started from a purely 'artistic' premise and have taken time to emerge into the realities of modern career-development methods.

The sooner the student becomes motivated towards acquiring the functions of the professional musician, the easier he will find the transition. A useful value check to make is that of identity and goals, put simply as:

Who am I?
What am I?
What is my function?

The musical child may say:
Who am I? – a child.
What am I? – nothing, but I like playing music.
What is my function? – to have fun, learn things and please my parents.

The student in transition may say:
Who am I? – a student.
What am I? – a musician.
What is my function? – to learn things and become good enough to earn a living.

The professional musician may say:
Who am I? – a sensitive and imaginative person/partner/parent.
What am I? – a professional musician.
What is my function? – to entertain/go down in history/earn a living/feed a family.

Teachers in music colleges may have a strategic plan for gifted students, holding them back until they can make maximum impact in the right circumstances. For the average musician, however, early reality testing in terms of public playing will give an idea of what repertoire is needed and works well, what style of music holds the most appeal, including both classical and popular, what combinations of fellow musicians seem to work well and how well present technique and confidence holds up to the rigours of performance. During the period where teachers are there to give guidance, they can be of invaluable help with this progressive initiation into the business, and frequently pass work on to students as they become ready to cope with it.

The other crucial part of developing the musician's confidence and autonomy is money. Money in the pocket is a powerful incentive to play more and better, and a confirmation that music-making is a 'real job' with real rewards. It will not be long after the musician leaves college before money becomes a whole issue in what kind of work to do and how to get as much as possible out of it. Further guidance with this is given in Chapter Eight.

3 Motivation and Commitment

Questionnaire

Working through the following questions will help you to get the most out of the rest of the chapter.

Why Be a Musician?

All sorts of reasons have been put forward for being a musician. What reasons do you have? Do they seem good enough to justify a whole career in music, or is music likely to be a temporary satisfaction or lifetime hobby? See which of the following apply to you:

Being on stage or television, or being an exhibitionist.
Being in a glamorous profession, making it easy to meet sexual partners.
Doing the same thing as friends do.
Being so besotted by music that it is hard to exist without it.
Having an unstoppable urge to create things.
Rebelling and doing something antisocial.
Getting the attention of parents or others.
Following in family footsteps.
Being able to express feelings, jump about or make loud noises.
Having an outside chance of making lots of money quickly.
Avoiding a nine-to-five job.

Where is the Pleasure and Love in Music?

What is really good about music?
What are the things that cause satisfaction in playing?
Is it good being a musician?
Is the life OK?

What are the Negative Sides of Music Making?

Is there anxiety attached to some aspects of music?
Who disapproved of music when you were young?

Your 'Life Script'

Can you identify any hunches or convictions you have about how you see your life developing?
Do you see yourself in the years ahead as rich/poor, single/family person, performer/creator, staying in music/getting another job, getting to the top/staying at an average level, etc.?
Can you trace any elements of this 'life script' back to things other people said to you which you then absorbed into your own belief system?

• Making a Commitment

Motivation is the dynamo behind all healthy self-activated action, goal-setting and career-planning. Maximum motivation comes from total commitment. As the decision to go into music-making is typically one that arouses more controversy than becoming a doctor or a lawyer, there is more likelihood of the musician picking up a range of ambivalent attitudes to his choice. Some conflicts are internalised, and some are creatively resolved in the musician's artistic work.

Our personal motivation can be seen as a balance between positive and negative drives. The positive feelings are like the vital motor behind music-making; the negative forces are like the brakes. To achieve full forward momentum, the brakes need to be released.

The transition into music as a career introduces a whole new series of 'reality' factors which test and question our commitment. Commitment is partly about how well we deal with these reality factors. Difficulty in meeting the demands of reality can result in:

- Ruining performances in order to achieve an unconscious aim or 'secondary benefit', such as getting sympathy for failing.
- Prolonging early rebellions against the over-expectations of family and teachers.
- Not believing in, or taking personal responsibility for, succeeding.
- Carrying out a negative life-script based on put-downs instilled in childhood.
- Falling into a self-image of vulnerability based on memories of past failures.

Life Scripts

The way people react to reality demands and the positive and negative factors in their inner motivations tends to give them a characteristic 'style' of thought and action. This style generally determines how they react to life events and shape their lives and ambitions. Because their particular internal make-up tends to be 'played out' on the stage of life, it can be called a 'life script'. This is a term often used in Transactional Analysis (*see page 28*). TA analyses such Life Scripts, and gives them titles to identify easily their characteristics, such as 'yes but' or 'if only'. Such identifiers are sometimes uncannily accurate. The person that frequently says 'yes but...' or 'if only...' may be characteristically acting out this assumption.

Typical examples of the inner conflicts of musicians expressed as life scripts are given below. Although they are meant to give an overview of some of the characteristic motivations of the professional musician, they are frequently found in performing artists of all kinds. The basic mechanisms at work here are quite normal and should be no cause for alarm. Musicians have a good tolerance of ambiguity and conflict, and are often clever at resolving it or turning it into a sharp sense of humour. If conflict is perceived as a worry, then some insight and suggestions for improvement may be gained from these examples.

The 'Unfulfilled Greatness' Model

This is a common model. As a child, the musician will have been rewarded for being clever, creative and musical. The musical child, when developing these gifts further, can easily feel all-powerful through the uncritical rewards he has been given in early stages. The child may feel 'I'm the greatest', within the limited reality framework an infant possesses *(see page 25)*.

Later, the child starts to think in a more advanced way and make comparisons with other musicians and musical children. In all but the exceptionally gifted and precocious, this 'reality-testing' is likely to produce the natural realisation that 'I'm not the greatest'. The musician will then, on the one hand, try to play better in order to justify his belief that he is 'the greatest', while on the other hand feeling frustrated at the growing idea of not actually being likely to become 'the greatest'.

The resulting internal contradiction causes conflict. The unconscious, in a narcissistic way, needs and expects more praise than is ever possible in the real world, and may drive the musician on. The musician may experience a low-level feeling of anxiety, accompanied by the feeling that 'I don't know why I sometimes feel I can succeed and sometimes feel I'm useless'.

If unreasonably high expectations are set at a primitive age, they are difficult to maintain in reality. This leads to feelings of inferiority, which are mixed in with the original feelings of superiority, resulting in a vacillation between the 'grandiose' and the 'inadequate'. This can result in difficulty in handling criticism from others, because criticism does not seem to fit into this exaggerated sense of 'scale'. Praise may be received as either insufficient or unbelievable, and criticism may be taken very personally.

If the musician dismisses the criticisms of others as hostile and uncomprehending, and blames audiences and others for not appreciating his real talent, it may be possible to preserve an illusion of superiority. In this way the performer may never really improve or indeed come to value the constructive comments of friends and teachers. He may hear his inner voice telling him to play better, and then sabotage it.

How do we deal with this double-bind? By accepting such inner feelings as fairly typical, the musician can then argue with them and accept a realistic level of achievement in proportion to his goals and talents. This means that it may then become possible to feel real satisfaction for a realistic level of achievement, rather than listening to the fantasy voices of greatness and inadequacy.

This starts the process of positive self-criticism, and improvement from the bottom up rather than from the top down. The unattainable goal of being 'the best pianist in the world', which results in hopelessness, can be replaced by a short-term goal of being, say, 'the third best pianist in my street'. If this is attainable, then one can move on, set a further attainable goal and then reach that. By progressively attaining and then surpassing goals, the musician feels real satisfaction, and bases his career on solid gains which are recognised and rewarded by others. He may later say of his success 'I've been lucky', disguising the real effort that went into attaining these goals. His inner voice may add 'and I think I deserved it too'. Other musicians recognise this as 'paying one's dues'.

'If Only' and 'Yes But' Scripts

This is a close variation on the unfulfilled greatness model (*above*). It describes ways of putting off actual achievements by constructing plausible arguments why they cannot be carried out, for example:

If only I had a better instrument I could audition for an orchestra.
I'd like to join a band but first I have to play perfectly.

To avoid having our real talent put on the line and made obvious to ourselves and others, it is hidden by all sorts of mechanisms which stall it. On the face of it illogical, this procedure is actually quite clever and practised by many musicians. It avoids the unpleasant anxiety of having to expose ourselves, and creates the illusion that we are really playing 'beneath our potential'. This makes us feel secure that we really could do better if we tried.

This is like trying to have our cake and eat it. Nobody knows what this 'real hidden talent' is because nobody ever sees it. Playing below our potential has the emotional value of self-protection, but the actual effect of endlessly postponing our real-life career. In this case the secondary benefit of avoiding criticism has sabotaged the primary benefit of playing as well as we can.

The 'Rebel' Script

Musicians are often associated with rebellious behaviour. This is particularly, but not always, the case with popular and jazz musicians because of their perceived image as radical and against social norms. Rebellion is partly self-defence against aggressive criticism from others, such as 'when are you going to get a proper job?' and accusations of being 'arty' and bad at games at school. Hard-rock and heavy-metal musicians become used to defending themselves from a public image 'only slightly above that of rapists and muggers' as one musician put it. Rebelling is a 'young person's thing' naturally associated with teens and beyond. It is part of the lifestyle of creative people who experiment with and change the popular state of mass culture at any moment in time. Rebellion preserves the need to perform, which the child has made a lifelong priority through its earlier rewards of love and praise.

The problem with rebellion is that it alienates people by provoking disapproval and hostility. Musicians, being more 'feeling' than average, need to be loved by at least somebody. This creates a situation in need of some kind of resolution. The 'betrayed' teenager tries to show he is independent of parental approval, and seeks support in like-minded rebels, but this means that he is now dependent on the approval of his peers. The performer may consciously think 'I'm independent of people's reactions', but unconsciously the opposite may in fact be true. He may have exchanged one support mechanism for another.

The perceived loss of parental love and approval normally causes some degree of angry reaction, since anger is itself one of the fundamental stages of loss. Such anger fuels the rebellion. All rebellion, however, needs a cause – just as showing off is dependent on some visible reaction, so the child who rebels against his parents may be depending on some reaction from them. The 'rebel' may consciously maintain that he is independent of parental approval, and reinforces this by rejecting establishment or parental values. Inside, however, there may be some degree of yearning for the reinstatement of parental love. Such inner sensitivity can be felt when parents show no interest, do not attend gigs or concerts, or constantly suggest other ways of earning a living.

This can all be quite confusing. Rebellious behaviour can lead to fame, scandal and recognition – all types of approval. But the same behaviour can leave the inner feeling that the people we most want to please – usually parents – do not love, understand or approve of us. Such was the typical story line and basic psychology of the Hollywood 'misfit', typified by James Dean and early Marlon Brando films.

As we have seen, 'sabotage' scripts, such as 'Yes but' or 'If only' have some clear uses. The standpoint of the rebel shares this: the real self need not be shown to anybody or brought to account because there is no need to modify behaviour to make others approve. Freed of the intent to seek approval, the performer can predict that people will not approve, and feels in control of other people's reactions. The performer can then go on to blame others for disapproving of him because they do not understand his real self: nothing is his fault, it is all theirs. The real approval-seeking inner self, meanwhile, need never be shown or brought to account.

The musician may desire to please people, but feel that those same people cannot be pleased. Realistically, the people who matter in his adult career may be quite different from the ones that he is still trying to please and whose approval is of no actual consequence. Parents, for example, may have no direct connection with the musician's career. It greatly helps the musician's peace of mind to have a realistic idea of who matters and who does not. This makes it easier not to blame other people for the original problems they had nothing to do with.

By progressively becoming emotionally mature and self-dependent the musician tends naturally to reduce this need for the approval of others. When this is done, he can start to play for himself and to his own standards without worrying unduly about those who are indifferent or interested in other things. The independent musician can then become less concerned with rebellion as a reaction to others. The main concern will be in getting on with his career, and enlisting the help and support of all sorts of useful people, rather than alienating them. Older musicians tend to do this a lot more easily.

Succeeding can be a complex process. It exposes us to other people's evaluations, and it demands the emotional maturity to ignore irrelevant criticism and get by with only the essential approval of those who matter and are close to our aims.

The 'I'm a Fraud' Script

The term 'fraud' is used loosely here to express the idea of 'not typical'. This script is found particularly in the musical careers of 'outsiders' or those who are naturally slightly different from the 'norm'. It tends to affect late starters, foreigners and children who do not follow the same path as their peers, such as those who do not enter county and national youth orchestras, do not sight-read well or sit grade exams. Since the wide spectrum of musicians includes the 'typical' and the 'individual' this idea is quite natural.

Part of the blame for feeling a 'fraud' can be accounted for by the standardisation of classical-music education. There is an accepted path to follow through instrumental training, exams, recitals, orchestras, college and later master classes. Sometimes this is so rigid that musicians become very sensitive to their progress along the path – they may worry about whether or when their teacher will enter them for an exam, or about their position in the hierarchy of an orchestra.

Teachers may, in some instances, be guilty of directly giving musicians the message that they are a 'fraud' by making them believe that they have not really got what it takes. When the musician proves such teachers wrong, they may cover their tracks by saying 'it must all have been due to hard work' or 'you were lucky that time, but I'm sure it won't continue to be so easy'.

Sometimes these feelings of being a 'fraud' are due to the late development of musical ability in someone who has abundant intelligence, creativity and musicality. Such a person has all it takes to do well, but may still have fixed in his mind the memories of early disasters and being behind his peers in ability.

In terms of inner psychology, feelings of being a 'fraud' are again closely linked to the 'unfulfilled greatness' model (*see page 44*). An inner fear of success can lead to a musician not giving his best; this in turn can cause feelings of dishonesty or fraudulence. The musician then feels guilt at being 'a fraud' and worries that people will find out that he is not the greatest but in fact quite ordinary. In this way his own self doubt is projected on to other people, and he starts to imagine that they are constantly thinking 'is he the greatest or is he really rather ordinary as we all suspected – maybe he can't play properly at all'.

While musicians themselves may use the word 'fraud' in therapy, this is an extreme exaggeration of what is happening. The musician's talents and abilities are quite real – he is not a spy or impostor in any sense, and is typically much more able than these negative inner voices may suggest. Many late starters go on to do well because they have a richness of life experience that transfers positively into their musical qualities.

The Guilt and Punishment Script

Musicians grow up in a world where there is constant criticism on all levels – of their playing, lifestyle and achievements. The musician internalises criticism from early years and carries it in his head as the 'internal critic' or censor. This is the 'superego' of psychoanalysis, or the 'critical parent' of Transactional Analysis. The censor mimics parents and authority figures in criticising poor practice, showing off, flirting or having too much fun, and when basic desires for gratification contradict the Puritanism of the censor, the result is guilt.

Some of this guilt goes right back to simplistic associations made by children:

- The feeling that hands themselves are naughty because they get smacked in childhood. Hands that play an instrument may then be naughty.
- Play may also be naughty because it is not serious. If it is forbidden by parents, the child may then imagine that 'mummy and daddy don't like me to play'. Practice, by contrast, is serious.
- Showing off may become an ambivalent, confusing issue. Initially this behaviour may have been greeted with fun and rewards, but later with 'stop showing off'. The child may not know whether it is right or wrong to show off. He may become anxious because showing off in public by performing may be 'clever', 'bad' or 'likely to get rewards or anger randomly, or both together'.

Showing off is also 'being looked at'. The child associates this with higher states of excitement – when other people are there and new things happen, or the child is asked to perform in some way. Being looked at later becomes associated with higher adrenalin levels typical of the 'fight or flight' mechanism – the alertness reaction all living beings have when faced with danger and have to decide whether to flee from it or stay and confront it. It is exciting and nerve-racking at the same time. As well as carrying memories of being criticised, showing off becomes simultaneously exciting, naughty and liable to bring punishment. Later in life there are no parents to punish the child, so the musical performer may punish himself with stress and feelings of anxiety just to fulfil the familiar and expected consequences.

Such 'self-punishment' is also meant to make the guilt 'go away'. One way of doing this is sabotaging his playing to make sure that he is somehow 'found out'. This is the sort of unconscious saboteur that tells criminals to drop hints as to their identity or guilt. In the performer, this may mean playing quite well, but putting in one small mistake so that the 'critic' can enact its little procedure of crime and punishment. Solo performers such as concert pianists may be quite familiar with this and wonder why such a 'token mistake' is really necessary.

Self-punishment may happen in more general ways by drinking, drug-taking or self-induced vomiting before concerts. The aim is to feel that the 'crime' has been properly punished. Part of this ritual can be the excitement of the sin, which becomes mixed in with the thrill of the performance and the pre-performance nerves, creating a sinfully self-destructive cocktail. In the case of vomiting or excessive drinking and drug-taking, the physical effects can be quite dangerous and should be stopped with some determination and help.

In a deeper way, the censor can act like an undertow on the whole essence of the musician's self-confidence. Even if the musician's career is going exceptionally well, the censor may still remind the unconscious of past sins and the hostility or indifference of others. In this way, the internal critic sends up danger warnings which bring to light all the old primitive anxieties in otherwise successful performances. Such danger warnings are historical, and should be consciously phased out.

The 'God-given Talent' Script

It can be particularly difficult to deal with parents or teachers who tell you that you have a 'God-given talent'. This is a heavy responsibility if it is taken literally. As we know, children are prone to exactly that – taking things literally. If it is 'the wish of God' how do you go against it? Do you have to be the best in the world for God to love you? Do you get sent to hell if you play wrong notes?

It is difficult enough to be a good musician without God taking sides in the proceedings. Such comments may in fact be made by older people who love both God and music, and tend to fuse them into the idea that God loves music and wants his followers to be musical – an idea supported by the amount of music that enters into religion. Younger musicians may simply find this incomprehensible.

One outcome of the 'God given talent' scenario is the idea that 'God has chosen ones'. This is like the elite or 'insiders' that religion in many of its forms tends to propose. The dilemma for the musician then becomes 'am I in or am I out?'. Speculation then continues as to whether fellow students or brothers and sisters are 'chosen ones' or not. All this loses sight of musical talent and learning how to play as a continuous process, with all possible shades of ability, styles, preferences and levels of enjoyment, and almost certainly does a lot more harm than good.

Projections that Distort Reality

Associations of guilt are one reality distortion. Another is projection: the feeling that other people are experiencing the same emotions and thoughts as yourself, particularly critical thoughts. When the musician's internal censor is intense, he may feel that he has played abominably badly on occasions when the audience has not even noticed any shortcomings. He may feel audiences are aggressive and hostile if this represents his own inner feelings of self-criticism. He may exaggerate the natural envy that audiences can and do feel into something stronger. He may even feel, through this projection, that the audience actually wants him to play badly. Such feelings are not real, and again should be phased out.

Approach-avoidance

Desire to reach a goal may well conflict with doubts and fears which try to avoid that goal. This is called 'approach-avoidance', because the closer you get to the goal, the more it holds you up. This is like snooker players who miss on the black ball, footballers who shoot wide at the goal mouth itself, or a partner that fails to turn up at the church on the day of the wedding.

The problem is that desire for a goal remains relatively constant: it is felt both far away and close to the goal. Avoidance, however, may be weak at a distance, where the goal seems mainly attractive, but much stronger close to it, where actual avoidance mechanisms may operate with increasing intensity. A musician may plan to do an audition months ahead, then back out suddenly just before it. This may be for practical reasons such as lack of preparation, but it may also happen when preparation is quite good.

Dealing with this requires two steps. The first is analysing feelings for and against, taking them realistically into account, and deciding whether the action to be taken is the right one. If it is not, then postpone or abandon it. The second step is then making the decision to go ahead. The maximum fear tends to occur at the actual 'agonising over the decision' stage. Once a decision is made, the avoidance fear tends to decrease naturally.

Knowing this helps us accept the heightened internal 'bargaining' that goes on just before something like an audition. It happens to performers at all levels of competence, including the most talented. Once this period has been successfully put behind us, the commitment to action is positive and the emotions relax as the course of action becomes increasingly clear.

Dealing with Life Scripts

Life scripts are part of Transactional Analysis, and to understand them it is strongly recommended that you do some further reading. All the books by Eric Berne, its founder, are accessible and easily readable self-help texts. So is *Born to Win*, which is also a good beginner's book. Detailed examples of life scripts are given in *What Do You Say After You Say Hello*, and illustrations include some fascinating 'scripts' of fairy tales like Cinderella and Little Red Riding Hood. These books are given at the end of the last chapter.

Some other essential things need to be borne in mind:

- We probably all have elements of these life scripts in our inner motivational patterns. Since they are commonplace in musicians and other performing artists, the presence of some of their aspects is normal and no cause for alarm. They are only worth dealing with when they become exaggerated out of proportion. Do not suddenly 'discover' that you are one thing or the other and fall into the trap of exaggerating it yourself. The scripts are meant for guidance into natural tendencies, not as a 'diagnosis' of who you are.
- The whole of human existence in biological terms represents the development of ever more complex forms which have the skills to survive in their environments. The complexities within creative artists may partly account for the richness of their talent. Some degree of inner conflict represents the symbolic 'chaos' out of which creativity creates 'order'. This may be particularly valuable to songwriters, as it is to novelists and scriptwriters. Without such complexities there may even be a reduced creative desire.
- There is always the option of talking over some of the 'unconscious' aspects of our inner make-up with a third party, such as a counsellor. If this seems a good course of action, try it. Details of counselling are given in Chapter Twelve.
- Musicians have a tendency towards the dramatic – music itself is dramatic. The tendency to dramatise may be fine for artistic work, but avoid dramatising your own failings as much as possible. Working with musicians in counselling overwhelmingly shows that motivation conflicts exist even in those at the very top of the profession. They do not stop you playing or becoming successful.

4 Ambition and Self-confidence

Having looked at early motivations and barriers to commitment, the next stage is to examine our musical ambitions and see how they fit into the reality of our careers. Matching ambition with reality in this way is the cornerstone of success – it relegates unproductive fantasies to where they can have no direct effect on music-making; it ensures that we get real satisfaction from seeing our actual career reflecting our ambitions; and it reinforces our self-esteem as we reach our goals. Once we have started to attain the musical standards we have set for ourselves, it then helps us achieve them consistently.

• Developing a Sense of Scale

Musicians are ambitious. They are constantly motivating themselves to attain greater levels of technical and musical achievement, or play as well as their peers or heroes. The problem is that there is a difference between ambition that is unreal and likely to remain a fantasy, and ambition which is real and can be achieved in our actual playing careers. To differentiate between the real and the unreal, it is essential to develop a proper sense of scale.

To start at the top of the scale, perfection in music is not an absolute, unless we are referring to 'perfect intervals' which have a definite mathematical formula. It is a construction inside the mind of the musician, which has no more existence in reality than 'total imperfection' has. It would be extremely difficult to imagine a piece of music that could not be made worse in any way, and it is equally futile to imagine any music that could not be improved upon in any detail. Even mathematicians have difficulty with absolutes – if you have infinity, which is infinite, then can you or can you not have an 'infinity' of infinities?

If we take out the idea of perfection, which is a helpful start, then we are still left with some sort of scale. In athletics we could construct a descending scale of existing achievement: 'world record', 'Olympic record', 'national record', 'local record' etc. The problem is that there are no such reliable measurements for music, any more than there are for emotional states such as love and happiness. Even the idea of 'the highest paid musician' does not reflect musical attainment, unless you believe that 'the most popular must be the best' as Harold Robbins once remarked when he was the highest paid writer in the world. Titles are equally misleading – 'pianist of the century' has been given by the press to Richter, Horowitz and Schiff as well as probably countless others. And for how long does success have to last – for one hit, one year, ten years, or for long enough to qualify for a 'lifetime achievement' award, or to go down in history as a legend?

Some degree of measurement for a musical performance is, however, possible, such as:

- Legendary performance – critics still rave about it.
- Very satisfying performance – critics loved it.
- Variable performance – good and bad bits.
- Technically correct performance, but musically disappointing.
- Performance errors noticed by trained musicians.
- Performance errors noticed by general public.
- Gross performance errors but piece completed.
- Performance breaks down completely and is abandoned.

Another way of scaling musical attainment is to use 'acceptable standards' for certain playing situations. For a classical musician this might be:

- International soloist.
- National soloist.
- Featured ensemble player, e.g. principal or member of small ensemble (string quartet or chamber group).
- Rank and file in leading orchestra.

- Extra or occasional player in leading orchestra.
- Freelance in less well-known orchestras.
- Member of semi-professional or amateur group.

We could also scale musicians on whether they:

- Regularly play on major recording sessions as named player.
- Play on major recording sessions as part of regular orchestra.
- Play on major recording sessions on an occasional basis.
- Do not play on major recording sessions.

Though unreliable, these sorts of scales do make sense to the musician because there is usually some recognisable 'rite of passage' between one level and another. This is frequently an audition – such as for entry into a major orchestra, for principal or for one of the top desks in a string section – and players plan carefully as to whether they should or should not audition at their present level of playing and confidence.

Setting Your Optimum Performance Range

The range of performing ability varies between musicians. Some, like session musicians, have the reputation of working to tight tolerances, or predictably small ranges of difference. Others have the reputation of being 'inspired or awful'. Consistent musicians may be disciplined or conscientious by nature, or they may have become mature and more confident of their mastery. 'Inspired or awful' musicians may be highly gifted, but are likely to have problems with such things as:

- Self-image: there may be cracks in confidence that sabotage playing.
- High-risk 'brinkmanship' tactics: arriving just before the music starts; drinking alcohol just short of, or indeed beyond, the point where it noticeably worsens playing.
- Lack of pride in themselves, with a laissez-faire approach to getting all aspects of the music correct. This can result from laziness or confused motivation.

- High dependency on other musicians to make things happen, and low playing autonomy.
- A truly creative and 'inspirational' personality which has peaks and troughs of concentration and engagement in the music.

Raising the Top of Your Range

Raising the top of your performing range is helped by matching your inner musical voice to your performing ability and by admitting your full potential to yourself.

Using Your Inner Musical Voice

Music is not only what you play, it is also what you hear in your head. It can be 'real' to you before it is played, written or recorded, existing in the imagination as melody lines or snatches of mental arrangements. Your maximum possible performance range is partly determined by your capacity to deal with this potential richness and reproduce it in performance or composition. This is an achievable goal and a good means to self-improvement. It has been valued by a number of jazz musicians, such as Charlie Parker, Sonny Rollins and John Coltrane, all of whom worked intensely on their 'inner sounds' until they found the means to reproduce them. Your musical imagination deserves the greatest respect.

Owning Your Talent

Another vital part in realising the upper limits of your potential is 'owning' and admitting it. This may mean 'buying back' parts of your ego that you may have wrongly attributed to the inspiration of others. The feeling that others 'inspire you' is commonly experienced when you fall deeply in love with someone and they leave you. You feel that person 'was' the heightened awareness you felt when in love, that the person 'gave' you something you did not have, that the reasons for your enhanced state came from 'outside' yourself and not from your own qualities.

If you analyse this a little, you can see that the inspiration actually came from within yourself. You contain the capacity for such an experience. Such experiences are within your own power, ability and emotional range. If you are able to rescue and 'own' your inspiration it is yours to use freely and when you need it. It can be quite difficult to convince yourself that this is true, but it also shows that anything you have done at any time has been within your range. The range of any person may be considerably greater than expected. To get some concept of this, imagine how fast you would run for a bus compared with how fast you would run if chased by a lion.

Our best shot is hard to measure. We do not have the opportunity that athletes have to record their ability in thousandths of a second and record the best times. We have our own measurement – partly external in terms of technique and standard of work – but mainly internal in terms of our self-conceptions. Because of this difficulty in measuring ability, it is important we try to get it right.

Raising the Bottom of Your Range

Raising the bottom of your performing range is helped by eliminating bad habits and outdated criticisms and learning how to deal with failure.

Eliminating Bad Habits

The bottom of your performing range is usually indicated by things that go wrong. One part of dealing with this is maintaining instruments and equipment in a professionally reliable state, and if necessary carrying appropriate spares. Another part is eliminating unreliable elements of your general conduct such as:

- Arriving late for rehearsals or gigs, or late enough to make other band members uncomfortable.
- Drinking too much or generally being in an 'altered' state of perception which may mean an unpredictable level of performance.

This may be a hard exercise for many musicians who somehow

'hope that it will be alright on the night'. Confidence is *knowing* that it will. Many musicians rely on their ability to pull a good performance out of the bag, but as they take more and more risks there may come a point where there is a serious danger of sabotaging a performance and maybe a career opportunity. This applies especially to drinking, where the amount drunk may gradually increase until one day it becomes almost impossible to play correctly.

Being superhuman is a fantasy cultivated by alcoholics, possibly because they think 'If I can do that drunk, then I must really be good – think how well I could do it sober!' Doing it sober may, however, be just a memory. Tempting fate means that you are constantly gambling, sometimes winning small victories which give hope of greater gains. The sting in the tail comes the moment you meet forces stronger than your own. Alcoholics in recovery are the first to testify to this.

Professional standards impose enough discipline on the self to create the sort of freedom that consistency allows. This is not discipline for the sake of rigid control – it is the way to make spontaneous expression easiest.

Eliminating Outdated Criticisms and Humiliations

The memory of any performer includes unpleasant thoughts of:

- A time when he played badly.
- One or a number of musical disasters in performing situations.
- Criticism by others of his poor standard.

Such memories may be few or many, recent or early. Since nobody is born with the ability to play it is achieved by making a large number of mistakes. When these mistakes or humiliations are in public, the memory may be a particularly difficult one to eradicate. The major steps towards dealing with this are:

1) Accepting that mistakes are part of the process of learning.
2) Accepting that critical or sadistic people exist and may tend to pick on people without considering their feelings. This is your problem only if you let it be. You can either take steps to avoid such people or, if this is impossible, take steps to cut yourself off emotionally from them. This is done by consistently reminding yourself that this is their problem.
3) Dealing with stage fright to eliminate or neutralise the memories of unpleasant performing situations (*see Chapter Six*).
4) Thoroughly familiarising yourself with your present standard of performance and musicianship, and not allowing yourself to be dragged down by memories of past insufficiencies. These belong in their rightful place – the past.

Learning How to Deal with Failure

The first step in dealing with failure is to put it into perspective. A 'bad performance' is not a catastrophe – it cannot be compared to a real catastrophe such as an earthquake, war, sudden heart attack, or destructive fire.

The second step is to know how to manage failure. When learning to sail a dinghy, you practise capsizing then righting it; in judo, you learn to fall; and regular fire drills are essential in all large buildings. Situations are manageable – even predictable – when you know the routine for dealing with failure. They start to become nerve-racking or dangerous when you have not read the 'how to fail' manual from cover to cover.

It is unfortunate that the idea of 'the pursuit of excellence' proclaimed by music colleges and others does not start with a thorough training in how to fail and start again, how to rationalise failure and go forward rather than panicking and being knocked sideways. The same applies to parents who reward cleverness and achievement but who may simply not have the ability to deal with setbacks or failures or pass on this knowledge to their children.

Do not be afraid of failure – like wrong notes when improvising it can lead you in more constructive directions. The capacity to see failures in scale, to accept them and then go forward to greater things is one of the key qualities of winners – whether in music, in sport or in life.

• Matching Expectations to Reality

When your own expectations match the reality of your work, you achieve maximum harmony. This applies not only to your career expectations but also to each gig. On any level, from Carnegie Hall to village hall, if the musicians and the audience all feel that something of value has been given and gratefully received, then satisfaction is appropriate. Perhaps the goal of the musician is 'beyond' present reality, but do not underestimate the pleasure people get out of coming to hear live music. Nor should you underestimate the part they play in determining what aspects of the musician's playing get the best responses. If audiences laugh, we have a Victor Borge in the making, if they applaud elegance, a Liberace, if they go for rebelliousness, a Nigel Kennedy, if they like the grand gesture, a Paganini. Such shaping is realistic because it is in tune with objective reality. If the performer is happy with that direction, then it is clear that it works.

Other People

The difficulty comes when you try to match your expectations not to reality but to the expectations of other people who are frequently far from objective. The true arbiter of performance is the music itself, and the only expectation should be to play it right. When expectations are set by people, they can be encouraging but they can equally well be very damaging. The musician is expected to enter a sort of musical league table, competing against sisters, cousins, the boy in the next class up, fellow students listening at the door of practice rooms, a famous parent, a teacher with a 'method', an insatiable mother, a biased critic, a sensation-seeking journalist...the list goes on and on.

The musician is all too easily 'shaped' by expectations. He may know, for example, that the musicians he respects the most – his role models – believe that 'Bach should be played on original instruments'. He then internalises their opinion, and applies it to others in a critical way without really questioning why.

The worst shaping comes from the subjective comments of others who ignore the personal tastes and ambitions of the musician. This can be imposed by parents who say 'jazz is just a horrible noise' to the jazz-loving child, or by teachers with strongly held views who do not bother to find out what the musician's natural likes are before moulding him into another shape. It can be done by well-meaning people saying 'I can see you at your dressing table, ready to walk onto the stage and sing', when the actual steps to that goal (practice, rehearsal, badly paid gigs, better-paid gigs and so on) have been completely overlooked.

Throughout his career the musician will experience comments for and against his playing. Some are constructive, some biased nonsense. Following your own gut feelings and getting your musical direction right early in your career is vital to building on the strengths of you own vision – after all, neither parents, teachers nor anyone else can play the music for you.

Self-expectations

It is natural to set high self-expectations, but there is a difference between an achievable high point and a fantasy. The wish 'if only I could play like... (best in profession)' is basically hero worship. Although this may have some function in setting levels of ambition, make sure that such ambitions are constructive ones and not delusions. An inner conviction that you are wonderful, based on childhood expectations, is pointless if it does not correspond to achievable levels of performance. Such fantasies are a handicap, and should be confronted fairly ruthlessly. This may also mean taking decisive steps to disbelieve irrational ideas of superiority that you have learned from your family. These may simply be hopes that you would go further than they ever did, or quite uncritical levels of praise compared to your own reality.

When stripped of fantasy, reality may look pretty disappointing, but it is a crucial basis from which to improve. Simply repeating to yourself 'this is what I can do now – tomorrow I could do more' sets standards for self-improvement. Nobody is born playing the scale of C-major. Reality means learning first one level of playing then a higher level.

Is there a problem with admitting reality? Being constantly open to improvement seems a very attractive and open-ended idea. Maybe the word 'reality' itself is difficult for imaginative people. Getting an imaginative artist to accept the virtues of reality may be like asking a claustrophobic person to enjoy potholing. Is there some rebellious part of us that finds reality distasteful and restrictive? The maximum potential of what we can do ('how fast we can run when pursued by a lion') is in fact a lot higher than we imagine, so a consistent response to reality does not in itself imply anything 'average'.

The problem is with something else – fantasy and perfectionism. If we reserve the 'upper levels' of our talent for our fantasy, then a consistent reality of performance will be worse than our fantasy. By maintaining our actual standard of reality we are admitting to ourselves that 'this is how we actually play'. Reality is our 'best shot'. When we put this to the test we find that others use us as musicians for our actual playing, not our fantasy, and there are no real ways around this. Internally we may want more, but we are judged by what we deliver. In international competitions, consistency is further stressed, as doing well involves the career reality of producing reliable results over a long string of engagements.

When you have decided what you want to do, then build the house from the bottom up, not the top down. Whatever your present level of work, accept it as reality, and then set about making it better. Wherever you are you can improve. Forget perfection and abstract ideas of who you 'ought to be in an ideal world'. Match your self-esteem to the actual reality of your work. If your self-esteem is lower than the level of your work, then it should be higher. If it is higher, then you may be deluding yourself. If – as is usual – it is sometimes higher and sometimes lower, then fixing it on the level of reality avoids at the same time the pain of self-doubt and the delusion of grandeur.

• Maintaining Self-confidence

Musicians are particularly concerned with their standard of playing, for obvious reasons. According to a survey of popular musicians carried out by British psychologist and musician Geoff Wills*, the most stressful factor they encountered was 'Feeling you must reach or maintain the standards of musicianship that you set for yourself'. Over half the musicians surveyed claimed to suffer in this way. This simple fact tells us an important thing: musicians strive for high standards, and feel they are inconsistent in reaching them.

Reaching the standards you set for yourself is a question of maximising your motivation and matching your ambitions to reality. Maintaining it is a matter of having confidence in your ability, so that you are put off as little as possible by the constant variations in performing situations and the ups and downs of a musical career.

Maintaining a professionally satisfying standard brings us to the idea of consistency – being able to rely on a 'constant' source of ability which is always at your disposal.

Creating the Constant Self

It may not occur to musicians to 'create' a part of themselves which can be defined and relied on, yet others will already have done this. Musicians are employed regularly by others for the qualities with which they are uniquely associated. To others, they produce these qualities over and over again in their performances. Acquiring a 'constant' self-image is therefore part of reality.

The idea of consistency has another virtue: it directly confronts many of the problems inherent in anxiety, which is:

- Vague – we 'cannot fight what we do not know'.
- Internal and subjective, so does not accurately predict reality.
- Increased by the unpredictability of life events.
- Vulnerable to the ups and downs of our moods and surroundings.

*See *Pressure Sensitive* (Sage Books)

The 'constant' self is used as a defence against all the external and internal variables the musician usually feels so vulnerable to: the variables encountered in performance, and the variable nature of one's own self-esteem.

To identify our 'constant' qualities we can turn them into a list, then contrast this list with another list of the 'variable' factors we see as disturbing the consistency of our music-making.

The constant self is built around:

- Ability and technique.
- Talent, inspiration, musicality and creativity.
- Self-esteem and inner conviction of worth.
- Peer rating: feedback of our standards by fellow musicians.
- Career rating: assessment by the standard of work we are offered.
- Capacity consistently to reproduce something near our ability.
- Personal qualities and the ability to deal with life events.

Unstable variables consist of both internal and external factors. Internal ones measure our own areas of vulnerability, such as:

- Variables in own performing state: tiredness, stress, jet-lag, alcohol or drugs, how we react to life events on the day of performance.
- Variable personal effectiveness: difficulties in coping with life events, susceptibility to career stresses or stage fright, health and general stress.

External variables include specific performance stressors such as acoustics, instrument, stage placing, equipment, touring factors, overall loudness or the inability to hear properly. A particular stressor is the presence of critical or disturbing human elements in or outside the band: conductor, fellow musicians, members of audience, partner, friends, family and teachers. These people usually fall into three categories:

- Disturbing: negative or critical people. It sometimes requires considerable vigilance to detach yourself from their influence.
- Neutral: these people may not give positive feedback, but nei-

ther do they give destructive criticism.

- Inspirational: these people make life easier for those around them, and are often sought after as fellow musicians and indeed friends. The importance of inspirational people is that they allow you to be yourself.

CASE HISTORY

Here is an illustration of the factors that make up the 'constant self' and 'unstable variables'. The musician concerned is a principal player in a professional orchestra who also does freelance work. He suffers from intermittent performance anxiety but has played through many nervous performances with at worst some occasional missed notes. For many years he has played at the top of his profession. What is perceived as a weakness is in reality an ability to cope with high stress levels. While these should be reduced for the sake of comfort, the capacity to survive them is still worthy of note, and therefore an ability.

The musician's 'constant self' comprises the following:

- Technique: good.
- Sight-reading: good. Prefers to see part sometimes, but can read first time.
- Leadership ability: good. Can do principal parts.
- Musicality: good. Complemented by peers and others.
- Reliability: good. High coping skills, recognised by others.
- Experience: good. Thousands of performances.
- Versatility: good. Clarinets, saxes and flute, plus light music, bands etc.
- Competitiveness: good. Determined not to be put off.
- Capacity for dealing with crises: good. Can play through feelings of considerable distress.

The variables that this musician needs to guard against are:

- Venue: certain concert halls cause discomfort.
- Conductors and personalities: some work still needs to be done to banish memories of humiliations at the hands of over-critical conductors and to avoid internalising their

negativity.

- Rehearsals: there are some bad memories of rehearsals which need to be forgotten.
- Catastrophising: he has a tendency to perfectionism and over-dramatising mistakes. The reality is not nearly as bad as fantasy suggests. Disasters have never occurred, and bad performances have been rare.
- Long struggle to become established: the response to this is 'you made it in the end. Well done'.
- Perfectionism: there is a need to concentrate more on talent and less on failings. Everyone makes mistakes, and in this case mistakes are rare.
- Lack of pleasure in music-making: Too much concentration on duty, control and accuracy has meant some sacrifice of pleasure in the performing situation. In addition, some boredom and lack of motivation may be the result of heavy schedules, repetitive or superficial repertoire and several years in the business. Freshness needs to be brought into music-making by better listening and a more open and relaxed awareness.
- Tiredness and stress: Heavy schedules and a family at home have meant frequent rehearsals where concentration has been a struggle. This has contributed to the lack of freshness and to feelings of being below potential, which have been misinterpreted as ability-related performance anxiety.

Maximising the Constant Self

After making up two such lists, the next step is to maximise the constant self and minimise the variables. This can be done by moving parts of the 'variable' list into the 'constant' list when the variables are sufficiently controllable. The result is confidence built around a realistic self-image corresponding to your typical level of performance, and one which should closely mirror the image others have of your ability and playing.

When doing this, try to remain objective by neither overestimating nor underestimating yourself. Many of us are optimists, believing like Mr Micawber that 'something will always turn up', or like Dr Pangloss that 'all is for the best'. Many of us are pessimists, tending to dwell on our shortcomings and turn physical ailments into hypochondria. Try to be a realist. If you have a tendency to 'fake good', allow for it by questioning your positive qualities – are they real and evident in your playing and career? If you have a tendency to 'fake bad', look carefully at your negative qualities – are they really that bad? And look again at your positive qualities – have you left some out?

Dealing with Unstable Variables

In a healthy order of priorities, music, the profession and yourself come before other people and audiences. The priorities for a musician are remarkably similar to those taught in many professions, particularly health care:

1) The Profession: loyalty and respect for the art and profession of being a musician comes first. This represents its standards, ethics, history and personalities, and the simple joy of music itself. Good music-making is an ideal to live up to and a reference when in doubt.
2) Yourself: loyalty to your own goals and artistic direction comes second to the ideal of being a musician – this is what keeps your standards high and your heart in the right place. Your priorities towards yourself include mental, physical and artistic self-preservation, and fulfilment of your career plan. You are irreplaceable, and are more important to yourself than audiences who come and go. As Timothy Gallwey says, 'the person should play the game, not the game the person'.
3) Other people: other musicians, audiences, audition panels, teachers, agents, managers and critics come last. Although they play their part, they should not dominate you or the quality of your music.

The reason for this hierarchy is that the profession represents the most constant set of values, followed by your own values. The most variable and unreliable standards are those represented by other people. A professional musician is loyal to the music and to himself. An unprofessional musician with no respect for the music and a poor sense of self is of little use to his public or anyone else. Realising this enables the musician to set boundaries such as not playing without professional preparation, not overusing or misusing the body, and not allowing himself to be needlessly intimidated by fellow musicians, audiences, audition panels, critics and agents.

Dealing with Anxiety over Fellow Musicians

One of the most stressful environmental factors in the musician's life can be dealing with difficult fellow professionals. This applies not only within the general pool of freelance players but also, and in particular, when touring and spending a lot of time with a regular band or classical orchestra. Typical of this is the tendency for critical or aggressive fellow players to get 'under your skin' and cause feelings of anxious insecurity.

Dealing with feelings of being criticised or put down brings us into the sphere of suspiciousness and criticism. We know from the 16PF (*see page 7*) that musicians have elevated critical tendencies and mild-to-pronounced suspicious feelings of others. We also know that criticism is internalised as self-criticism, directed onto other musicians, and then projected back as a feeling that others are constantly critical of you. Experience of counselling a number of orchestral players shows that friction between personalities is a very prevalent problem area, and can undermine a whole section of an orchestra.

Popular musicians are also sensitive to 'attitude problems' because they already have a history of being manipulated, tricked and exploited. On top of this is professional envy, jealousy and the worry that other players are after your work. At worst, musicians can see each other as 'cynical', 'two-faced', 'greedy', 'ego-tripping' or simply 'always taking the piss'. Extraverts are wary of introverts; poor, idealistic musicians are wary of rich, commercial ones; piss-takers of serious types; laid-back ones of those that are well-organised. In addition, musicians are collectively wary about band-leaders, management, agents, record companies and so on – often for the good reason that their goal is to make money out of musicians. So the criticism and suspicion goes round and round – everyone complains and everyone suffers but little effort is made actually to reduce the general pool of criticism or make the musical world a less paranoid place to live in.

THE FUNDAMENTAL ATTRIBUTION ERROR

One way of dealing with this problem is by seeing all these opinions, attitudes and suspicions as 'attributions'. An attribution describes any behaviour that you 'attribute' to somebody or something. Behaviour can on the one hand be attributed to a set of circumstances – 'he's angry because his car was towed away this morning' or on the other hand to a person's inner motives – 'he's angry because he thinks I can't play the music correctly'.

The problem occurs when situational reasons are confused with people's motives. We interpret people's anger as displeasure with us, their tired looks as boredom with us, their failure to make contact as rejection of us. All too often these assumptions are wrong, as the following true story illustrates.

A New York actor was auditioning for a musical, and came on stage just before lunchtime on the last day of auditioning. As soon as he reached the front of the stage the producer groaned and said 'Oh No!' very audibly. The actor fled the stage on the spot, and remained angry and distressed until he happened to meet the producer a few days later. 'How could you humiliate me like that in front of everybody,' he said angrily, recounting what he thought he had witnessed. The producer looked blank for a while, then his face suddenly lit up. 'Oh my God – I know what that was! We'd sent the messenger boy out for some takeaway lunch and told him on no account to bring back the tasteless junk food we'd had all week. I turned round as you came on and saw him coming towards us with yet another pile of junk-food takeaways. I must have said "Oh No!" pretty loudly – I guess you thought I meant you. Now you mention it, you auditioned very well a few months ago, and we had our eye on you for the part.'

Apart from being ridiculous when wrong, attribution errors cause us self-doubt we can well do without. The worst problem is the 'fundamental' attribution error – that of blaming ourselves for what we assume is our fault, rather than looking for causes outside ourselves. When the conductor is ratty, we assume we are playing badly. We do not realise his car was towed away that morning.

Other people's moods are known by a number of familiar terms such as 'vibes' or 'attitude problems'. We have an instinctive feeling that we do not want do deal with 'their stuff', but we may need to really train ourselves to disconnect our own feelings from the moods of others.

As little children we will have blamed mummy's bad moods on our 'naughty' behaviour, and we have a lot of unlearning to do to be free of this almost unconscious self-blaming tendency.

DEALING WITH ATTRIBUTION ERRORS

The first stage in retraining is simply to remind ourselves constantly that there are all sorts of possible reasons for the moods or actions of others. Had the New York actor done so he might have got the part. So do not start with the assumption you are in the wrong.

The second stage is to find out what other people's motivations actually are. Ask them, interpret their actions, look for reasons. Find alternative attributions for your feelings.

The third stage is to create 'boundaries' between the moods of others and yourself. See fellow musicians as 'inside their skins'. Do this by visualising their emotions and personality 'contained' inside their skin, so they stop at the boundary of their skins. When you do this they will seem life-size, and will not 'spill over' or 'spread' towards you. Constantly remind yourself of this.

When other people seem angry, negative or critical, this may first and foremost be a function of their own situation and feelings, and possibly their own inability to cope with their problems. People in the grip of inner problems are naturally inflexible, unsociable, defensive or aggressive. By not responding to their bad moods you not only save yourself unnecessary grief, you are also more likely to bring them out of their negative emotions into the more positive emotion that you are projecting. All this helps cut out the negative feedback that can go round and round when the performing environment seems loaded with bad feelings.

CRITICISM AND GENEROSITY

The highly developed internal critic in each musician has two usual functions:

1) Setting standards for himself and judging whether he lives up to them.
2) Criticising other musicians for not reaching standards.

The second function is a 'projection' of self-criticism onto others, and comes from the same source. Musicians paradoxically under-rate how much they are critical of others, just as they underrate their own competitiveness.

Generosity is the complete antidote to criticism. By positively allowing other musicians to play as they feel inclined to, and supporting them in the directions in which they want to go, much can be contributed to the collective happiness of music-making. Duke Ellington demonstrated this to the world in his uniquely generous band arrangements. Generosity is not just one of the fundamentals of ego-less performing and a non-judgemental attitude, it is the main secret of making other musicians 'feel good'. And as American saxophonist Cannonball Adderley used to say, 'fun is what happens when everything is mellow'. Feeling good is often the reason that lies behind hiring certain musicians time and time again. Musicians who 'feel bad' are doing something to decrease everyone's ability to play – 'if you are not part of the solution you are part of the problem', as black Americans succinctly put it.

Putting down other musicians can be deliberately avoided. This was demonstrated in a *Downbeat* magazine 'blindfold test' in which American saxophonist Sam Rivers awarded five stars to every piece of music 'because the musicians deserve that much for surviving in this business'. His interviewer was perplexed with his 'uncritical' response because it was unprecedented. There is a need for standards in music-making, if only to establish goals towards which to strive. Respecting such goals can, however, go together with supporting fellow musicians.

Close Proximity

Life can be distressing when it involves spending a lot of time with someone you don't get on with at all. A musician may find himself touring with such a person, and having to put up with him at rehearsals, concerts and social situations, and perhaps having to listen to criticism from him as well. Musicians in major orchestras have been known to walk off stage, argue out loud and even have recurring nightmares as a result of having to spend long hours right next to someone whose behaviour they find impossible.

Besides creating emotional boundaries it may also be necessary to create working boundaries between what you will and will not stand for, so that the other person knows your limits; and between his time and yours, so he does not interfere with you off the bandstand.

It is difficult to say what is the most effective way of dealing with the consistently annoying fellow musician. One way is the 'short sharp shock' of confronting the musician face to face, alone or in front of others, and telling him exactly what he is doing, and what you are not prepared to tolerate. Another way is constant lack of response, or the 'silent treatment' used by the Inuit to discipline their children. To be effective the latter has to be completely consistent and predictable, so that the lack of response extinguishes any point in the behaviour. Perhaps the best approach is a mixture of assertiveness and negotiating skills, which are included in Chapter Nine.

Other issues relevant to this chapter are discussed in more detail later. For dealing with stressful performance factors, *see Chapter Six*; for dealing with internal conflicts, *see Chapter Three* ; and for dealing with career stressors, *see Chapter Seven.*

Affirming Your Personal Effectiveness

The essential self-affirmations of confidence are:

- Reminding yourself that genuine catastrophes practically never occur.
- Reminding yourself that some level of discomfort can be coped with and is not in itself a 'disaster' in the making.
- Reminding yourself that it is quite possible to 'grow out of' earlier mistakes and inadequacies as these are progressively dealt with in counselling and self-help procedures, and that past mistakes will not materialise like ghosts to haunt performances.
- Rewarding your progress and telling yourself 'well done' more often.
- Reminding yourself regularly of the pleasure of music-making by allowing yourself to experience real joy in music. If necessary this may mean playing favourite music in your free time simply for the pleasure it gives.

Positive Psyching-up

By reminding yourself of your 'constant' self you can psych yourself up against the presence of fellow musicians who put you off your playing. The internal conversation may go: 'I feel nervous. He puts me off my playing. He has always been critical of me. I feel this affecting my playing already. My bow-arm is unsteady. I'm sure I'll start to shake and my bow will jump.'

In response to this external stressor, you defend yourself with what you know to be your constant abilities: 'I could play this morning when I practised. I was asked to do the gig because I can play it. Other musicians think I'm a good player. If I really think about it, I'm better than he thinks I am. That's his problem if he's critical. I'm going to play this like I usually do.'

The timing of this reaction is important; to avoid any build up of insecurity it should occur almost simultaneously with the thoughts that are disturbing you. Otherwise mental anxiety may translate into physical nervousness, travel down the neck and arm, and cause effects like bow-shake.

The same rationalisation can be made for audiences: 'The audience puts me off. However, when I think about, it I can still play this better than anyone in the audience can. That's why I'm on the stage and they aren't.' It can also be made for audition panels: 'What if some of the audition panel can play better than me? So what? They are not playing – I am.'

Using Practice to Improve Self-esteem

Practice is the key not only to playing ability but to self-confidence, and those who attempt to do without it are tempting fate. Practice is a particularly 'conscious' time, unlike performing, which may be trance-like in quality. During this period of consciousness it is possible to accomplish several important things:

- Work on technical variables so they can constantly be produced correctly.
- Develop confidence through playing passages several times correctly, so reinforcing self-awareness of having succeeded.
- Practise several possible variations on a piece which is going to be performed, so allowing the choice of how to play it on

the night to be made spontaneously according to what feels best and fits with the other musicians as they are playing it.
- Work on positive cognitive beliefs, starting with 'I am good at this' and 'I can do this' and taking in 'I am a meaningful and good person' and 'people will appreciate me and like me, as well as liking what I do'.

Eliminating technical variables means practising vulnerable parts of your playing deliberately and slowly until they improve to the point where they can be depended on. This means owning up to weaknesses and working on them, and abandoning thoughts that 'if it were not for certain aspects of my playing I would be really good'. There is no place for 'if only' excuses in consistency. On the contrary, it has to be assumed that in performance any movements must be automatic, so in practice all details have to be correctly rehearsed. Performance must take place in a state of total readiness. Only in this state can the performer hope to access the higher levels of trance-like 'peak' performance where all details are magically correct and fit into a spontaneous flow of inspiration.

The goal of practice is to eliminate stress, so any expected stress points in a performance must be eliminated in practice. At the end of practice periods there should be a good feeling, not an anticipation of disaster. This good feeling has a cumulative effect, the point of which is to reinforce the self-belief of being OK in performance. So practise confidence – do not practise stress. Practice periods that end in gloom and despondency must be avoided – they have the opposite effect of reinforcing or 'conditioning' helplessness.

Positive practice is a habit that many professionals – including older orchestral players – have fallen out of. This is unwise because practice is needed to keep limbs and mind fluent; and lack of practice breaks down the intimate contact between the self and the music. Confidence is very effective when built up in the intimate hours of practice and self-communication. This is also the best time to rehearse feelings of self-worth and self-affirmation, when your ability and stylistic identity can be thoroughly felt and internalised in the comfort of your home or rehearsal studio. Professionals with heavy touring schedules may be tempted to leave out practice due to travelling arrangements, but a number of top professionals make a habit of getting in at least an hour of practice before going on stage, in order to feel ready mentally, and fluent in their fingers (or vocal cords). If top people like guitarist Pat Metheny do this, it is making a statement about how beneficial it is to affirm your ability constantly.

• The Template for Self-confidence

This following template (*see Figure 4.1*) is to help you draw up your own list of your constant coping qualities, on the one hand, and the unstable characteristics of career and life events on the other. By using it you can monitor how well you are coping at any moment in your career.

Your constant qualities should typically remain stable or improve. The unstable factors should go up or down. At some moments you will need to cope more, at others you should feel naturally confident. Use the constant self to affirm your abilities to yourself. Use the unstable variables to determine accurately what you have to deal with. Do not overestimate their power to unsettle you, but at the same time allow for their existence. If, for example, you simultaneously have to cope with a number of destabilising factors – say, tiredness, stress and relationship problems – then deal with these problems separately.

Do not assume that natural life events can 'destroy' your constant abilities. Your talent and personal effectiveness are always with you. Trust them, and allow them to work in your favour.

THE CONSTANT SELF	UNSTABLE VARIABLES
Personality Traits	**Anxiety**
Management qualities	Stress and tiredness
Awareness qualities	
Musical ability	**Career stresses**
Intonation	Fame
Technique	Lack of artistic fulfilment
Sight-reading	Professional insecurity
Rhythm	Financial insecurity
Aural ability	
Creative expressive ability	**Life Stresses**
Creativity	Health problems
Musicality	Relationship problems
	Family problems
	Loss or bereavement
Personal Effectiveness	**Motivation Problems**
Leadership	Catastrophising
Independence	Childhood curses and injunctions
Judgement	Fear of success or failure
Experience	Approach-avoidance
Energy	Low self-esteem
Competitiveness	Other people's expectations
Commitment	
Versatility	
Team spirit	**Interpersonal difficulties**
Reliability	Discomfort with fellow musicians
Coping Strategies	Career clashes with others
Humour	Sensitivity to criticism
Control	Difficult conductors
Tolerance of ambiguity	
Toughing it out	**Performance Variables**
	Tours
Business Qualities	Equipment malfunction
Assertiveness	Venues
Negotiating ability	Acoustics
Financial ability	Instrument malfunction
Promotional ability	
Self-management	

Figure 4.1. This template lists both constant and variable qualities. Use it to draw up a list of your own strengths and weaknesses.

5 Self-management, Zen and the Inner Game

There are two main philosophies, both with a long cultural history, that are important to the musician. One is based on control and management and is largely favoured in the West; the other is based on awareness and openness, and has been made popular by Eastern schools of thought. Both have strong benefits for particular aspects of the musical profession, and certain drawbacks for others.

• Management and Awareness Models

The 'Management' style gives us the self-management skills we need: assertiveness, negotiation, career-planning, book-keeping, musical technique, and the ability to analyse and solve our problems objectively. The 'Awareness' style gives us the performance skills that depend on listening to and taking in the whole playing experience, not just our part in it. These are found in the 'Inner Game' technique and 'Zen' attitudes.

The Awareness model, from which Zen and the Inner Game are derived, is defined by many philosophies and methods that emphasise two main elements:

1) A 'holistic' view of the world, stressing the interaction of all elements, and the 'flow' of such interactions and events over time.
2) The need for all individual elements in this holistic activity to understand and be 'aware' of the nature and consequences of their actions.

Holistic activity is like an 'ant hill' where individual ants are aware of their part in the complexity of their overall culture. It is also like the 'horizontal' or non-hierarchical example of a team game. This interdependence is sometimes called a 'bootstrap' model – when we pull the straps on a boot, one end tightens everything else up, and if we pull in the middle it pulls the ends in. Any activity anywhere in the process 'acts on' and changes all the rest of the process. No man is an island – everything in the universe is connected to everything else. The relevance of this to collective music-making is obvious.

Further aspects of this holistic model can be found in all the Zen literature, and in philosophers such as Hegel and Heraclitus (*c.*500 BC) whose surviving fragments include sayings such as 'everything flows and nothing stays' and 'you cannot step twice into the same river' (i.e. the water in a river is constantly changing). It has found a lot of favour recently within the ecological and holistic movements. *

This model is often contrasted with the cause-and-effect approach, sometimes referred to as the 'Western' model. Because it forms the basis of European science and thought, it is also called a Newtonian model (after Isaac Newton) or a Cartesian model (after Descartes). It conforms to the scientist's desire to control or manage events, and produce predictable and repeatable experimental results which are 'isolated' as much as possible from external factors or 'variables'.

Such a 'cause-and-effect' model is easier to deal with than the holistic one since it tries to be as focused as possible, to eliminate 'everything else'. The problem is that 'everything else' is still going on and may be partly unaccounted for. This is like the performing situation where the musician is aware of the 'cause and effect' of his own playing but less so of 'everything else going on'.

For those who like simple solutions, and to 'control' events to get predictable results, it is difficult to move from the cause-and-effect approach to a more complex conceptual model. This is also a difficult step for those in the 'pursuit of excellence' culture, which puts less emphasis on 'equality and fraternity' and more on the 'freedom' of the individual. Despite the rise of a substantial ecological movement, our prevailing philosophy is still a 'vertical' or hier-

*Another source that may be of interest is Kapra's *The Tao of Physics* (Fontana, 1975), in which the holistic model is applied to sub-atomic particle theory.

archical one, expressed as 'anyone can be President of the United States', or 'there are winners and losers in life'.

In terms of the performer, this Management model contains some of the following ideas:

- I act on things.
- The better I get at acting on things the more I influence things in my favour.
- As I become more successful than others at acting on things, I acquire more power and influence than they do.
- My superior power and influence give me control over my life, my goals and my environment.

This emphasis on the person controlling the environment is typical of psychologist J. Rotter's 'internal locus of control', whereby a person feels that life events are directed mainly by his choices, rather than by the environment or the 'external locus of control'. The importance of being a 'winner' is very prevalent in the United States, and can also be found in other societies where individual wealth and success are valued. In a holistic model, however, there is a loser for every winner. One of the cornerstone philosophies of Western business practice is to make individual gains (or 'profit') at the expense of the total environment.

The Awareness model contains some of the following ideas:

- Things act on me.
- The more aware I become of the infinite flow and wholeness of all parts of the experience called 'life', the more my awareness and understanding of it increases.
- Increased awareness and understanding makes me more 'in tune with' natural events.
- Being in tune with natural events makes my actions right for both myself and my environment.
- Harmony between all elements in the natural world increases the overall quality of life of these individual elements, and is more likely to satisfy their collective needs.

Such a model is 'passively aware' rather than controlling, and proceeds via listening, noticing and understanding. It responds to events by creating new elements that fit into the whole, and emphasises self-knowledge, study and an 'ego-less' state of humility as the means of achieving 'mastery' over one's environment. It emphasises the way things naturally happen, as in the Buddhist term 'karma'.

The Awareness model, like the Management one, has many additional philosophic, scientific, cultural and religious variations and flavours. Associated belief systems include:

- Reincarnation – all beings are connected to each other through the flow of time.
- Astrology – we are influenced by the position and movement of elements in the universe.
- Paranormal or ESP (extrasensory perception) phenomena – there are forms of communication that have been subjectively experienced which have no objective explanation.

These additional beliefs are a matter of personal taste, and can be treated on a 'take it or leave it' basis. You can choose not to believe in a number of the spiritual expressions of this model while still adhering in its essential core: that life is a complex inter-related activity, and that passive awareness of it produces understanding and harmony.

• The Awareness or Zen Personality

The Zen personality is much the same as that suggested by W. Timothy Gallwey in his 'Inner Game' method*. Significantly, it is also the commonest 'artistic' personality found in the Myers–Briggs Type Indicator (*see Chapter One*):

- Introvert – introspective, passive, understanding.
- Intuitive – complex, imaginative, holistic.
- Feeling – non-verbal, subjective, non-analytical.
- Perceptive – open, spontaneous, non-judgemental, non-planning.

*See the *Inner Game of Music*, and other *Inner Game* books by Timothy Gallwey (published by Pan).

The first two preferences are slightly paradoxical. Although the introverted personality is thought to be more conducive to creativity and more common in meditative pursuits, Zen would strictly speaking not consider that this duality existed: it would state that there is no internal or external, no inside or outside to the mind. It favours both inner meditative awareness and awareness of the whole outer world of the senses. In meditation, for example, the eyes are half-closed, focusing neither inward nor outward. The Inner Game tends to share this.

In the artistic personality the second preference is very strongly for Intuition, which provides the creativity and imagination that underlies practically all art. The philosophic nature of Zen, and its sudden creative insights, is also nearer to the 'intuitive' preference. Paradoxically, however, Zen appears to favour the senses heavily. Since enlightenment may involve difficult conceptual leaps into the unknown, the journey towards it may actually be through the imagination and meditative contemplation back to the senses.

Zen is certainly not about materialism in the sense of permanent objects with independent forms for which people feel greed. Its fundamental idea that all nature is a complex system or whole made of 'ten thousand' particles, all in a state of flow, is simple but at the same time more abstract than many would be able to grasp. So the world of sensation means 'every level of sensation, emotion, intuition and reason at one time' (*Zen for Beginner's*, referred to from now on as *ZFB*). Strictly speaking, Zen would again not admit there could be a dualism between Sensing and Intuition: 'To see dualism in life is due to confusion of thought. The enlightened see into the reality of things unhampered by ideas' (Hui-neng).

In Zen, intellectual analysis is one of the principal traps of the mind, and much effort is made to free one of it in favour of the actual living experience, so the preference here is for 'feeling'. This is also true of the Inner Game, in which 'thinking' is close to Self 1 (interference), while 'feeling' is nearer to Self 2 (naturalness, trust).

Zen clearly favours the spontaneous attitude, and the concept of the universe in a constant state of flow and change. It also teaches openness to this flow as the means of true understanding of and being at one with the universe. In terms of Inner Game theory, there is an equally strong bias towards the 'open and absorbing attitude'. Judging is nearer to Self 1 (interference), while 'perceiving' is close to Self 2 (awareness).

The Managing Personality

Typically esteemed in Western culture, the Managing personality is most commonly found in high-school males in the United States and, not surprisingly, in managers. It is a typical 'managerial' or 'controlling' personality, and the 'thinking' part of it is typically masculine (as opposed to the 'feeling' preference which is more common in American females). The Managing personality is the following, in terms of the Myers–Briggs Type Indicator:

- Extravert – outer-directed.
- Sensing – realistic, objective, favouring tried-and-tested, step-by-step procedures.
- Thinking – analytical, favouring logic over feelings.
- Judging – making judgements and decisions to achieve goals.

Management skills have heavily permeated the culture of business and free enterprise, and show more signs of increasing than of decreasing in a world of technology and intensive trade. The success of the East in world trade, however, shows that Western cultures are far from achieving a monopoly of business supremacy, particularly in respect of the holistic working environments of the Japanese.

Zen and the Peak Performing Experience

Zen is probably the best explanation yet of the musical 'peak experience'. This happens during certain special performances when the flow of the music has a magical rightness, the mind seems to have a heightened awareness of the music itself, and nothing else seems to intrude on concentration. The following quotes are from *ZFB*.

The true Zen state has been described as:

Always master of the situation, completely free to respond in any way, but at the same time totally involved in what is happening. In what is seen there must just be the seen; in what is heard there must just be the heard; in what is sensed there must just be the sensed; in what is thought there must just be the thought.

Through this state one can reach the ultimate state of absorption:

There are simply two degrees of absorption. Mindfulness is a state wherein one is totally aware in any situation and so always able to respond appropriately – yet one is aware of being aware. Mindlessness, on the other hand, or 'no-mindedness' as it has been called, is a condition of such complete absorption that there is no vestige of self-awareness.

While the mind may start by focusing on certain elements, it passes to a holistic awareness:

Try not to localise the mind anywhere, but let it fill up the whole body, let it flow throughout the totality of your being. When this happens you use the hands where they are needed, you use the legs or the eyes where they are needed, and no time or energy will go to waste.

Zen emphasises the 'once only' nature of experience. Every performance is a once-only event – if we experience it fully our actions are 100-per-cent meaningful. It also emphasises the 'ego-less' quality of the perfect experience. The 'I' does not interfere in enlightenment, in which the death of those psychological patterns called the 'ego' is referred to as the 'great death'. Without the ego there is no division of experience into subject and object – 'because the mind has no definite form it can so freely act in every form'.

• Awareness and the Inner Game

The *Inner Game* series of books has been a great help to sportspeople and musicians. Designed for sportspeople, its theories were first applied by W. Timothy Gallwey to golf and tennis, and later to skiing. In the meantime they were applied to musicians by the American classical double-bass player Barry Green in *The Inner Game of Music*. We all owe a debt of gratitude to what is an accepted and effective way of improving skills and attitudes for performers of all disciplines.

Like many aspects of human knowledge, the Inner Game technique owes, in its turn, a debt of gratitude to its precursors, particularly to Zen and its centuries of tradition, and may be seen as a contemporary adaptation of its essential precepts.

The term 'awareness' is chosen in the Inner Game to describe the passively aware state similar to what is achieved by Zen meditation and by musicians who listen in an ego-less way. This global awareness is called Self 2, and the 'interference' mental activity is called Self 1. The preferred self, Self 2, is therefore open, non-judgemental and takes in the whole external experience, not just parts of it mixed in with one's internal brain activity. It responds to the flow of the music and its overall shape, and so tends to be right-brain spatial rather than left-brain analytic. It also focuses on the moment, being in the 'now' rather than the 'what if'.

In sporting activities, such as golf and tennis, external awareness is simpler because all the external cues are visual. It is easy to 'watch the ball' and see the whole game revolve around it. The position and flight of the ball carry most of the cues needed to hit it accurately, and there is no need for internal dialogues and speculations in playing it. In the moment of hitting the ball, where it is going, what the opponent is doing or how the racket is being held are distractions to the 'flow' of the ball. The same is true of visual awareness in driving – watching the road ahead shows the flow of the traffic and how you need to react to it.

In driving, awareness of the flow of traffic also reduces the ego to a passive state. The focus is on others, not the self. The exercise of 'power and control' by the automaniac is ultimately self-destructive because all the danger signals are in the external environment. The wise driver watches constantly, realising that he is vulnerable at all times. This vulnerability is one of our basic biological instincts: the animal in the jungle is constantly monitoring the sound of birds and other animals for the presence of the tiger; the animal drinking at a water hole is constantly looking around. The illusion that we are all-powerful leads to arrogance and disasters, and the whole of the martial arts emphasises exactly the same silencing of the ego and awareness of the action around us. The same is true of skiing, which is the subject of a further *Inner Game* book.

External Awareness and Music

How, then, does this external awareness relate to music? Unlike driving or skiing, music is not a dangerous activity, but it does require vigilance to external cues. The difference between music and all of the above, however, is that it is not exclusively visual, but auditory as well. The visual cues are, nevertheless, complex – if you are reading a score in an orchestra, your eyes may be partly on the conductor, partly on the score, and your vision may be taking in the instrument or the audience. Then there is the added element of sound, on which a much larger percentage of concentration needs to be focused. So 'listen to the music' is for the musician what 'watch the ball' is for the tennis player.

While 'listen to the music' works best for popular musicians, who do not have a score or a conductor to distract their visual focus, in classical musicians it needs to work together with ongoing sight-reading and attention to the conductor. In this case, the score is like a constant 'carrier frequency' around which the external music is 'modulated': the score carries the supply of information, and the player's performance is continually adjusted to the cues coming in from listening to the sounds around him.

What part of the music, then, should be listened to? Certainly not yourself to the exclusion of others (unless playing solo and unaccompanied). Many performers listen too much to themselves and too little to the overall music. They even go into collective music-making with a 'blueprint' of what they are going to play, based on what they have been working on or want to try out, regardless of what their fellow performers want to do.

Particularly in jazz, such 'ego-trippers' destroy the flow of performance and conflict with other musicians. Such a musician is effectively 'in a tunnel'. This tunnel-hearing not only cuts out essential cues in the music, it also deprives the musician of the ability to react to the flow of the music and respond with creative and unexpected solutions which fit into what others are playing. It destroys teamwork and diminishes the ability of others to be creative. Ego-tripping may result in flashy individual shows of technique, but it disables the 'best' creative ideas of the whole band. Audiences know this and respond best to the collective atmosphere of the band when it is really 'cooking'.

Great listening can mean great performances, as testimony from all styles of musicians overwhelmingly indicates. It also reduces vulnerability to stage fright and self-doubt, because shifting the focus from the internal to the external takes the weight off inner dialogues and anxieties.

WHERE TO FOCUS AWARENESS

If 'listen to the music' is the first step in awareness, 'listen to what?' is the next. The easiest and probably best answer would be 'to everything'. Some things, however, have obvious importance in themselves. These include:

1) The emotions in the music. The four main human emotions are happiness, sadness, anger and fear – most other emotions are variations on these. Some music has little obvious emotional state, the richness being in the musical 'argument'. Other music has obvious emotional content, and to make sense of it the musician needs to be aware of it and respond with the same emotion – examples are the works of Mendelssohn (happy), Rachmaninov (sad), Stravinsky's *Rite of Spring* (angry), Sibelius (afraid).
2) The rhythm in the music. In popular and jazz music, flowing with the rhythm means the difference between 'flying home' and 'trying to row the Queen Mary through an ocean of Mars bars'. In classical music, where dance rhythms underlie many compositions, it makes the difference between taut, natural rhythms with a spring to them – as Rubinstein plays Chopin – and shapeless, sentimental meanderings around a basic pulse, as some others do.

Expressiveness does not need to be outside rhythm – awareness of the rhythm can place phrases expressively within it, as Billie Holiday shows. Rhythm is not the same as tempo either – inside a fixed jazz tempo it is the individual components of the beat that matter – where the backbeat is and where the drummer is playing the hi-hat and ride cymbal. Within the same tempo, two musicians can be totally out of rhythm with each other, and the way to get the actual rhythm right is to listen. A Chicago shuffle is not the same as a New Orleans one, a Brazilian samba is not the same as a Los Angeles one. Certain beats need practice, like reggae and salsa, and practice starts with listening.

3) The sound and dynamics of the music, and the balance between instruments.
4) The meaning of the music. This may be expressed in words, with the meaning and emotions they contain; in the 'programme' content of the music, such as in Strauss's *Till Eulenspiegel*; or in the social and historical content of the music. Besides this, music itself has a natural structure with suspense and resolution, and a series of 'arguments' with phrases that question, elaborate, digress, modify or answer. This is just as true of a Beethoven sonata as it is of a 32-bar jazz tune or a 12-bar blues. This 'language' of music often brings us closest to what the music is saying.

Besides the whole listening focus, global awareness also encompasses the body functions that produce music. This includes posture, response to phrases, relaxed suppleness, breathing in relation to the music and the physical movements of other players.

One of the essential ideas of the Inner Game is taking your focus away from what is inhibiting performance (Self 1), and transferring it onto what enhances performance. Any of the above essential elements in music can be a worthwhile focus, and trial end error will show which is best in different situations.

A further finding of the Inner Game technique is that certain functions are better carried out semi-automatically – without constantly trying to monitor and control them. An example is drumming out a rhythm on a table-top with your fingers while listening to music on the hi-fi or radio. If you try to control the precise activity of every finger, the process gets harder. If you let your awareness expand to 'feel' the overall rhythm within the global context of what else is going on in the music, it gets simpler. It also seems to use less physical effort, as just the right amount of effort is automatically put into the movement.

The other interesting finding is that it can help to focus not on the global environment but on one single thing. While drumming with the fingers, for example, feeling elbow movement makes it easier. Like a mantra in meditation, this is useful in the first stage of diverting attention from unproductive interference. Once the mind is more relaxed – as in meditation – attention can become more global and take in the holistic experience. Try these things out and see the effects for yourself.

TRYING AND TRUST

The passive nature of awareness and its 'ego-less' quality may be a problem for some musicians. Those who instinctively want to be 'in control' may feel that they are losing their power over their playing. They may believe that the harder they try, the better the results. This may be one way of playing, but it has many things against it. The act of 'trying' tenses the muscles and occupies the mind with distracting self-admonishments about doing better, not making mistakes, getting through this bit or doing that right. It takes up mental energy and space which is better used in listening and awareness. Sportspeople who 'psych themselves up' repeatedly during performances may find they are on a downward continuum where the harder they try the worse they perform. Trying may aid power sports, such as weightlifting, where the muscles have to tense up, but does little for delicate finger movements. In addition:

- Trying causes panic when it is the only method and fails.
- Trying causes 'blanking out' of the memory, as often happens when trying to remember names or when doing tests.
- Trying can have an obsessive quality to it which is attention consuming.
- Trying is antagonistic to trusting your ability – if you can do it why do you need to try? Zen teaches that we have inside ourselves all the natural ability we need – we simply need to remove the obstacles to using it. Tao says the same, calling it 'doing without trying'.
- Trying makes us aware of the difference between succeeding through trying, and failing through not trying – as in the

popular expression 'you're just not trying'. Success and failure divides music into a totally arbitrary set of opposing values which it does not contain in the first place. Failure, anyway, is something that should be positively explored as a dynamic situation with several means of escape, rather than as a static dead-end entity in itself. Permission to fail allows you to succeed (*see also page 61*).

- Trying is a form of desire, allied to envy, ambition and many other forms of self-fulfilment which are essentially selfish in nature. 'Can't you see how hard I'm trying?' is a defensive stance, not an open one.
- Trying is allied to 'force' and 'strain', and assumes difficulty. Like success and failure, this introduces the negative element of 'not trying hard enough', as in 'if at first you don't succeed, try, try and try again'. This in itself is dangerous, since over-strain ('no pain, no gain') can lead to injury. If at first you don't succeed, sit back and take a look at the problem, then wait for a different form of inspiration. As Fritz Perls says, 'trying fails, awareness cures'.

The Zen master Rinzai said 'there is nothing extraordinary for you to perform – you just live as usual without even trying to do anything in particular'. The Inner Game theory equally points out such negative effects of 'trying', and suggests the term 'trust' as an alternative means of letting things happen naturally. Such trust is both physical and mental.

Physical trust is synonymous with economy of effort. Muscle power is not the basis of performance – it is the correct use of muscles that counts. Trusting your body without imposing the tension of 'trying' allows muscles to work within their optimum range. This is the range from total relaxation to somewhere below maximum tension. Within this range they are flexible and responsive, and raising the threshold of tension progressively cuts down flexibility and brings muscles closer to their non-functional limits.

The more relaxed you are to begin with, the more muscle range you have, and the more you are able to use the tiny forces necessary to play pianissimo, because even pianissimo should be above the lowest threshold of muscle movement. Economy of movement also keeps muscle power in reserve, increasing stamina and long-term effectiveness. The correct amount of power is 'just enough to do the job', and leaves reserves to play true fortissimos where they are needed. Such muscle power is not a function of extra 'trying' in performance, but of regular practice to build up stamina. In performance, power can be achieved better by timing its release, as in karate. Again, 'effectiveness' is more important than 'trying'.

Such physical trust is the key to the violin playing method of Kato Havas, the Hungarian soloist and educator. The way of holding the violin and bow is loose, as Gypsy violinists do. The more the player can trust that the violin and bow are safe and will not fall, the more the body can become relaxed, expressive and flexible. This flexibility spreads from the left thumb through the arm, shoulder, neck and torso to the right bow hold, arm, shoulder and body.

Mental trust is equally about letting the mind do what it does best with the minimum of interference. Like the body, the mind is a marvel of exquisitely fine capabilities. It contains instincts, memories, learned processes and a whole wealth of subconscious powers which, like the iceberg, are far greater than they appear on the surface.

Memory – one of the key elements in solo recitals – is a hugely underestimated power. Under hypnosis, memory is known to be capable of retrieving vast amounts of unrealised information. It works best when you are relaxed and can positively trust it. The term 'sleep on it' describes the problem-solving ability of the brain when asleep.

Your memory not only stores information, it also indexes and cross-references it. The mind is constantly rearranging thoughts towards conscious goals, and improving memory by 'understanding' what needs to be memorised and storing it into more easily retrievable forms. Anyone who has crammed hours of notes into their heads the day before an exam and found that they are sorted out into a recognisable form in the morning will have noticed this. So let self-doubt interfere as little as possible – trust your memory, and let it work for you.

Intuition is another mental power that works best when trusted. We do not need to analyse everything consciously to stay in control. Intuition contains its own 'analysis' of events, sounds and feelings, and is processed outside the rational brain. Again, our capacity for intuition hugely exceeds our estimations, and can supply a whole wealth of information that lies outside the processes of verbal logic. As Pascal puts it, 'Le coeur a ses raisons que la raison ne connait pas' – our feelings reason in ways that lie outside the awareness of our logical brain.

The difficulty with trust is that it goes against so many of the ways in which we are educated to think. We believe we are functioning best when we are 'in control' through constant vigilance to our wishes and plans. We ignore that we may have more control through constant awareness of our surroundings and the flow of experiences of which we are a part. We force our brain to work hard. We ignore the ability of our brain to take care of itself. We try to manage ourselves without delegating our essential functions to the natural instincts of our minds and bodies. We become at times so over-managed that we are unaware not only of our surroundings and the messages they are constantly giving us, but also of our own inner space and how it naturally reacts to our environment.

A further difficulty with trust is with bad learned events. When once bitten, we are twice shy. If we are conditioned to believe we will throw up during performances we try to control it rather than trust that we will not. The same applies to our 'beliefs' that we will play out of tempo, forget the music, drop the bow, play wrong notes or lose our place in the music. We do not see trust as a way out of this dilemma because we do not 'trust' trust. We can say, paradoxically, 'I don't mind losing control as long as I don't actually lose control'. In other words, abandonment of control is not an option. And so we fill our minds with all sorts of controlling mechanisms which interfere with the whole process of awareness, and raise our ego to centre stage rather than letting it tick over in the background. Such over-management becomes obsessional, and we occupy mental space with its checking procedures. Where this occurs, there may be a long way to climb down to a level of ego-less awareness. Any steps towards such trust are steps that will be rewarded with increased satisfaction in performance, even though the process may feel at first like 'the unbearable lightness of being'.

Will

Will is the least defined of the Inner Game terms because it is closer to the management concept. As such it has a much lesser role in actual performance, and a much greater role in all aspects of the music profession that exist around performance – goal-setting, practice, career progress. It is fundamentally about 'shaping', a term applied by psychologists to describe the act of modifying behaviour in a desired direction. At its simplest, it works in a trial-and-error form – the process of selecting the results that work, and correcting the errors that do not. It describes the constant modification of potential goals in the light of goals achieved in the desired direction. Like the progress of a long-term career, it selects the useful and productive, and rejects the useless and unproductive. The steps to the desired goal are modified in the direction of the steps that yield the best results. Will is therefore enhanced by:

- Goal clarity – have a good idea of what you want to achieve; 'no aim, no game'.
- Goal direction – set goals, then modify them progressively.
- Goal steps – goals for today, this week, this year, the next five years...

• Zen and Creative Thought

The Inner Game of Music is an excellent way of acquiring some of the basic ideas that would be present in a Zen approach to performing music. It concerns itself not so much with the career management of the musician as with the actual performing experience. All those aspects of awareness, openness, intuition, trust and ego-less involvement are present in 'Self 2', the desired performance state. This relaxed concentration is called 'the master skill'. All that interferes is called 'Self 1'. The equation of the Inner Game states that total performance ability is the 'performance' minus the interference.

As in Zen, interference is characterised by 'thinking'. It is this exclusion of thinking that may not give a complete picture of music-making, or indeed of creative activity in general. Many others have placed a high priority on brainwork, such as British poet and painter Dante Gabriel Rossetti: 'Conception, fundamental brainwork, is what makes the difference in all art'. The sort of 'brainwork' that interferes with performance in the Inner Game or enlightenment in Zen needs more careful definition if it is to be meaningful.

Zen is not entirely against thinking: 'thoughts themselves are not a problem, it is possible to let the thoughts come and go without being distracted by them' (*ZFB*). It does, however, demote thinking to a background activity, and is against getting 'stuck' in thoughts. The interfering thoughts which intrude into Zen being are referred to as 'babble' or 'the mad monkey'. This is fairly close to the Inner Game description of 'traffic' – the running commentary which talks back and focuses on small parts rather than the whole.

It is easy to see that musical performance is diminished by mental digressions, anxieties that question confidence and self-criticisms that impose 'shoulds' and 'should nots'. But what of the sort of brainwork that actually shapes the flow of our ideas and forms the foundation for our instincts and intuitions? What of the creative trial-and-error process which orders our music into logical artistic structures rather than in random, goal-less directions? Without it we would play without talent, and improvise nonsense. Our total musical activity takes in both right-brain spatial awareness and left-brain analysis.

The thinking Self 1 may in reality be composed of two parts – interfering analysis and constructive analysis. Constructive analysis is something more than the passive awareness of Self 2 because while some of it is unconscious, other parts of it are conscious. It is true that this conscious analysis works best in a mental environment of trust and goal-direction, and relies on cues from awareness of the external flow of music. But the state of 'no-mindedness', as in meditation, has two drawbacks:

1) It silences the creative-speculative thought processes which are constantly throwing up 'what if?' suggestions.
2) It roots experience in the here-and-now, while creativity is jumping constantly into the future.

The roots of the Inner Game in performance sports can prioritise the moment of play. But this is not the same as, for example, jazz improvisation which is constantly speculative and idea-oriented. It may be that in the Inner Game's transition from sport to music the added 'compositional' element of jazz has been insufficiently allowed for, particularly given the author's natural bias towards the 'interpretive' aspects of classical music. Being in the moment may work better for interpretive music-making, but how does it allow for creativity?

Zen enlightenment has some elements of the creative process – it is a process of awareness which also contains germination, incubation and sudden insight. But again, the emphasis in Zen enlightenment is also on interpretation – understanding the universe and one's part in it.

The truly creative mind is not just concerned with interpreting what exists. It is actively innovative. It does not passively wait for awareness – it constantly jostles with ideas, jumping from the first idea to a string of related ones. It does not think 'apple, apple, apple, apple, appleness...'; it thinks 'apple, William Tell, Austria, skiing, I need a holiday...'.

Creative speculation jumps ahead in a series of moves, just as in chess. The chess-player's mind is not in the 'now' at all – it is constantly several moves ahead, and being 'at one with the chess board and the playing environment' is not really of much help to the precise analysis of consequences, however much an instinctive global awareness of a situation may give strong hunches.

To be free to create, the mind needs to go where it wants to go – to access thoughts, feelings, analysis or the external environment. It needs to proceed via trial and error, integration, synthesis, symbol and metaphor. At times it gains insights from the 'now'; at other times it speculates into the future and feeds back the results to the present.

So there is a place for rational problem-solving procedures within music, and in creative performance this need not be totally disabled. At the same time, listening skills in performance should always be present as a parallel awareness – mental 'management' alone is not sufficient to give the best playing experience. This is where musicians with a planning preference may have most difficulty, and this includes the majority of classical performers. Demoting 'managing' mental activity during performance may need a 'quantum shift' from preferred Western cultural norms prioritising control, to a 'letting go', within which brainwork is a more free and relaxed activity. Musicians with a naturally open attitude, such as most jazz musicians, may find this part easy. Classical musicians who allow themselves to embrace this attitude may find, like Lord Yehudi Menuhin, that 'our control is best when we are least aware of it'.

6 Stage Fright and the Fear of Auditions

• Questionnaire

Working through the following exercises will help you to get the most out of the rest of the chapter.

1) Make a full list of all the causes that trigger stage fright. This might include people, situations, places and certain types of music.
2) Categorise each cause of anxiety as one of the following:

   Paralysing terror
   Extreme unease
   Moderate fear and anxiety
   Some anxiety but controllable
   Mild unease, fairly easily controlled

3) Indicate what type of anxiety each cause provokes – free-floating or specific.
4) Note down your best and worst musical experiences.
5) Note any of the following fears you particularly suffer from:

   Doubting your own ability
   Fear of losing control
   Fear of not having practised enough
   Fear of not seeing/hearing properly
   Anxiety about accompanist/backing

Fear equipment might malfunction
Fear of losing your place in the music
Doubts that audience will like the performance
Fear of forgetting what has been memorised
Fear that others may be critical of you

6) What physical effects accompany the fear?

Loss of breath
Dry mouth
Increased heartbeat
Sweaty hands
Shaking fingers/arms/knees
Inability to see/hear clearly
Loss of sensitivity in the fingers
Tension
Stiff body movement
Dizziness
Nausea

7) What other things actually happen when you are anxious?
8) What thoughts go through your head? Are there any repeti tive fantasies, like being sick on stage, passing out or drop ping your instrument?

• Stage Fright

Stage fright is the common term for fear of audiences and auditions. It is also called performance anxiety, since it can happen in many other locations besides stages. Athletes get it at the trackside, snooker players at the snooker table, politicians before important speeches. Musicians get stage fright when going on stage, and this is usually worst just before and in the first moments of the performance. They also get it when being 'judged' in competitions and auditions, and when doing music that is being recorded or broadcast. Some get it in rehearsals, particularly where there is the possibility of having to play parts alone in front of others, and some even experience it when practising within earshot of others. Stage fright is thus associated with diverse situations of being 'listened to', of being 'criticised' and of being 'looked at'.

The predisposing causes of such anxiety can be many and varied, and can go back to our earliest years. It is triggered off by different things in different people, and what the fear itself is about can also be different. It may be mainly situational – being on stage or in front of people. It may be motivational – allowing inner doubts to affect playing. It may be interpersonal – being oversensitive to the criticisms and expectations of other people. Stage fright is not just one distinct problem with one distinct solution. Its overriding characteristic is fear and anxiety, but its origins and treatment can cover quite a bit of ground.

Typical Physical Symptoms

Stage fright mimics the 'fight or flight' reflex in the body, and consequently produces all the typical features of preparing the body for action:

- Increased heartbeat and blood pressure to pump blood around the body.
- Increased blood flow to muscles and away from extremities, causing cold fingers, hands and feet.
- Major muscles stiffen ready for action.
- Sweaty hands and body to cool overheating.
- Increased breathing rate to supply more oxygen.
- Inhibited digestion causing dry mouth, lack of appetite and sometimes desire to vomit.
- Heightened awareness to outside stimuli.

Any performer will tell you that such changes to the body are often completely inappropriate: sweaty fingers slip on piano keys, bows bounce, arousal turns into panic when no natural outcome can be achieved (neither fight nor flight). In fact, all these changes are directly antagonistic to relaxation. What is useful for an 'action state' is not useful for a state of paralysis, which occurs in an animal when escape is barred or the animal is confused about what to do. Under these circumstances the animal experiences loss of breath and extreme shaking, and it is this 'aborted flight' state that is most typical of the performer struck by stage fright in the centre of the stage, like an animal caught in a car's headlights.

Emotional and Mental Characteristics

Some of the most common emotional features and 'maladaptive thoughts' associated with stage fright are the following:

- Advance experience of anxiety preceding a performance.
- Disturbed sleep, restlessness and stress before the event.
- A sense of catastrophe in which there is no proportion to the threat.
- An inability to think constructively and analyse problems objectively.
- Disorientation and inability to focus attention on the beat or where you are in the music.
- A feeling of having forgotten your technique, fingering, bowing or the actual notes.
- Subjective feeling of loss of control: the brain 'goes blank', and the head is 'swimming'.
- Constant worry about the inability to perform successfully.
- A feeling of being alone or deserted.
- A sense of desperation at not having the power to deal with the event.
- A feeling of paralysis and inability to act, in which the body feels inert.
- A desire to escape or sabotage the performance.
- An anticipation of failure and humiliation in front of others who expect success.

Behavioural Disturbances

The presence of stage fright in the performer produces a range of behaviour which is maladaptive and makes the problem worse. Examples are:

- Vomiting before performances, sometimes self-induced to avoid doing it on stage.
- Cancelling gigs for no reason other than the fear of not being able to cope.
- Turning up late or drunk in an effort to 'escape' the problem.
- Walking off stage during performances.
- Refusing to play lead parts or exposed passages.

- 'Faking' playing when parts are doubled up by other players.
- Waiting for other players to come in at cues and entries before playing.

The Inner Mechanics of Stage Fright

Stage fright, as an inner process, has some of the following features:

- Fear of personal self-exposure and humiliation, sometimes with a sexual undertone of being 'looked at'. It is typified by the feeling that 'people will expose me, laugh at me and ridicule me'.
- Fear of appearing professionally inadequate or a fraud, frequently in front of fellow musicians, and fear of being criticised or made to feel guilty for not meeting expectations. This is typified by the feeling that 'people will discover I'm really not as good as I ought to be'.
- Self-sabotage and fear of success – ruining a performance in order to get sympathy for failing; rebelling against the expectations of family and teachers; or 'living up' to a background of musical failures or adverse criticism.
- A paradoxical thrill at somehow getting through the fear and facing an audience. People who suffer from stage fright, after all, go on stage again and again knowing that they will feel nervous. On a lower level this can go on for a long time. If, however, the discomfort escalates, it can turn into a real state of desperation and a desire to quit the profession to preserve one's health and mental wellbeing.

Effects of Stress during Performance

Stress inhibits our ability to function on top form, causing:

- Mistakes
- Inability to focus on several things at once
- Periodic loss of attention
- Untypical behaviour reactions designed to avoid stress

Causes of Stage Fright

Predisposing Causes (Learned Responses)

Stage fright is often the result of a sequence of bad experiences. These are frequently 'first time' experiences, such as your first day in school, the first time you had to stand up and recite something to the class from memory, or your first time in the local youth orchestra. Such experiences can 'condition' our behaviour to associate fear and the prospect of failure with performing in public. This is known as a 'learned response'. Such conditioning can either be general, as in feeling a generalised anxiety, or can express itself as a repetition of particular facets of performance which have gone badly in the past. Such fears commonly include:

- Singing flat or out of tune
- Forgetting words
- Passing out
- Being sick
- Ruining the performance at the start, in the middle or at the end
- Always making at least one mistake which becomes unavoidable
- Having to walk off stage in mid-concert

Another cause of stage fright can be linked to childhood. An overprotective family member who constantly worries about the child, whatever he does, vividly imparts this fear to the child. This figure is usually a parent, and often the mother. The child then becomes afraid of the consequences of actions by empathising with the fear being expressed to him. Such fear can be of being away from home, mixing with strangers, eating certain types of food, going on aeroplanes or being in a big city. Since touring often involves all of these elements, it can be a debilitating experience if such imparted fears have not been extinguished.

Early this century, the Russian psychologist Ivan Pavlov did some pioneering experiments with conditioning and learned responses. These are just as meaningful today for explaining and treating stage fright. Pavlov's experiments with dogs showed that a dog will salivate when expecting food. This he regarded as a normal or usual response, regardless of any other conditions present at the time, so he called it an 'unconditioned' response. He then rang a bell each time that the dog was presented with food. The dog 'learned' to associate the bell with food. After repeatedly associating food with a bell ringing, the dog then started to salivate each time the bell was rung, whether there was food or not. It had 'learned' to salivate to the sound of a bell. Since this was a particular 'condition' that Pavlov had imposed on the dog, he called the dog's salivation a 'conditioned' response. The dog had been 'conditioned' to salivate to the sound of a bell.

Exactly the same happens with musical performances. Music in itself is not something that causes panic. We practise music without panic for hours and hours. Performing in general may be a slightly nervous experience but not one which causes panic. We talk to groups of people without panic and the large majority of us can manage to speak to a group of strangers competently when reading from notes. For feelings of panic to be present we must look for some association or 'learned response'.

Such an association suggests that at some time or other we have been exposed to another event which happened at the same time as music was taking place. The following case histories illustrate this association.

Musician A

This violinist had a bad experience during a school play. A member of a string quartet, she had to perform a short piece at the top of a tower. She was terrified of heights, and because it was also a very cold day she froze up and made a complete mess of her part. All her friends and teachers were listening, and from then on she associated this feeling of panic and loss of control with playing in an exposed situation in front of an audience.

Musician B

This clarinet player had bad food poisoning while playing in the school orchestra, and passed out during a rehearsal. When he came to he was on the floor, looking up at members of the orchestra standing over him and the conductor panicking and calling for the school nurse. He later developed a fear of passing out during a rehearsal, associated with the fear of dropping his clarinet and losing control.

Musician C

This girl had to run in a long-distance race at her school sports day. She arrived in a panic only seconds before the start of the race, directly after eating a large lunch and making a fairly long journey by car. After running a short distance she was violently sick, and fell on the side of the track, retching. Some days later she had to sing in front of the school, and again arrived late after having eaten a heavy lunch. She panicked, and ran off to the toilets where she was, again, very sick. As a result she developed a fear of being sick every time she had to stand up and sing in front of an audience.

The first thing that is apparent from these case histories is the real sense of drama we feel as we read them. It is not the music-making that is dramatic, it is the 'catastrophic' fear of falling off a tower, losing consciousness or being violently sick. They illustrate how such fears can be overlaid on music-making. It is as if a bell goes off during performance and brings back an old historical panic that was the result of one freak experience. This old experience will not quite go away and haunts the unconscious as a reminder that things could get totally out of control. Such panics are irrational. They are only rational in the sense that something like it actually happened once. But the chances of those exact circumstances being repeated are as unlikely as bells going off every time we eat a bowl of cereal. These responses were conditioned by a particular set of events and a freak association between two utterly dissimilar things.

Subjectively, anyone who has fallen victim to such freak occurrences while making music will ask himself 'how do I know it won't happen again?'. We do not *know* that another world war will never happen again, but we do not plan our lives around it. If we did everyone would have a bunker at the bottom of the garden with enough food to last a year or more. We carry on with our lives under the assumption that if freak events actually happen, we will deal with them as and when they occur. We do not allow them to stop us carrying on with the normal processes of living. Life itself is an unpredictable event, but it is overwhelmingly safer than it is catastrophic. If the natural life-expectancy is about 70 years, then this is what we base our assumptions on. And if our natural performing expectancy is making music in a professional way, this is the actual reality on which we should base our assumptions.

Situational Causes

Performing requires not only skill and good preparation but also the ability to deal with audiences and the performing environment. As such, part of the causes of anxiety are 'internal' and lie in the musician's mastery over the tasks he faces, and part are 'external' and dependent on stressors present around him. Confidence is achieved when the task-mastery of the musician is greater than the sum of the environmental stressors. Anxiety is induced when the task-mastery is inadequate to deal with the complexity of the music or when the ability to cope is inadequate to meet the degree of environmental stress.

There are many situational causes of different origins:

TECHNIQUE

Playing an instrument in public requires a high degree of physical and mental co-ordination. Any lapse in technique can disrupt your grasp of the music and cause loss of concentration and confidence.

MEMORY

Playing in public also requires control over your memory. If you have a memory lapse it disrupts playing. Some musicians are particularly fearful of memory lapses and believe, often wrongly, that they are prone to them. Not trusting your memory can further predispose you to nervousness, which itself increases the likelihood of memory lapses – a vicious circle. There are several memory techniques that help musicians, one being to learn music backwards so that in performance it becomes progressively more familiar.

PLAYING UP TO PERSONAL EXPECTATIONS

The musician has an inner expectation of how the music ought to sound. When it fails to sound as it should, the result is self-criticism and worry.

EQUIPMENT FAILURE

Many musicians need to master complex mechanical or electrical problems, from shaping oboe reeds to programming synthesisers.

Equipment is prone to occasional failure, causing a lurking insecurity that unpredictable things may go wrong.

BAD FEELINGS ABOUT YOUR INSTRUMENT

Your instrument may have unpleasant associations, be difficult or awkward to play, have wolf notes, be badly set up or out of tune or have a sliding strap, all of which prevent playing comfort. This is particularly true when a musician often has to play different instruments from his own, as is the case with pianists.

BAD SITUATIONAL VARIABLES

These include the following:

- Cramped conditions where you cannot play properly
- Interrupted line of sight to the conductor
- Bad acoustics
- Wrong chairs
- Humidity or dryness
- Mood of audiences and fellow musicians
- Emotional and physical state (tiredness, jet-lag, alcohol consumption, drugs)
- Inner preoccupations
- What is happening in the world in general.

This is the anxiety associated with 'not being able to predict for certain how things will go on the night'.

PERFORMING CONDITIONS

Performing creates conditions which are quite different from practising and rehearsing the music in the privacy of home or rehearsal studio. This means that music will not necessarily sound the way you expect it to.

CRITICAL AUDIENCES

Audiences can at times show criticism, envy or hostility towards performers. The performer who is built up to appear 'different', 'super-talented' or 'exhibitionist', such as violinist Nigel Kennedy, may meet with both positive and negative reactions. Some people in the audience may feel inner satisfaction in belittling the performer and making him more commonplace.

NOTE-PERFECT PERFORMANCE

The classical performer is bound by the written page just like the actor is – there is only one correct set of notes. The great advantage with popular music and jazz is that you can improvise and play within your means – you do not have to constantly read and memorise unfamiliar work whose difficulties may at times be at the edge of your technique.

FORMALISED RITUAL

It seems paradoxical that music itself is an expression of the most profound and unrestrained human emotions, but that in the classical concert hall this is carried out in an atmosphere more reminiscent of the reading of a will, with all the interested parties looking critically on and waiting for the essential details to be unfurled. The performer is expected to express all the raw emotion in the music in circumstances of great decorum.

The popular club musician works in a much more relaxed environment. Since he can start again if he wishes, get up and walk out for a few minutes, eat a sandwich, have a glass of beer or talk to the audience a little, he generally suffers a lot less from stage fright. In the world of classical music the audiences generally have money and social status, and behave in public with commensurate restraint. Occasions like the extremely informal and patriotic Last Night at The Proms in London show how pleasant music making is when it takes place in an atmosphere of fun. Such evenings of entertainment were much more typical of concerts before the twentieth century, when programmes were longer with more breaks and included varied and popular items. It may be that the formality of modern classical concerts 'heightens the occasion', and that audiences enjoy this elevated mood, just as they enjoy dressing up and state pageantry; but moves back to more informal dress and behaviour have by common consent resulted in a more relaxed atmosphere which means less stage fright for the musicians.

Performance Anxiety in Orchestras

For classical musicians the greatest stressor appears to be stage fright during performance, claimed by 58 per cent in a survey by W. Schulz of members of the Vienna Symphony Orchestra. This survey also indicated that 24 per cent suffered from nerves before performances. A survey of orchestral members by British clinical pharmacologist Dr Ian James showed that while 15 per cent thought nerves improved their performance and 9 per cent thought they made no difference, they were seen as detrimental to performance by a considerably larger 60 per cent. So the idea that nerves help performance is only true for a minority of musicians, and by definition those that can deal positively with them.

When we break down the performance anxieties of orchestral musicians we discover the following typical factors:

- Classical musicians are particularly reluctant to talk about problems with their colleagues because they see them every day. If we do not 'talk away' feelings of fear and anger, they can be converted into physical symptoms. Fear becomes stage fright, while anger turns into fantasies of revenge, such as sabotaging a concert by throwing up, dropping your instrument or walking off stage. Musicians can mentally rehearse the fear that this unexpressed anger will blurt out dramatically in front of others, sabotaging their place in the delicate political balance of the orchestra.

- If artificial additives (beta-blockers, alcohol, drugs) are used to counter fear, musicians may become dependent on them because of the dread of 'what it might be like playing cold'. Note that frequent cups of coffee and tea may provide elevated levels of the stimulant caffeine, and the musician may underestimate the effect this has on 'nerves'.
- Since orchestras have a reputation of not expressing approval, but of implying criticism, there is the added tension that the criticism and rejection is embodied in the orchestra as a whole. The musician may feel that the whole orchestra, or a section, is against him. The fear of not belonging is often inherited from school where the pupils that went off to practise music were the ones left out of games and team activities. In some brass sections there can be a similar implied acceptance of rowdy

behaviour and a rejection of shyness and sensitivity.

- Orchestral playing is a very public activity and is particularly hard on shy people who are sensitive to exposure or shrink from leading. During trials, players may be moved up quite unpredictably to front desks and find themselves playing solo passages.

- A number of successful musicians start early (at around six to ten years of age) and follow a predictable 'training programme' through a succession of increasingly competent orchestras – school, town, county, National Youth, etc. They became familiar with orchestral playing, the repertoire and a number of colleagues who later reappear as friendly faces. All this makes it harder for the talented late starter, who may feel gauche, unfamiliar and vulnerable to learning his trade in public without the support of friends. This can easily undermine the quality of his playing and his natural ambitions to do well and be accepted. He may feel 'they are a team, but I'm not in it'.
- Orchestral music making is dramatic by nature. One consequence of this is that failures are subjectively seen as dramatic. One or more early incidents of 'failing' dramatically in public – often highly exaggerated by the musician – can lead to a tendency to inwardly manufacture a drama out of a crisis, and turn surmountable difficulties into a subjective feeling of 'catastrophe'.

- Musicians are generally 'feeling' people who try hard to please. When attempts to please meet with indifference or criticism from the orchestra, section leaders or conductor, feelings of frustration and anger may be turned inwards and precipitate the feeling that 'nobody accepts and loves me for who I really am: they just say nothing or imply criticism'.

- Fear at playing in public can become associated with high adrenalin, which is then associated with excitement and elation. In a paradoxical way, the orchestral musician can thus become addicted to excitement, even though this is mentally debilitating and emotionally draining. This produces the long-term fear that life in the profession will 'destroy me', with the consequent feeling of dread at being on an unstoppable path to self-damage. Again, this fear is often exaggerated by musicians.

Psychological Causes

STAGE FRIGHT AS A PHOBIA

In some musicians stage fright has the character of a phobia. A phobia is a fear habitually brought about by exposure to 'objects' in the environment, such as spiders, heights or confined spaces. In this way stage fright could be called 'audience and audition phobia' in that it is the presence of the audience or the audition panel that inevitably brings on the fear. Take away the external trigger and you take away the fear.

There is a strong similarity between stage fright and claustrophobia in that once a performance starts it is delimited in both space and time – you cannot get off the stage and you cannot get out of the performance. It is like being on a train stuck in a tunnel, and likewise venues often have no windows with a view of the outside world. Those who experience stage fright as a phobia can also suffer from claustrophobia, and particularly dislike stages without doors in the wings through which they could escape.

Overseas concert tours are notorious for exacerbating claustrophobia: you have to deal with the confines of aeroplanes and small hotel rooms; there is no escape route back to your family and the warmth of your own living room and bed; and you are surrounded by a wall of strangers speaking incomprehensible languages. Then, on top of this, you have to go on to a stage from which you cannot escape. Fear escalates as escape routes back to familiarity and emotional safety appear progressively cut off.

STAGE FRIGHT AS A PANIC ATTACK

Stage fright can also be experienced as a panic attack. This differs from a phobia in that there is no obvious external trigger – it seems to be brought on unexpectedly or in different circumstances by something internal, and results in a generalised feeling of unexplained anxiety. Some experienced performers will say that playing to an audience of 2,000 people gives them a good feeling, whereas having to play their instrument in a television studio in front of two or three well-known musicians is emotional torture. Rock musicians who tour regularly will often say that stage fright, like good and bad gigs, occurs quite unpredictably: it may be on the third night of an otherwise good week, for no apparent reason.

STAGE FRIGHT AS A DEFENSIVE TACTIC

There is a paradoxical way in which fear of one particular aspect of playing is used to eliminate fears of the whole playing situation. You would reasonably expect a top professional to be conscious of potential difficulties in any number of areas: fast tempos, long slow tempos, pianissimo playing or modern scores. What one typically finds, however, is that one isolated area of playing is used as a symbol or trigger for stage fright. In violinists it may be playing quietly at the tip or the heel, or playing in the middle of the bow; in wind players it may be playing quiet exposed entries; in brass players it may be finding the perfect embouchure for certain passages.

Typically, such top professionals will say 'If I don't get that particular thing in a piece I'm alright', like a driver might say 'If I don't go over 70 miles an hour I feel there's no real risk', or a child might say 'I'm not afraid of any animals as long as they are not snakes'. Since the risk is associated with just one thing, it is eliminated from everything else. In practice, this may result in the musician anticipating with dread 'the bottom of page 5' in the score, but as soon as that is past, everything becomes alright again.

Logic tells us that, when driving, there are risks other than speed, and that many animals besides snakes are dangerous. Focusing on one fear may be a lot easier than being engulfed by a whole number of potential threats. This rather clever mechanism is like the Inner Game technique of focusing on one thing to take one's attention off other fears.

The paradox here is why there is just one fear and not several, and why that particular fear can go on for years and years of a successful professional career where the musician in question says 'I'm not really worried about the rest of my playing'. This paradox is not at all apparent to musicians, and is concealed by the fact that the 'particular stressor' is a real and genuine fear. If one *has* to worry as a matter of principle, surely it is better to choose just one thing rather than worrying about everything, particularly when that one thing (quiet exposed passages, unaccompanied entries) occurs relatively infrequently.

Physical Causes

TIREDNESS AND STRESS

A particular cause of performance anxiety is stress and tiredness. This is caused during the actual day of performance by:

- Travelling long distances on the day before a gig. Touring can be quite energy-draining, especially when it involves long-distance travel with many transport changes and shifts of luggage. A major tour can cover over 20,000 miles.
- Jet lag.
- Having to drive to gigs, typically for two hours or more.
- Overexertion during the day, such as carrying heavy instruments or musical gear.
- Too much musical activity in the day, such as teaching and rehearsals.
- Low energy from hunger and irregular eating because of crowded schedules.
- Playing late gigs, such as in clubs open to 2 a.m. or later.

Stress and anxiety caused by the above can easily lead to insomnia or early waking, and therefore tiredness. Sleep problems tend to cause further stress, a vicious circle leading to consistently inadequate sleep – 4 to 6 hours instead of 7 to 9 hours. This is worse when touring, in all-night recording sessions or in late-finishing gigs where the body has to readjust from a nervous hyped-up state to normal sleep patterns. Touring musicians often say that true tiredness only hits them at the end of the tour.

The after-effects of a performance can contribute a great deal to sleep disturbance – the musician is physically, mentally and emotionally aroused by performing and may need some time to calm down:

- The musician's brain is likely to 'run over' events or mistakes repeatedly, or the music itself will not stop going round in his head.
- Over-concentration can cause irritability, and this contributes to insomnia.
- Pressure is often put on musicians to party and socialise after gigs, putting off sleep for many more hours, or even leaving sleep to a nap on the bus.

A further problem is that the frustration of not performing to your best standards due to tiredness leads to further stress.

Disturbed or Inadequate Sleep

New research has shown that some people repeatedly stop breathing during sleep, then start again suddenly as if recovering from choking (sleep apnoea). Sleep is constantly disrupted, and the sufferer may feel very tired the next day without knowing why. This is made worse by age, which makes the palette less firm, by over-consumption of alcohol before sleep, and by obesity. The most at risk are overweight older musicians who regularly 'drink to relax' before sleep and who in fact end up getting less sleep as a result. This problem is alleviated by reducing weight and alcohol consumption.

'Tiredness' as Depression or Frustration

Psychologically speaking, 'tired' is a loaded concept or umbrella word. 'I'm tired' simultaneously connects up with:

- Tiredness as general depression: tired of what you are doing; the work you get; being rank and file; having an unresolved career; having no money; things in general; state of the world; state of your health; ongoing problems.
- Tiredness as unresolved anger turned inwards, when there is no way of releasing it among fellow professionals without creating a scene or risking your job.
- Tiredness from bad health, smoking, drinking and no exercise or fresh air. Any run-down physical state is likely to result in stress and low self-regard.

This sort of 'futile tiredness' is more a feature of work underload than the nervous tiredness experienced by touring musicians, which is clearly a result of work overload. Tiredness can be cured by sleep, but anxiety or a poor physical state may inhibit sleep. There are a number of theories that people can get by on fewer than eight hours of sleep, but in stressed people there is one other factor to consider: if your waking hours are stressful, every increase in sleeping hours decreases correspondingly the hours spent in waking states of stress. So in stressed subjects, sleep may be more important than for the general population.

The general effects of tiredness on performance may be consistently underestimated by musicians who take punishing schedules as a matter of course, and research has shown that this is particularly a 'British phenomenon' in the world of classical orchestras.

Pre-performance Stress

A recent survey by British psychologist Dr Elizabeth Valentine showed that the best indicator of good performance is a subjective evaluation of ability immediately prior to performance – 'feeling in a good state to perform'. A musician in a tired state is much more likely to have a pre-performance expectation of reduced ability. This may then act as a psychological programmer of a poor performance unless it is deliberately counteracted by positive 'psyching up'. We have seen that Wills found the greatest stressor of musicians was 'feeling that you must reach or maintain the standards of musicianship that you set for yourself', and tired and stressed musicians may get further depressed by the belief that they cannot reach the basic performing goals they set for themselves.

Disorientation

Besides depressive tiredness and active over-exhaustion, there is a further factor of disorientation which can cause havoc in performance. This can come about:

- Through drugs or alcohol
- Through panic and loss of an external reality reference
- Through over-concentration on controlling inner disorganisation

Such disorientation affects multiple attention span and the ability to listen. The musician may be able to cope only with certain musical cues, when he really needs to continuously monitor his playing, listen to others, watch the conductor or read the score. He may only be able to do some of these things or attention may vacilate between one or the other. Take as an example a jazz bass player (*see Figure 6.1*).

Typically, the bassist will strive to get these right in the order of priority listed. If he can only achieve steps 1–3, the music will suffer but still sound together. If only 1–2, then the music will start to sound wrong. If either 1 or 2 goes, the other musicians will start to panic, change the beat to compensate, drop out or simply stop playing altogether or signal a drum solo and return to the final theme. Such a substantial disruption can ruin an evening and may

CONCENTRATION NEED	IF THIS FAILS
1) Place in musical structure	Lose place; be in wrong bar; double/halve beat
2) Place in the beat	Lose the beat; play 1 on 2/3 etc.
3) Get harmony right	Play wrong notes
4) Listen to drummer	Poor integration in beat
5) Listen to pianist	Poor response to chords used
6) Listen to soloist	Inability to follow soloist's argument

Figure 6.1. **Examples of what happens when concentration is lost.**

pass the word around that the bassist is too unreliable to be used.

General effects of disorientation are:

- Uncertain rhythm or falling behind the beat, which is particularly sensitive to tiredness
- Memory lapses
- Personal problems intruding on consciousness
- Confusion and panic: What is going on? Can I play? Can I follow the music at all?

The 'optimum' level of nerves for performing is something that musicians interpret in different ways: a minority claim that stress helps 'psych them up' for a performance; many prefer to feel 'just right'; and some like to feel relaxed. Our typical reaction to increases in arousal level looks like an inverted U (*see Figure 6.2*). Performing ability steadily rises until it reaches the top 'plateau' of the inverted U, which represents the optimum level for performing. After that it drops down into disorganisation and distress.

A successful performance clearly needs some degree of arousal and energy or it will be sluggish and inattentive, and tiredness progressively inhibits us from reaching this optimum level. On the other hand, the energy in a dynamic performance should not have a stress level which runs serious risks of disorientation. The worst case is a positive feedback of tiredness and stress on each other: the musician does not have the real physical energy to cope, and the mind is constantly 'stressing up' the arousal level, leaving little

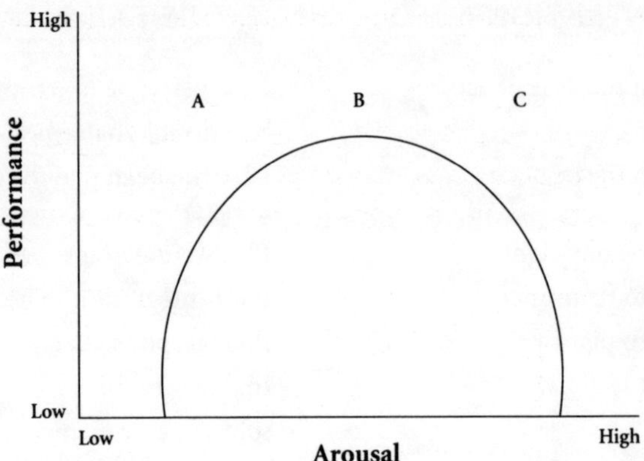

Figure 6.2. **Performance – Arousal Curve. It is possible for musicians to have differing performance 'styles' – some liking to be in the 'low risk' back area of the plateau (A), some at the very centre (B), and some in the 'high risk' front end (C), where the 'buzz' of performance nerves are just short of the cliff edge leading down to disorientation.**

concentration for the external needs of the music. This is like the tired driver who tries to stay awake at the wheel, constantly psyching himself up to prevent losing his attention on the road.

Effect on Fellow Musicians

As no man is an island, so no musical performance can exist without the contribution of each musician involved. This is Heisenberg's uncertainty principle – you can only assess the effects of an event in the measure that you are part of it. Effects on the collective band of an individual's tiredness and stress are likely to be:

- The fundamental attribution error (*see page 71*) of passing bad vibes on to the band. If the musician does not explain his poor performing state to his colleagues, they may start to blame themselves and start a collective panic situation.
- If the musician does complain about feeling lousy this may start a collective 'isn't everything awful' reaction in the band, with general cashing in of bad feelings.
- The band may become supportive and psych up the musician, turning around his state of mind. Musicians tend to do this because of their sympathetic person-centred personalities and

their innate counselling skills. The musician may then relax enough to overcome the tiredness.
- A critical reaction from some of the musicians may split the collective personality of the band. They may begin taking sides ('scapegoating', rescuing etc.). This can happen before or during the performance, or in the interval.

Dealing with Stage Fright

Warren Brodsky, the American–Israeli music research psychologist, suggests that some of the factors in stage fright can be generalised into a 'Performing Anxiety Syndrome'. This may include:

- Performing technically difficult material.
- Expecting to be criticised for not playing 'note-perfect'.
- Coping with a number of unpredictable situational variables.
- Having to rely heavily on concentration and memory.
- Dealing with personality difficulties ('attitude problems') among fellow musicians.
- Having to be constantly on top form despite rehearsals, travelling and transporting gear.
- Having to cope with very exacting studio situations involving large sums of money.
- Having to deal with highly-skilled tasks in real time for three hours or more without stopping.

For each individual musician, however, the particular combination of stressors may vary considerably. Some are no problem, whereas others are. Dealing with stage fright is therefore a matter of identifying the particular elements that cause maximum discomfort, then finding the best ways of dealing with them.

Practical Measures

Basic practical measures to lessen the predisposing fear include the following:

- Enlist the help of the accompanist or fellow musicians. Make friends with them and use them as your emotional anchor during performance. Maintain good eye contact. Talk through the performance together, and decide on aims and how to achieve them. You will then feel supported and not alone.

- As the concert or audition approaches, visualise what the room will be like, who will be in it, what is likely to happen, and how to cope with any problems that may arise. It is often effective to visualise a 'worst case' scenario, both as a rehearsal of what to do should it actually occur, and more generally to remove the hidden 'catastrophe' at the back of the mind and turn it into a practical problem which can be dealt with.

Relaxation and Stress-reduction Techniques

The first rule of combating acute anxiety and panic is to deliberately drop the shoulders and then breathe out. This should be done deeply, slowly and repeatedly until an improvement is noticed. Thereafter concentrate on regular outward breaths, keeping the shoulders dropped to reduce tension in the neck and arms. The fundamental principle of anxiety reduction is that you cannot feel relaxed and tense at the same time – the one blocks out the other. Be careful not to over-breathe or 'hyperventilate' (quick and repeated deep intakes of breath) which is the opposite of this and makes the situation worse.

As the body relaxes, you can then sit still, let your eyelids gradually close, and imagine a pleasant and happy scene. Often this will be a childhood memory, which is filled out in detail until it becomes a vivid source of tranquillity. An example would be:

> *I'm reclining in the back of a boat, gently rocking on the river on a sunny summer's day. The sky is blue and I can hear the water lapping at the sides of the boat as I quietly doze in the heat.*

Another rapid relaxation technique is exercise. Some musicians like to walk about before a performance to release tension. This is a logical response to the bodily changes involved in the 'fight or flight' mechanism, and tends to lessen some of the anxiety by using muscles that are charged for action. If you feel particularly 'charged up' with adrenalin it is not unreasonable to actually run up and down stairs or do some sort of physical workout for a few minutes.

This should be timed to finish between 20 and 10 minutes prior to going on stage, so that the body has time to regain its balance.

If tension occurs suddenly in the middle of music-making use either the technique of 'stopping', which simply means putting the unpleasant thought deliberately out of your head, or use the Inner Game technique of 'shifting' the external focus. Shift quickly from the 'stressor', such as fear of sight-reading a particular page or the presence of the audience, to one particular non-stressful element. Immediate shifts of focus can be onto the rhythm, harmony or melody of the music. More generally useful ones are the feelings of the composer in writing the music, or in a song the meaning of the words and what the lyricist was feeling when writing them. When you start to feel better, gradually enlarge your focus to the whole music.

As well as the short-term methods above, there are other relaxation techniques which should take place at more distance from the moment of going on stage. One widely favoured general trend is cutting down the amount of outside stimulation before important performances. This reduces irrelevant distractions and focuses the mind on preparation. During the pre-performance period some kind of distracting or routine physical activity may also be helpful, such as making reeds, changing strings or polishing your instrument. While some find television viewing and phone calls relaxing, others see them as annoying distractions and prefer to avoid them. Where there is a need for actual relaxation techniques, the following ones may be used.

BIOFEEDBACK

Biofeedback techniques can be learned from an appropriate teacher, and include the following steps:

- Rate the tension in your body on a scale of one to ten.
- Focus on the problem you want to deal with, such as a tense neck.
- Rate the problem in its present state between one and ten.
- Try to make the problem worse.
- Make a note of which muscles stiffen.
- Still focusing on the same muscles, try to decrease the tension.
- Make a note of anything or any movement that decreases the problem.

• Remember what you did and apply it again when the problem occurs.

PROGRESSIVE RELAXATION TECHNIQUES

There is a fairly standard relaxation method of tensing and releasing muscles one by one, from the feet up to the head, while breathing out deliberately and telling yourself to relax.

To do this sit in a comfortable chair, drop your shoulders and breathe regularly. Then start with the left calf muscle. Tense it as much as you can, breathing in. As you contract your muscles say to yourself 'my muscles feel very tense'. Count to five and then let go quickly, breathing out at the same time. Count to five with your breath exhaled and tell yourself 'I feel warm, soft and relaxed'. Then repeat the same thing with the right calf muscle. Go on to the thighs, stomach, chest, back, arms, shoulders and jaw. When you have finished, carry on sitting in the chair for a little while in a relaxed state and with a blank mind.

SOMATRON RECLINER

The Somatron recliner is a sophisticated reclining chair containing speakers that vibrate the body of the chair. This music generated 'vibro-tactile' environment is used to enhance the treatment of performance anxiety and career stresses. Its use with musicians is currently being developed by Warren Brodsky and Professor John Sloboda in the Unit for the Study of Musical Skill and Development at Keele University, England, in conjunction with a number of Britain's leading orchestral musicians. Using sound for therapeutic purposes should favour natural 'auditives' such as musicians, and this current research holds interesting future possibilities.

'Unlearning' Panic Responses

We have seen illustrations of how panic responses can be overlaid on performing situations. For musicians who suffer predominantly from feelings of fright, the following measures apply. The essential parts of unlearning these responses are:

- Identify how the panic response became associated with performing in the first place.
- Dissociate the added panic situation from the essential process of making music. The two are not the same.
- Remind yourself that the 'catastrophe' that caused the panic happened only as a result of a freak event, and that it will not be repeated in the normal process of making music.
- Remind yourself that the particular 'catastrophe' or panic-causing event is firmly in the past – that it is history not reality.

The goal of unlearning panic responses is not necessarily to extinguish all fear in all circumstances since this would be plainly unrealistic – playing music is technically difficult and a large audience is a slightly awesome phenomenon. But a goal of 'reducing fear to manageable levels' is attainable and can have permanent effects. Musicians regard this as an acceptable solution because the biggest fear is not of 'being a bit nervous' but of being 'out of control'. Musicians are used to playing through some degree of nerves, but the idea of not being able to perform – of not being able to keep the bow on the string, of fingers slipping off piano keys, of not being able to keep up a quiet and controlled flow of breath – is subjectively threatening.

This goal is reached when new learned responses consistently show that catastrophes do not happen any more, even though they may have taken place under freak circumstances in the past. There is usually a period of disbelief during which feeling better alternates with feelings of increased nervousness ('what if something goes wrong?', 'how do I know this is really going to work?'); but this gradually becomes a new feeling of security and a new self-image: 'I'm alright now – my bad problems are a thing of the past, and I know how to control states of rising anxiety if they should occur'.

Cognitive Techniques

Cognitive therapy consists, at its simplest, of finding out the beliefs and thoughts of the musician, analysing them, and replacing inappropriate or negative beliefs with positive ones that stand up to reality. The order of doing this is:

- Identify the troublesome belief, e.g. 'If I make one mistake, the

whole piece is ruined'.
- Analyse it and examine the evidence, e.g. 'What do I mean by "ruined", and what do people really want in a performance?'
- Challenge the belief in the light of reality, e.g. 'Will people even notice it? Is perfection possible again and again in real life? Do people really put one note before the musicality of the whole performance?'
- Change the irrational belief to a better one, e.g. 'A few fluffs, though better avoided, are less important than the quality of the whole performance'.

This type of intervention is popular in counselling at present. Real gains can be achieved in relatively few sessions by concentrating on the problem itself, rather than the general background of the person.

Since musicians are often emotional people who come to conclusions through gut reactions, a 'cognitive' approach may at first seem foreign, since it means using the 'thinking' or 'analytical' part of your being. Even after a problem has been analysed, a new belief system will only really work after it has been 'internalised', or translated into your inner language. It needs to be allowed into your 'inner room', and treated with trust and familiarity.

Because they use the analytic functions, cognitive techniques can supply the objective reality that a musician's 'feeling' world may need in order to see exactly what is going on. Seeing all sides of a question enables us to 'attribute' the problem to the right causes. Ask yourself whether the problem is:

1) Internal or external. Is what is going on:
   - *Inside me – my reaction, my feeling, my fault?*
   - *Or outside – the band, someone else, external circumstances?*
2) Permanent or temporary:
   - *Do I always need to have these feelings?*
   - *Or am I really experiencing something temporary that may go away if I make it?*
3) Global or specific:
   - *Does this feeling of unease affect everything – I will fall apart completely?*
   - *Or does it affect just part of me – I will feel more nervous than usual but this will not stop me playing the music successfully?*

From the above, it can be seen that musicians who narrow down anxiety to specific things are far less likely to feel 'engulfed'. This is to say that an external explanation should be preferred to an internal one, a temporary occurrence preferred to a permanent one, and a specific reason preferred to a global one.

A musician applying this approach and concentrating on external, temporary and specific factors might say: 'I'm feeling a bit stressed at the moment because I didn't get enough sleep, but I am confident that I can still play up to a professional standard, and it is quite likely that things will improve as I get more into the performance.' On the other hand, a musician concentrating on internal, permanent and global factors might say: 'I feel stress engulfing me for no reason – my whole performance is doomed from here on, and I don't know how I'll get to the end'.

When building up your confidence, however, the opposite is true. You try to build up internal ways of coping that are as permanent as possible and apply to as much of your musical life as possible. This may seem a paradox, but global self-belief builds up self-assurance and positive motivation. By narrowing down the problem, but generalising the solution we are loading the dice heavily in our favour. We are making our expected task-mastery greater than the problem.

To bring problems 'down to scale', you are particularly encouraged to avoid catastrophising (*see page 61*). Learn to distinguish between anxiety and panic. One clever piece of self-persuasion is to divide stage fright into two distinct types:

1) Anxiety, which is uncomfortable but manageable and does not prevent performance.
2) Panic, which is very debilitating and causes shaking, rapid heartbeat and dizziness.

You then persuade yourself that extreme 'panic', where playing is impossible, is in fact most unlikely, and so all that remains is that sort of anxiety which is manageable. Consequently, when there is an increase in anxiety levels, the message to yourself is 'this is just fear, and I can deal with it'.

Remind yourself that you have lived through several performances in which you were uncomfortable but in which you actually played all the notes and in which no real disaster or 'catastrophe' actually happened. Maybe your performance was not perfect, but maybe nobody noticed anything particularly wrong. In other words you are capable of surviving performances of great stress.

At this point you can make the surprising but true realisation that you may actually be more capable of surviving fear and stress than other musicians. Far from being 'unable to cope' – which is your subjective feeling – you are in fact surprisingly good at coping with stress. What you are afraid of is the effects of fear, like dizziness, increased heartbeat etc. In other words you are afraid of fear itself.

Now, by constantly reminding yourself that you can play through fear, you are telling yourself that you do not need to be afraid of fear. This means that you do not need to be afraid, and can start to play with confidence again.

Some other cognitive readjustments to typical belief systems are worth looking at and understanding. An example is adjusting your style of performance to suit your personality type:

- Extraverts – Make good contact with the people in the audience, and allow yourself to feel good when they pay attention to you and show interest.
- Introverts – Create a dialogue with the composer when you play. Perform to the wishes and spirit of the composer. Tell yourself that the audience is there to hear the composer, not to look at you. You are 'not there', merely the vessel through which the spirit of the music flows.
- Teachers (and those with didactic tendencies) – Think of the audience as children. Show them what the music is all about.

Think through what audiences and audition panels really are, and restructure your opinions accordingly. The musician's emotional vulnerability to authority symbols has a direct bearing on fear of audiences and audition panels. It can be a great help to restructure cognitively what these represent in real terms, and contrast this with the 'perceived' image:

THE AUDIENCE

- Perceived as: an awesome mass of critical people who have high expectations and who are are looking to pick tiny holes in the performer's technique and presentation.

- In reality: the source of the musician's income. The more numerous they are, the higher the standard of living of the musician. The more they are entertained, the more likely they are to come again.

THE AUDITION PANEL

- Perceived as: a bored and critical collection of professionals who are likely to look for reasons to reject an applicant and pick tiny holes in technique.
- In reality: a group of people whose aim is to find somebody who can play with the right degree of talent. Since they have to choose someone, the applicant must persuade the panel he is the one by using the usual arts of persuasion: sound and well-prepared arguments, pleasing presentation and proper research into what the panel is looking for. Analysis of how audition panels make decisions reveals that they generally respond to positive all-round quality of interpretation rather

than cold and stiff technique and nothing else – we are talking about music, not mathematics. It is hardly surprising that audition panels are affected by the music – they are there because they love music, not because they hate you.

Banishing Old Spells and Curses

In Chapter Two we saw how internal criticisms originate in childhood 'spells and curses' cast by parents and other figures of authority. Under the stress of facing auditions and audiences we become more vulnerable to these inner voices. Even worse, audition panels can easily have the emotional effect of bringing back situations where you were 'talked to' or scolded. In the stress of trying to perform at your best the slightest frown or sign of disinterest may trigger an internal conviction that 'I've done something wrong and they are going to punish me'. Reassure yourself that audiences and audition panels are just a bunch of people listening to music, not parental figures with awesome powers.

Failing an audition can be worse. It can trigger the internal conviction that 'I'm really no good – they said I wouldn't make it and they were right'. This also has to be reinterpreted. The reality will be more like 'they auditioned a number of people and for reasons I don't really know, they chose someone else. There will be more chances to audition, and the circumstances and outcomes will be just as impossible to determine. All I know for certain is that I can try my best'. A certain amount of disappointment is understandable. Morbid fatalism that nothing will ever go right is not.

Toughing it Out

This is a solution to stage fright which is all too often ignored by counselling, but nevertheless an important one to consider. Playing through a technically difficult programme for three hours is not dissimilar to an airline pilot flying a plane or a surgeon performing an operation. These are fairly exact comparisons in terms of performing difficult tasks without stopping or making bad mistakes. It is widely known that pilots and surgeons are required to be physically and mentally fit, and able at all times during work to apply total concentration and physical co-ordination. Musicians are well advised to keep in the same mental and physical shape – the symphony orchestra is no place for alcoholics and physical wrecks, and neither is the rock circuit where tours are exceptionally demanding of physical and mental fitness.

While music is partly the realm of prematurely dead heroes, more careful musicians realise that physical fitness tells in the long run: drugged, drunk and unfit musicians that have bragged about being able to 'make it' are either gone or unnecessarily unemployed. Either way, the profession has revealed them as unable to cope with its exceptional set of demands.

Mental fitness is partly the strength to accept and deal with challenge – life can be quite demanding on our human resources. As M. Scott Peck writes, 'It is only because of problems that we grow. It is for this reason that wise people learn not to dread but actually welcome problems'. Music is a highly skilled profession where some degree of challenge and controllable anxiety goes with the territory. The more easily we can accept this basic fact and incorporate it into our 'normal' reactions, the better the tolerance we will have for the predictable ups and downs of our careers.

Responding to Physical Cues

One particularly interesting fact that has come to light during research is that rapid heartbeat is experienced just as much by performers who do not admit to stage fright as by performers who do. This immediately suggests that rapid heartbeat is an 'automatic' response to performing in front of others. How, then, do performers actually interpret this rapid heartbeat?. Those who get a 'buzz' out of nerves prior to performing may interpret it positively as a heightened sense of occasion. Others may simply accept it and not be either put off or more than mildly aroused. The problem with those who suffer from stage fright is that they interpret rapid heartbeat as a trigger for fear and loss of control, and then proceed to live out the consequences by becoming anxious and disorientated.

In psychology, the James–Lange Theory states that our emotions actually follow our bodily changes – 'we are afraid because we run away', for example, or 'we are angry because we strike'. In a similar way we could say that 'we are anxious because our heart is beating fast' or 'we feel fear because our bow arm shakes slightly'. While bodily states do not vary much from person to person, their actual emotional interpretation does vary considerably. This emotional reaction, in turn, is filtered by our beliefs about what is happening and what this will result in. So while one performer can feel elation and confidence in response to a rapid heartbeat, another may feel fear and an expectation of failure. While one violinist may not be too put off by a slight shake, another may go into a state of panic, and believe the whole performance is ruined.

The point of this for the musician is that anxiety in response to rapid heartbeat may be a 'learned' response. If it is 'learned', then it can be unlearned. The negative response would probably be something like: 'Oh dear, my heart is beating fast – I feel nervous and I'm sure my playing will suffer'. The positive response, on the other hand, would be something like: 'Ah yes, I notice my heartbeat is a little more rapid, just as I would expect – I'm sure that as I get into the performance it will go back to normal fairly quickly'.

Panic is an infectious emotion, and easily invades the system, so the more rapid the 'normalising' interpretation the better. There can be a progressive 'positive feedback' effect between physical cues, emotional response and the beliefs and interpretations we give to what is going on. This is illustrated in Figure 6.3.

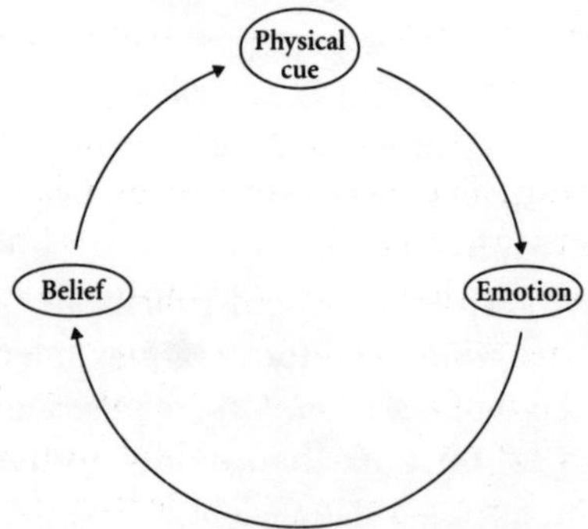

Figure 6.3. **The cycle of positive feedback.**

In an invasive state of anxiety our alertness to signs of distress can act like a 'hypervigilance'. The onset of even a tiny signal – sluggish digestion, slight shaking, changes in concentration – can be highly magnified by the emotions and interpreted as a 'worst' belief, which is then confirmed by further physical effects. Our attention becomes 'selectively' filtered to let in those physical, emotional or mental distress cues which 'fit' our current concerns, and tends to ignore cues outside this feedback circle. Ambiguous cues like raised heartbeat are thus interpreted as 'fear' rather than 'invigoration', because priority will be given in a state of fear to cues which fit a 'fearful' interpretation. In depression the same thing happens – we give much more attention to sad thoughts and reminiscences because our physical inactivity and depressed mood filters our thought patterns. In both fear and depression our thought patterns become progressively more 'personalised' and removed from the world outside our intimate circle of concern – reality recedes and everything seems to be focused on oneself, causing yet further distortions of what may really be happening.

Thoughts of imminent catastrophe are grossly misinterpreted and exaggerated in moods of fear, just as thoughts of failure are in moods of depression. Much recent research indicates that panic attacks can be initially triggered by 'catastrophic' misinterpretations of bodily symptoms. The remedy for this is to destroy the positive feedback effect of the circle by reversing one of the elements. We can reverse arousal by relaxation techniques, which in turn create a more tranquil mood. We can also reverse such misinterpretations of body changes by first understanding what bodily changes are natural – such as those of the adrenalin response to performing – and then deliberately re-interpreting our belief system to accept such changes as normal. The brain then ignores the 'false' panic trigger, sees that there is no cause for alarm and passes the signal to relax on to the body. The body responds by relaxing and the rapid heartbeat and physical tremor declines.

Heartbeat and 'the shakes' are the most obviously exaggerated cues in performers, but some are 'hypervigilant' to other physical effects of the adrenalin response, such as inhibited digestion. Digestive cues are largely ignored by the majority of us, but can act like a trigger in those particularly sensitive to their digestion, causing them to feel sick or want to be sick. The same coping response should be made: 'Ah yes, I notice my digestion is a little more inhibited, just as I would expect – I'm sure that as I get into the performance it will go back to normal fairly quickly'.

The effects of nervousness on digestion raises the whole question of what to eat before performances and when. The worst foods are those, like sugar, chocolate or alcohol, which very quickly raise the blood sugar level, but then let it drop down below the original level, giving a perceived drop in energy. This leaves a choice between fibre-containing foods like bananas and oatmeal biscuits which are still easily digestible, and starchy foods which stay longer in the stomach and release energy more gradually. The performer may want to experiment to see how much of which kind of food works best – high-energy diets for stamina or reduced eating before performing to leave the stomach with less to digest. One favoured food seems to be fish.

Many bodily cues can be misinterpreted to cause fear – tiredness and common colds are two obvious examples that cause feelings of vulnerability. The importance is not to attribute mental anxiety to factors which can be correctly explained away by a physical symptom. The 'automatic' anxiety reaction then becomes a 'strategic' reaction which successfully explains away false panic signals. By practising such strategic reactions, performers can return to a relatively relaxed and confident performing state typical of those who tend to give little special awareness to raised heartbeat or other such physical cues.

Postural Therapies

A number of posture methods promoting correct balance have been used for performers, chiefly Alexander and Feldenkreis. They tend to put the body into a more ergonomic and relaxed state for performing, which decreases some of the tension in the mind–body feedback loop that we have seen above. The message from the body to the brain is 'I feel relaxed', and the brain responds.

Body language for performers can also help to 'ground' the mental fears by physically 'grounding' the body. When working with musicians , British psychologist Martin Lloyd-Elliott encourages flat shoes and keeping both feet on the floor, as well as balancing the body to offset playing any side-weighted instrument such as the violin.

Beta-blockers

Beta-blockers are drugs that 'block' the adrenalin reaction in the body, or the 'fight or flight' mechanism in which animals tense their bodies to danger to make them more alert to the likelihood of fleeing or fighting. In countering this, beta-blockers reduce some of the unpleasant effects of panic, such as rapid heartbeat and trembling. They are used by orchestral musicians to some degree (probably 5–10 per cent) and have also been used in sports like snooker where a steady hand is vitally important.

Modern medical opinion is that their benefit is that of 'buying time', since they are particularly useful as a quick remedy for states of acute anxiety. In cases where performances have to be got through immediately and before any alternative psychological therapy can take effect, their use has been seen as one way of saving the musician from distress.

Musicians who take beta-blockers are usually aware that their use is not the perfect solution, since all drugs have some degree of side-effects. They keep them in the pocket in case they need a 'quick fix', sometimes waiting until just before the performance to see if they are needed.

They thus take on the character of a 'rescue remedy'. In fact, 'Rescue Remedy' is the name of a Bach flower remedy which is claimed to have similar effects, and which some musicians take as they would a beta-blocker. If a sugar pill or placebo were substituted for either, there would be some emotional feeling of 'rescue' even if the drug itself did nothing, simply because the musician's mental response changes to 'I'm going to be alright now' on taking a pill. So the total effects of pill taking are both physical (what it does) and mental (what you are expecting it to do).

Musicians who do not want to become emotionally dependent on beta-blockers or who want to find non-drug-induced solutions tend to come into therapy with the specific goal of stopping their regular use. They already have the knowledge gained from using beta-blockers that they can perform without anxiety, and this in itself is useful. What they then want to do is find another way of predicting fairly confidently that they are not going to fall apart or experience acute distress. This can be done by psychological means which aim to replace 'controlling' the problem with 'understanding' it. As this takes effect the beta-blockers are either phased out, or confined to exceptional circumstances.

One fact about beta-blockers that musicians may not fully appreciate is that they are often ineffective in cases where anxiety is associated with depression, only working when the depression itself is tackled by some method such as counselling or anti-depressants.

Becoming 'Panic-free'

Stage fright has been described above as a whole variety of different and sometimes interlinked symptoms and beliefs. The more flexible the methods used to combat it, the greater the likelihood of success. Try out any or all of the methods described, choose those that work best for you and familiarise yourself with an anxiety-reducing routine that works predictably.

As your overall strategy for reducing stage fright starts to work, there is a typically enjoyable feeling that 'things are now better'. This is often, however, followed not only by the worry that 'maybe it will all come back again' but the paradoxical idea that 'the longer I go without a disaster happening, the more likely it is that a disaster will ultimately happen'. This is no more true than the likelihood of a coin coming up tails after it has come up heads five times: the odds are still exactly the same.

The odds of panic recurring are, in fact, infinitely less than flipping a coin because, in the overwhelming number of cases, the expectation of panic is built on isolated 'freak' occurrences which are extremely unlikely to happen again. Such paradoxical and habitual 'catastrophising' has been widely reported in studies of anxiety, and is part of the anxiety itself, not of reality. As the general anxiety lifts, the overall progress is to get steadily better in a sort of 'saw-tooth' recovery pattern. There are still ups and downs corresponding to difficult concerts and gigs, but these gradually flatten so that the worst cases are consistently less bad and the best cases are consistently better than before.

There is no such thing as a 'miracle cure' or 'getting better overnight just by doing this latest new technique'. Adjusting to reality means coping as well as possible with the constantly varying conditions of performing. The performer who becomes substantially more panic-free will, however, experience a new expectation. The old expectation that 'things will go wrong and I'll panic' becomes a new expectation that 'performing conditions may vary, but I sincerely believe and expect that I have what it takes to cope with that'.

What is needed to go with this new coping style is not just the new belief that 'I expect to be OK', it is also a new self-image. When you become confident you may practise saying to yourself and to others 'I don't panic unduly about stage fright'. Even better is to personalise this statement with a label – 'I'm a pretty panic-free sort of person'. Practising this label helps create the new self-image, just as saying 'I'm a non-smoker' is more definite than saying 'I don't smoke'. Both identify the new expectation, but personalising it really starts to make it sink in.

7 The Musician's Life and Career

The life of the musician is one of the most colourful of the self-employed careers. It is a fairly insecure and high-risk profession, offering both riches and poverty, but since musicians tend to work most weeks of the year, it also offers a steady amount of satisfying social and artistic feedback. Many are still working in the profession into their 70s and 80s, while those that give up full-time music tend to retain an amateur or semi-pro interest.

Despite the satisfactions of being in the music business there are a number of typical stressors which are acutely felt by some professionals.

• Stressors

Stressors regularly faced by popular musicians have been well documented by Geoff Wills in his book *Pressure Sensitive* (Sage, 1988). The following are his findings from a survey of musicians carried out through the Musicians' Union in Britain, showing the stressors listed by one fifth or more of those questioned. They have been divided for convenience into:

- Career or professional factors
- Situational factors in the actual working environment
- Personal factors, showing subjective perception of anxiety or low effectiveness.

The actual percentage of musicians listing the stressor is given in brackets.

Career Stressors

- Worrying because of lack of gigs (38.6%)
- Difficulty in getting a good recording/management deal (32.1%)
- Having to sack a musician if you are a bandleader (30.5%)
- Conflict with record/management/agency executives who do not share your musical ideals (28.5%)
- Waiting for payment to come through from a gig/session (27.2%)
- Having to play music you don't like to earn a living (26.4%)
- Doing an audition (24.4%)
- Having to work when it is available, making it difficult to take holidays (22.7%)
- Worrying about the lack of pensions and benefits in the music profession (22.0%)

Situational Stressors

- Instruments or equipment not working properly (44.8%)
- Having to read and play a difficult part at a recording session or gig (41.8%)
- Playing when there is inadequate rehearsal or preparation (38.2%)
- Effects of noise when the music is heavily amplified (37.4%)
- Endangering your life by having to drive a long distance after a gig when tired (33.3%)
- Having to play after travelling a long distance (30.1%)
- Doing sessions/rehearsals during the day then a gig at night (28.5%)
- Waiting around for long periods at the gig before it's time to play (27.6%)
- Getting musicians to deputise at short notice (27.2%)
- Playing a venue with bad conditions (23.5%)
- Doing a long tour (23.1%)
- Worrying about all the musicians getting to the gig on time (22.0%)
- Coping with an instrument that is physically difficult to play (21.5%)

Personal Stressors

- Feeling you must reach or maintain the standards of musicianship that you set for yourself (51.3%)
- Stress put upon personal relationships, e.g. marriage (30.5%)
- Feeling that you need to become better known and/or better paid (28.9%)
- Feeling lonely or bored in strange towns or hotels when on tour (23.2%)
- Feeling tense or nervous during recording sessions as a session musician (22.8%)
- Feeling tense or nervous doing a live gig as a session musician (21.5%)
- Worrying that your ability to play will leave you (20.4%)
- Feeling that your musical ability is not appreciated by a musically ignorant public (20.3%)

In the personal factors there is an obvious loading towards dissatisfaction with the quality of one's music-making, which is the highest overall stressor. This shows that musicians are particularly sensitive to how well they play and the overall quality of their gigs.

Music as a Career

A number of different studies suggest that the vast majority (typically 85 per cent or more) are happy with being a musician. Many other studies show a great number of detailed dissatisfactions with the 'profession' as opposed to music itself. This distinction between the 'artistic' and 'professional' sides of the business was well summarised by Berlioz as, roughly translated, 'Music – what a noble art, what a terrible profession'. A career in music works on a number of levels, including:

- Artistic satisfaction – the quality of work as perceived by yourself
- Financial satisfaction – whether it offers the desired or needed standard of living
- Social satisfaction – the whole image and status of musicians in society

The last point is one with which musicians have long been concerned. While many go into the profession because it can offer glamour and status, others feel society treats them as social lepers. As one experienced rock musician put it: 'Most people regard musicians as one step up the social ladder from rapists and muggers, and it's this alienation from the non-musician that I believe creates most of the problems. The public judge a musician only by the money he earns. If he's rich, he's a great man. If he's poor, he's a time-wasting parasite who should get a "real" job. Even despite the purely economic fact that Elton John has probably paid more tax than Wigan and brought in more foreign earnings than British Steel, it is not a "real" job!(from *Pressure Sensitive*, Wills & Cooper).

The 'worth' of a musician to society has always been an issue, because traditionally the musician is seen to do little 'labour' and produce no tangible 'product'. Friction between the 'average working person' and the artist includes:

- Jealousy of musicians, actors, television personalities and artists in general because their talent enables them to act, sing, play or entertain people.
- Jealousy of and curiosity about the artist's lifestyle, fame and publicity.

- Resentment that the artist appears to get up late and spend a leisurely day doing what passes through his head.
- Misunderstanding or disdain for the impractical imagination of the artist in which, as the proponents of Virtual Reality say 'fantasy has replaced money as the unit of currency'.
- Total underestimation of the long and unsociable hours musicians habitually work.

There has always been a conflict of values between realistic, material people whose lives are spent in administrative or physical work and 'artists' who live in a world where fantasy is the key to sudden wealth that would take years to earn by repetitive labour. The gains, if they come, may be enormous: it has been said that ABBA made more profit in one year than the whole of the Swedish economy. But music, like gambling, is a high-risk occupation, representing high gains or high losses. Secure jobs are low-risk strategies – moderate gains but low losses.

Since realistic people represent at least two-thirds of the population, artists rightly feel they are treated as a minority. This does not mean that musicians are not 'normal' – everything that exists is actually 'normal'. The 'normal curve' has a lot of 'middle values' in the centre and a smaller number of 'extreme values' at either end. Average-size people are normal, but so are short people and tall people – they all fit into the same 'normal curve'. Even if you took away the shortest and tallest and then redrew the normal curve, it would continue to have extremes at either end.

What is 'normal', however, is not what counts – it is the middle values of the majority that tend to become the norms of society. Having '2.4' children is 'in the middle'; being gay or having 12 children means being at one end or the other. Being a musician is normal. Twelve-tone or punk music is normal. It is just that the values of society tend to reflect low-risk 'middle of the road' values such as melodic love songs or romantic piano music.

Artistic integrity does, however, have a value. While there is always a healthy middle-of-the-road market, there is also a definite value in uniqueness, as with Frank Zappa or the Sex Pistols. Such uniqueness is very collectable, as art or antiques show, and society pays enormous sums for it. This is simple supply and demand – what is unique is in short supply, or is difficult to reproduce by anyone else. Such uniqueness may unfortunately only be valued when time has tamed it, which is small consolation to the likes of

Bela Bartók or Charlie Parker and those who, while living, were at the extreme end of what was acceptable.

A musical career is a constant choice of values. By and large, musicians rate musical satisfaction higher than money, so their first aim is to get the music right. Money can be the next value, but there is a well-known trap of getting caught in a 'money security situation' like a West-End show or a commercial band for year after year – the equivalent of an actor in a television soap. As in soaps, the minority break out to get more career prospects but the majority stay and take advantage of not having to deal with job insecurity.

There are stressors involved both in overachieving (fame) and underachieving. The latter can result from many factors:

- Being stuck in a purely commercial set of values
- Playing in a band with weak members in it
- Touring as a soloist, where the 'house band' may vary from good to diabolical

Stress can also result either from work overload or work underload. Overload can be travelling, rehearsing and playing two sets all in one day, not to mention hanging about for sound-checks. Since overload can last for days at a time, the musician may get chronically deprived of sleep and exist on a 'high' of excitement or stimulants, with a resulting 'come down' at the end of it. Underload can typically be long or regular periods of no work, where the musician can begin to doubt his whole value and ability to perform. The feelings of jealousy that 'other' musicians are getting the work because, for example, they are younger, more in vogue, more sycophantic, know the right fixers, does not help.

One particular career stressor is 'not getting the musical rewards you think you deserve' – another way of saying that the standards you set for yourself are not being realised in your career, whether these be financial, social or personal ones.

In terms of personal standards there is always the elusive 'peak experience' where you seem to be inspired beyond your usual playing. This happens at any level of the business from top to bottom: trumpeter Dizzy Gillespie claimed he only opened out and played to his full potential once or twice a year. It is, however, possible – as Dizzy showed – to maintain a high level of reliability and musical satisfaction by a good attitude and regular practice.

Coping with Attachment and Family Life

Musicians have a bad reputation for coping with commitments. Much of this criticism is unfair – like pilots and firefighters, musicians travel a lot, work unsociable hours and may be called out at the drop of a hat. This makes them 'environmentally' unstable, but not necessarily emotionally so. Musicians are frequently caring, sensitive and fun to be with, and have a justified reputation for attracting people to them. They may be slightly easier to live with than racing drivers, but they still have a certain set of values based on individual worth and performance, and these need to be shared or taken into consideration.

Some of the typical musician's values tend to help them integrate with other people: they are sensitive to others because they habitually moderate their behaviour to other musicians. They have team spirit because they work in teams. They believe in feelings because their work is non-verbal, and they tend to find creative ways out of difficulties.

Other parts of the musician's psyche are non-integrative. They are competitive and tend to think they are right. Rock, blues and jazz musicians in particular are used to alienation and can be defensive, nonconformist and react angrily to criticism. They tend to prefer their own values, friends, lifestyle and even jokes.

Such a generally defensive way of life sets a minimum value on commitment to social norms and a maximum value on individuality. Fitting this into the framework of commitment is not impossible, but may cause friction with partners and families who are left to take care of the day-to-day responsibilities of running a home. Likely consequences are that the musician will:

- Change partners where conflict arises.
- Find a partner in the profession and share values. For married musicians this can be one or more casual affairs.
- Have a family 'outside' the profession and live another set of values when not performing. In many cases this represents a valuable financial and emotional refuge.

Orchestral players who are inherently more stable, as is shown in a study of the Vienna Symphony Orchestra, seem largely content with family life. They nevertheless complain that work interferes with home and leisure life, and that holidays have to be rescheduled.

The early career of musicians – in their 20s and 30s – is often a pressure point where changes of direction or impulsive responses to events take place. Musicians become more stable as their careers progress, which may explain why later marriages can last longer than first ones. Later still, mid-life crises and anxiety over declining powers or looming retirement may cause a further stress point in relationships which partners have to negotiate.

The long or unsociable hours of musicians certainly put strains on families. Musicians may not want to travel as much as their schedules demand, and when home may only really see the family at lunch or weekends. When also rehearsing and doing sessions, they can wake to find nobody at home, go to work before anybody comes home and return when everyone is asleep. The effects on children and sex life are obvious.

It helps when partner and children feel committed to the musician's success, not only financially but socially. Children hear their parents on recordings, radio and television, get admired by other kids, and benefit from the stimulating and lively social environment of the musician. Many musicians make excellent parents, offering children a richness of fantasy that is particularly effective in early years. They may be often absent but they are rarely boring and may be much loved by their children.

Since arguments may be often about money, it helps when partners share a rather idealistic attitude to personal achievement at the expense of regular income. Poverty, however, is depressing and musicians who make no attempt to meet financial obligations may be simply seen as selfish. Periodic adjustments of values or temporary jobs are one way of avoiding total family breakdown and a lot of regret later.

• Fame and its Effects

The pinnacle of a musical career is fame. Or is it? Picasso is reputed to have said something along the lines of 'I have known poverty, disapproval, unhappiness and many other unpleasant things during my life. The worst thing of all has been fame – it is worse than all the other things put together'.

Fame is a notorious way of exposing potential weaknesses and opening cracks. If there are any conflicts in motivation between 'I'm the greatest' and 'I'm not really that good', fame exposes the doubt that 'I may be just a fraud – I'll be found out in the end'. This needs to be addressed and overcome.

In terms of friendships and relationships, fame may open new and sometimes exciting doors. But as one door opens, another tends to shut. Old friends drop away or are embarrassed to make contact, and relationships break up under the stress of conflicting lifestyles. The musician can suddenly be stranded with a whole new set of references. Sometimes all references are new: new management, new musicians, new relationship, new friends, new bank balance, new house, new country, new tour. Add to that the 'new' look in people's faces as they look straight at you and see someone else – a 'star' with a public image, not the person you see in the mirror. These are the 'yes' people – the ones that unconditionally accept your image, rather than the real person you are.

This can all be extremely confusing and a source of potential alienation. In the 'inner circle' of fame, reality may be even more distorted when things you normally take responsibility for yourself – your finances, clothes, musical direction and diary – are taken into the hands of others who make decisions for you 'in your best interests', meaning probably in theirs.

Many musicians have deliberately counteracted this by keeping their original bands together as much as possible – examples being Elvis, Sade and the Beatles. Others wisely try to keep control of their interests as much as possible, as the Beatles did after being manipulated by financiers. Many fail to keep relationships or marriages together, but many do manage to. It is likely that keeping at least some of the elements the same – like living in the same place or continuing to see old friends – counteracts the newness effect. Change in itself can be a stressor, and multiple change in terms of 'life stressors' has a cumulative stress effect. A table compiled by Holmes and Rahe suggests life-change values for a number of life events (*see page 144*).

To give a measurement of stress effects, these life changes were related to physical illness. When the total reached between 200 and 300 over a period of a year, more than half the people involved were found to show health problems the following year. For a total of over 300, this rose to about three-quarters. Admittedly, the subjects tested were not musicians, and also some of the factors tend to repeat themselves, but this scale does give some idea of how a number of sudden changes in basic living values can cause a stressful readjustment when they all come at once.

LIFE EVENT	LIFE-CHANGE VALUE
Marital separation	65
Business readjustment	39
Change in financial state	38
Change to different line of work	36
Change in responsibilities at work	29
Outstanding personal achievement	28
Change in living conditions	25
Revision of personal habits	24
Change in residence	20
Change in social activities	18

***Figure 7.1.* The 'life change' value of various events (Holmes and Rahe).**

Dealing with Fame

To avoid fame 'going to your head', make changes gradually where you can, and keep seeing familiar faces who act as a 'reference' – most often close friends and family. This helps you to digest mentally what is happening. Identify where it is important to say to yourself 'success won't change me'. And stay healthy – eat a healthy, balanced diet, take regular exercise, and build in periods of relaxation to your lifestyle.

It is also important to stay humble. The expression most commonly heard on chat shows when well-known actors are interviewed about their lives and work (apart from 'I'm currently appearing in...') is 'I've been very lucky'. Why is this distrust of the 'fickle finger of fame' the byline of the acting profession? Simply because it is quite possible to be here today and gone tomorrow, particularly if youth is a factor. You are indeed 'lucky' while you are in the public eye. Fame is an 'optional extra' in your career – the 'tinsel' that falls on you and then falls away again. This is true for all but the legends. Humility and realism in this way preserves a sense of scale and avoids the pride that goes before a fall. If you feel fame exceeds your expectations you will not be mortified to find that in the end it left you back where you expected. It will at least have given you a lot of experiences and useful contacts while it lasted.

Another thing about fame is that it signals reaching the top level of the profession. And from the top the journey may be down –

either slowly or, in some cases, quite suddenly. This may be difficult to cope with unless there is a 'plan B' for dealing with life after fame. Good examples are buying property, investing wisely, opening an interesting company, going into production, writing a book, starting a family or becoming a chat-show host. The most fulfilled of the ex-stars are the ones with new careers or families to occupy them.

On a purely financial level, keep mortgages and borrowing within realistic levels. A commitment for five, ten or twenty-five years can be a nightmare when money suddenly dries up unless you have the equity to survive it and sell up for a profit when the going gets rougher. Houses are a medium risk, instruments a good one (especially old stringed instruments like violins or even classic guitars), studio electronics an extremely bad one unless you are hiring equipment out for a profit, because it all goes out of date in months or years.

'Lifestyle' spending is the worst of all – running up debts to finance holidays, parties and shopping sprees with members of the 'jet set' whose money comes from much more predictable sources like business or family fortunes, and who may desert you as soon as your glitter or cash fades away.

Keeping a clear boundary between fantasy and reality is vitally important in handling your own self-image and your image in the eyes of fans. You may go 'into role' for a stage act, adopting particular clothes, image, even another name. Off-stage you can be confronted by fans or simply ordinary people who still see you in your 'role' rather than as yourself. Keeping a clear track of who you are to whom can help keep the inner self secure. To some fans you can be yourself, to others you will never be anything other than a public image.

To illustrate the last point, I remember sitting at a table with Chet Baker a few months before his death, just after he had played the first set at a jazz club. A journalist came over and asked for an interview, and Chet Baker asked him what he wanted to know. 'Oh, the usual things, why you sound like Miles Davis, why you have a reputation for hard living...' As he got up to sit with the journalist at a quieter table, I said 'It's a shame they never ask you anything personal like "what's your favourite colour". 'Yeah,' he said laconically. After the interview he went onto the bandstand and played the whole of the second set. An hour-and-a-half later he came back to the table, sat down, and said 'violet'.

Giving up Music

Surveys in America and Australia suggests that 60 per cent of orchestral players reach a point somewhere in their careers where they are unable to play. Typical crisis points include the following.

At College

The 'reality testing' (*see page 46*) of competitive playing situations can make musicians realise abruptly that it is harder than anticipated to keep up with the best. Changes in technique suggested or demanded by new teachers can be quite disturbing when they destroy a 'natural' or self-acquired way of playing, like an embouchure, a familiar way of holding an instrument or a fingering technique. The musician may find himself suddenly unable to play well or even anywhere near normal standards. Even when such changes work well in the long run, they are difficult at first. At worst they may cause an acute 'crisis' where anything and everything is tried out as a desperate way of getting back to a way of playing that works. This may cause such a drop in self confidence that giving up for a time is less stressful than continuing.

General small-talk in music colleges is often about who can do what, how many hours people practise, and who is doing what audition. Students are prone to checking up on each other by listening outside practice rooms and going to recitals, increasing the pressure that already comes from teachers and parental expectations. Pleasure from music-making may be lost in the stress of keeping up the expectations of everyone involved, particularly if parents are paying large sums of money for the course.

Another reason for dropping out at this stage is being pushed into music, or forced to play an instrument that is not really liked. It may be necessary simply to stop, for the sake of preserving your identity. There may then follow a period of reflection where a decision is made to play at an amateur level, to give up completely and do something else, or to take up a different instrument where there is less pressure. If there is a whole family history of violin playing and the musician really wants to play guitar, then a break may be a symbolic gesture that things have to change. This break is best made naturally, but can be made at the cost of a temporary emotional breakdown or a physical 'problem' that gives a reason for stopping that others can accept.

In Your Thirties

The reasons for burnout at this stage may be similar to those at music college in terms of ambiguous motivation. Pressures may, however, have built up gradually over a long period rather than coming to a head. Other reasons for problems at this stage are simply getting bored with performing, a dislike of constant touring, feeling you have reached your maximum potential and that it is time to pack it in, or finding that work is tailing off and other professions offer better career conditions. There may always have been a second potential career in the background, and this may eventually become that much more appealing. Musicians like variety and challenge, and may benefit from change, even when it means harbouring regrets about what they are losing.

Another reason for giving up in your thirties is loss of peak bodily function. This is typically the age when ballet dancers give up, and to a lesser degree it applies to singers or people who have a fairly strenuous stage act. Things start to work a little less well than before, then conspicuously less well. It becomes noticeable that you are no longer being hired for the same work, and then work may start to dry up completely. The answer to this may be – like boxers – to quit while you are on top. Physical factors may be felt by the artist in terms of loss of function, but they may also be perceived by the public in terms of getting older and losing the golden image of youth. You may suddenly start to realise – despite attempts to conceal or deny it – that the public has turned to younger artists. Time to become a chat-show host, journalist or record producer!

A further reason is starting a family, particularly for women. The break may be temporary or fairly permanent.

In Mid-life

By mid-life and beyond, almost all the above reasons may have been relevant. It is said that after the age of 40 one stops looking backwards to birth and starts looking forwards towards the end of life. This reassessment may be quite profound, prioritising the quality of your life and what you want to get done inside your lifetime. There may be some things that need to be done: writing books, travelling, moving house, visiting family. If there are adequate means available, musicians may retire early just so that other goals can be ensured.

Psychosomatic Reasons

There are a number of psychosomatic reasons for a breakdown in performing ability. The symptoms in these cases include physical ones, but there is a feeling among a number of health practitioners that psychological factors play some role. Some common conditions are:

- Brass players' 'lip'
- Violinists' 'wobble'
- Singers who lose their voices
- Repetitive Strain Injury (RSI)

These may be a bodily problem or may be 'a body in rebellion'. Often doctors cannot actually find anything wrong. The message inside the system may be 'this is too stressful – you must stop', and the indication to stop may come from the body if it does not come from the brain first.

External symptoms may reflect a larger unhappiness, like a marital problem, a sexual or financial frustration, a bereavement or something that destroys confidence or causes depression.

Attitudes of Other Musicians

Such attitudes are often expressed publicly as 'well, that's one less I have to compete with' – jokingly or seriously. Behind this is a secret feeling that 'there but for the grace of God go I'. Musicians have somewhere inside themselves the feeling that their lives and beings are always on the line, and that they are constantly teetering on the brink of failure. This makes musicians superstitious. Like actors they say 'I've been very lucky', and like actors they do not want to talk about failure or weaknesses.

Losses and Gains

Those who have had problems that have led to a period out of music may experience a mixture of losses and gains.

Losses can often be the 'breaking' of the unbroken thread of music-making and love of music that stretches right back to childhood. This thread is a source of great energy and sometimes has a sort of sacred quality to it – that of an unbroken commitment. Those who give up and return speak of a strong feeling that 'things will never feel the same', and report a wiser and sometimes more distant attitude to the profession. There are a number of distinct stages of loss. Typically these are:

- Denial – 'I can't believe it's happening'.
- Bargaining – 'If only I had...'; 'If only it had...'; 'Why did it have to..?'.
- Anger – 'It shouldn't have happened; I'm angry with it/everybody/the world/God...'.
- Depression – 'I feel down, lonely, sad, regretful...'.
- Acceptance – 'It's happened; I'm still here; I have friends and other things to do...'.

These stages do not necessarily happen in this order, and some reactions are stronger than others or may last longer. All the stages are normal, and experiencing them has a positive long-term effect of 'getting through' the loss. Understanding these stages can be helpful for musicians who have to give up playing for a period of time for reasons such as Repetitive Strain Injury. If any of the stages seem to be lasting too long, the help of a counsellor may make the process easier to get through.

Gains can be the result of substantial increases in self-confidence or objectivity. If one has become good at doing something else, that inner security can be transferred sideways into musical confidence. And being able to stand outside the profession may give all manner of useful insights that can be acted profitably on. Big problems become small; solutions become that much more obvious.

Like riding a bicycle, musical ability and talent do not really go away. It is possible to pick up music again – not at the same point in your career by any means, but with the same capacity to play, once limbs and joints have regained their flexibility.

Getting Older in the Profession

Getting older can mean a number of potential stresses for musicians:

- Becoming out of fashion or dated.
- Becoming bored, and 'coasting' rather than improving.
- Becoming disillusioned or 'bitter and twisted'.
- Having to defend your playing and job against a hungry new generation of players.
- Having to deal with natural physical decline, including loss of high-frequency hearing, weight gain, decline in absolute intelligence and responsiveness to new problems, plus a number of aches and pains.
- Having to deal with particular physical effects, such as contact dermatitis (common in cellists); varicose veins (common in bassists); shoulder, neck or back pain (common in drummers).
- Having the risk of your livelihood being stopped short through certain serious medical problems like arthritis, rheumatism, broken limbs, Multiple Sclerosis, Parkinson's Disease.
- Being exposed to situational hazards like high sound levels with resultant hearing problems like tinnitus (buzzing in the ears). The particular danger of high sound levels is that the full effects may only be experienced 3–4 years later, so there is no instant way of detecting damage (just as with smoking and drinking). Not only that, but levels above the permitted maximum (100 dbA for 2 hours or 5 dbA more for half that time) are regularly produced by both PA systems and some instruments themselves (drum-kit, amplified guitars, large brass section playing fortissimo). A drum kit, for instance, can reach 112 dbA, which in theory should only be experienced for about 30 minutes at a time. High sound levels have been linked not only to hearing damage but also to narrowing of the arteries, raised blood pressure and even some alteration of the chemical balance of the brain with possible personality effects.

• Unemployment

All musicians experience some fear of being unemployed. This can turn into fantasy and superstition. The telephone, for example, can take on 'magical' qualities for the freelancer; as one musician said: 'it controls my emotions – it can lift me from depression to elation in three minutes'. Many studio or freelance musicians feel a permanent fear of being unavailable or out when important calls come through, sometimes putting off holidays, even going out of the house. With an answering machine there is still the fear that the caller might be in a hurry and book someone else. Desperate musicians use pagers, mobile phones and diary services. Added to this are external factors for unemployment, such as economic recessions, cuts in orchestral grants, closure of clubs, and having no money while composing, putting together a band or rehearsing.

There are other reasons for unemployment that relate directly to the musician. As we have seen, musicians are typically ideas people with a future focus, whose strength is talent and creativity. Some of the main reasons for career failure or unemployment are:

- Lack of sustained planning. Musicians may be poor at carrying projects through, and are prone to putting off unpleasant tasks and working in binges or at the last minute.
- Love of variety and the life of a 'hobbyist'. Those with multiple skills may be unwilling or unable to choose which to pursue, ending up doing a lot of very little.
- Naivity. Musicians may be easily conned and have poor coping responses to life situations, particularly if in addition there is a dependence on drugs or alcohol.
- Rebelliousness. They may refuse work on principle, accepting unemployment rather than ideological compromise. In the most extreme case this is like painting oneself into a corner. This may be all the more so if the world of the entrepreneur, where most of the money changes hands, is viewed with disgust.
- Inability to internalise management concepts. The 'radical' dislike of authority or business also has the effect of preventing some musicians from accepting internal concepts of self-organisation which they desperately need to structure their careers.
- Sensitivity to stress may result in a tendency to withdraw from work if it seems too challenging. This can mean not phoning essential people, not going to auditions and generally succumbing to a feeling of uselessness which can paralyse action. At worst this can slide into depression where little or nothing is achieved.
- Feelings of distrust or mildly paranoid feelings about certain people or situations may lead to refusal to enter into certain work with certain people, again cutting down on the scope available.
- Extreme powers of imagination may result in self-delusions

about what is actually being accomplished and what needs to be done at the level of reality.

Musicians may have quite paradoxical powers of self-discipline. They may be able to concentrate for long periods on tasks that interest them and also keep up adequate amounts of practice – either regularly or in binges – but they may not be able to discipline themselves adequately to do everything needed to reach necessary goals. It is the 'necessary' parts rather than the pleasant parts that may hold up employment chances.

All these factors are mirrored in the musician's list of least-liked job values: predictable routines, well-known organisations, competition, persuading people, fast pace, working alone or under pressure, having to take responsibility for people and leading others. Since these values are those of the successful entrepreneur, this shows the difficulties the musician has in surviving under pressure.

All this seems like a long and sorry catalogue of 'unemployable qualities'. This is only part of the story since the musician's abilities are also considerable. But amongst the 'personality' reasons for unemployment, poor planning and self-management come very near the top, followed by inability to be assertive and negotiate the best career opportunities. Fortunately, these are skills that can be effectively learned.

Improving Your Life and Career

There are a number of general remedies for stress:

- Encouraging yourself to take holidays. This can be difficult as it goes against the whole ethos of the freelance musician as being always available for work. The freelancer fears that other musicians will get the work, that the fixers will promote others into his or her place on session and orchestral lists, and that work will dry up.
- Taking breaks with your spouse, boyfriend or girlfriend. To keep relationships working, both partners may have to arrange deliberately to synchronise time off.
- Getting into a regular band or orchestra. This makes life more predictable and so less stressed, but may mean more touring and more tiredness. It also means auditions and trials, which

are stressful in the short-term and a reason why some free-lancers do not apply for regular posts.

- Getting orchestras to arrange more sensible rehearsal patterns, with better preparation for gigs. Britain is particularly bad here compared to the rest of Europe.
- Learning to negotiate better and acquire financial and business skills. This would remove some of the stressors around being manipulated by fixers, managers and recording executives, and being unable to handle late or non-payment, tax, pension plans and personal promotion and marketing.
- Taking more responsibility for your own health, sleep patterns and time-management, prevention being part of the cure.

Practical measures for making life easier include:

- Checking instruments and equipment regularly and carrying spares.
- Preparing better for gigs and getting parts early.
- Turning down work that is clearly at the limit of or beyond your ability. Ask for details of gigs to assess the level of difficulty and stress
- Intervening positively to get ridiculously loud music turned down to safe levels.
- Leaving early for gigs.
- Talking more to fellow musicians on a personal level to monitor their subjective states, and adjusting your attitudes and expectations accordingly.
- Getting help when you feel you need it. Do not wait for a problem to become a crisis
- Structuring your life around work you enjoy as much as possible.
- Acquiring coping strategies for travel and touring situations.
- Increasing your overall confidence through self-help, and restructuring your belief patterns around your actual musical and personal abilities.
- Eliminating through therapy the particular stressors that lead to stage fright and personal feelings of anxiety, frustration and inadequacy.
- Learning to express anger, dissatisfaction and frustration in a positively assertive way, rather than turning frustrations inwards.
- Talking more to other musicians about musical performance

and your feelings around it.

- Acquiring short-term coping strategies for dealing with actual stress in performance, so that you can quickly psych yourself out of feelings of distress.
- Learning predictable relaxation techniques that you can use when you need them.

8 Succeeding in the Music Business

Success in the music business is not just about playing well and having a good professional attitude. As a working musician you also need to communicate often and effectively, by telephone, recordings or publicity material. You also have to manage yourself like a one-man business, and this means having some sort of career or business plan. Given the typically 'feeling' and spontaneous nature of many musicians, it is not surprising that management skills are foreign at first sight, but fears about not being able to cope are largely unfounded – musicians are adaptable, intelligent and resourceful. They are well able to learn computer skills or simple book-keeping, and may even design artwork or promotional material. And while musicians may dislike the ethics of marketing, they can be surprisingly good at it if they try.

The alternative to effective self-management is a 'can't cope' attitude, opting out of many essential aspects of the profession that could enhance your career. Being organised is a confidence booster, and proves to yourself you are on top of life, not that life is on top of you.

• Making a Business Plan

One of the best ways to plan for the future is to know who you are and what you want. Chapter One helps with the former, and goal-setting helps clarify the latter. To be fully effective, a career plan should be as detailed as a business plan – after all, as a self-employed person the musician is effectively a 'sole trader' in business terms.

Having a clear and achievable career plan is a motivation in itself – 'no aim, no gain'. This should be done as soon as possible, and preferably formulated at music college rather than in a sudden urgency upon leaving. Questions to be addressed are:

- What is the main area of choice: instrumental, orchestral, chamber, teaching, other? What secondary choices are involved?
- What are the styles of music envisaged: classical, baroque, contemporary, electronic, jazz, popular, West End musical, session? What mix is contemplated? Will lucrative styles subsidise chosen artistic ones?
- What is the main role or instrument? Composing, arranging; first and second instruments?
- What is the level of income aimed at? What is the lowest acceptable, and how is it achievable with the type of work envisaged? What level of income represents adequate motivation to stay in the profession or support a family?
- How will work be obtained? Joining an orchestra, diary service, fixer, agent, personal contacts, hanging out with other musicians and influential people, advertising and marketing oneself, responding to ads in the music press? All of these and more?
- What is the most artistically fulfilling choice? What is acceptable, and what is unacceptable?
- What is the expected scenario in 1, 2, 5, 10, 20 years and at retirement? Will there be a switch of career (e.g. 10 years as a performer before going into teaching or administration)?

Answering these questions first gives you chance of putting together an effective career. Ignoring them makes music a game of chance where you are at the mercy of anyone and any offer you get.

Promoting Yourself

Selling yourself requires a whole repertoire of promotional activity.

Publicity Material

PHOTOGRAPHS

Photographs should be:

- Recent.
- Of good detail and contrast, but with a variety of grey scales so that they will reproduce effectively on formats such as photocopiers.
- Probably black-and-white for economy, although colour has more impact and is getting cheaper with the introduction of affordable colour printers.
- Varied in their poses and attire, from the formal to the informal, and with or without instruments.
- Natural – particularly avoiding the terribly overworked cliché of 'expressive hands' framing the face – or if arty, then original and with genuine impact.
- Life size – the face and features must be right in the foreground unless an effective middle-distance shot is available.
- Done to a professional standard, whether by professional, enthusiast or yourself.
- Made over to you – you need to have copyright to reproduce publicity material at your convenience, not that of the photographer. This entails getting a letter of release and either the negatives or large prints that can be reduced/copied and reprinted. If the photographer wants to keep the negatives, get a signed agreement for terms and fees of reproduction.
- Ready to mail out, i.e. kept in sufficient numbers.

ARTWORK

A total publicity package can be put together by a graphic artist, and the benefit of this is that any logos or visual effects will be used throughout. The following are usually included:

- CV
- Business cards
- Letterheads
- Compliment slips
- Publicity brochure with photo(s)

- A4-size posters
- Larger posters (A3 plus) if required
- Artwork for cassettes, CDs, videos etc.
- Folders for packaging all the above

As with photographs, the same recommendation exists about getting a letter of release to give you the copyright, especially in the case of distinctive logos you will use as your trademark. The fee for the copyright should be agreed and paid at the same time as the first batch of printed material. If you keep the artwork yourself, this leaves you free to use different or cheaper printers. If the graphic artist keeps them and prints economically it can be more convenient. Be prepared to negotiate over artwork. Look for someone who does a lot of it and can show you a portfolio you like the look of and which includes the sort of material you want.

Beware of artists who have not done much of this type of work before, including friends of friends. They may have no idea of what to charge, what to do or who keeps copyright, and you may end up not speaking to each other or even suing. If you want to use them for their artistic merits or because they will 'do you a favour', then go ahead but make certain all arrangements are precise and mutually agreed from the start. Do not put up with any evasiveness, however good-natured in tone – no purchaser of a service should accept a vague 'we'll see how it turns out', or 'we'll cross that bridge when we come to it'. These are usually a sign of unprofessional conduct and can just as easily act against you as in your favour. This is a clear case for assertiveness and negotiating skills.

CURRICULUM VITAE (CV)

The CV of a musician is somewhat different from the usual one outlining education, work experience and hobbies. While it should be equally adult in tone (delete all minor teenage activities like 'president of the school stamp-collecting society'), it should give less emphasis to academic qualifications, such as exact exam grades, and more to actual musical experience. Where music colleges are mentioned, give names of teachers, particularly if they are well-known, and all recitals and prizes. With repertoire, start with a full list of all repertoire you have played and where, and from it make a working list which shows you in the best light. Include any commissions, own compositions, large venues and well-known fellow musicians. All material should be honest rather than exaggerated, but should also be assertive and complete. Understatement is of no use in a CV.

General rules for CV-type material is that it should be:

- On good grade paper, including glossy, textured or coloured paper where appropriate.
- A4-size, which is cheapest and easiest to print. Be a little wary of graphic artists who suggest impractical solutions because they want striking images for their own portfolios.
- Printed in a pleasant type face. 'Typewriter' style fonts like Courier are not effective. Serif fonts (with curls and squiggles) or sans-serif fonts (plain ones) give either a traditional or a modern image.
- Pleasantly set out on the page, using space as well as print for effect. Lists like dates and venues should be neatly arranged in regular columns down the page.
- Accompanied by photographic material. For a more professional look, incorporate pictures within the CV by scanning photos into a suitable computer and printing them inset in the CV. This is not at all difficult, and print outlets can do it quite cheaply. A hand-held scanner is now fairly cheap, so you could do it yourself.
- Chronological, either moving forwards in time – which shows a clearer artistic development – or backwards, starting with the most recent engagements. The latter is easier to read in a hurry and so has become accepted in the job market sector, but it may be more confusing in terms of a musical career.
- Relevant to the use to which it will be put. If work as a conductor is required, play down other work as violinist or pianist (list 'best results' only), but include arrangements and musical direction. In most cases list creative work, such as songs and compositions, particularly if recorded or played in public. This shows a valuable added dimension to a musical personality.
- Above all designed with the reader in mind. Put yourself in the position of someone opening your publicity package. Go through the actual motions of opening it and reading it, and note your objective reactions. Try this out with friends. Think of the typical working day of the person opening the package – how many such packages does that person get in a day, what

do they look like, what is likely to get noticed, what is likely to get thrown straight into the bin, what is the current state-of-the art technology (colour photos, CDs?), what is outdated, what is strikingly new? If you are quoting prices, what is the market like – are you expensive but good, overpriced, average or attractively cheap?

- Designed to take account of any change in status like address or telephone number. Get adequate copies printed at a time, with easy arrangements for change, rather than an 'economy package' of 2,500, of which 2,000 get thrown away when you move. You can 'design in' changes, by using small sticky address labels or putting addresses on the contents of folders rather than on the folder itself.
- Updated regularly, noting all the above.
- Particular items for inclusion are the following:

Personal information – *date of birth, nationality, driver's licence, brief family details plus any famous family members you want to include.*

Education – *schools and colleges plus private teachers and summer schools/special courses.*

Exam and competition results – *list all good results, or placings in important competitions. Restrict non-musical exams to the essentials.*

Hobbies and interests – *should be deliberately more 'human' and informal and designed to show that you are an interesting and well-rounded person. Active hobbies (oil painting, playing tennis) are more effective than passive ones (going to the cinema, reading), and interesting pastimes of an informal nature are fine ('presently renovating an old fisherman's house').*

Professional experience – *should easily fill half of the CV. If this is limited, cut down the rest and include every single engagement plus details of repertoire to pad it out. Repertoire should be playable at time of writing, since it may be asked for in response to your mail-out. Musicians with longer careers have more choice – the most prestigious venues, orchestras and fellow musicians in detail, and the rest in summary form* *('also toured Japan and Spain'; 'recent recitals include the complete Beethoven sonatas'). Future bookings should be included as far ahead as known.*

Repertoire – *can be included in the above or listed separately. It should be up to date and varied, and can include lighter as well as more serious work.*

Critics' quotes – *select quotes from major publications (newspapers, music magazines) rather than minor ones (parish newsletters) unless you are at the start of your career and that is all you have. Make friends with the press and inform them of all career moves, major recitals or recordings so you are likely to get maximum coverage.*

Agency – *If you have one, use this as your business address. If not, write 'Agency – self', and include either your home address or a post-office box number. List a professional telephone number, which can be ex-directory to protect your home address. A professional number should be different from your usual home number so you can put it on an answering machine with a proper, businesslike message (not 'this is the number for Ali, Marti and Snooky. Marti is on holiday until the 13th').*

Fees – *If you quote them, update them regularly and make it clear whether they include or exclude accompanist, travel or hotel. If you are VAT-registered, note this.*

Publicity and Marketing Aids

PRESS CUTTINGS

If you attach a lot of importance to press coverage, join a press-cuttings agency, which will collect all reviews and inform you of all occasions where you appear in print.

PUBLICITY AGENTS

Publicity agents are useful at key points in your career. They get concentrated media coverage by knowing people on first name terms and persuading them to use you in editorials, on covers or to fill empty space just before print deadlines. They are not cheap, but pay off if used wisely and sparingly, as in creating enough media exposure to get you a deal or good agent.

FAX MACHINES

These are increasingly common, and a way of getting printed material quickly to its destination.

DIARY SERVICES

These are useful when you are away from the telephone for long periods, since they accept work on your behalf. This often makes the difference between work going to you or going to someone else. If you have conditions for the work you accept, make this clear to the diary service – they usually accept anything within your usual professional field.

MOBILE PHONES AND PAGERS

These are one way of staying in control. Although expensive to run, they should justify their cost if you are truly busy.

COMPUTERS AND PRINTERS

Being equipped with your own computer and printer is a cheap and effective way of cutting down on costs. The computer should be a modern and widely used system, which effectively means that it should have IBM or Apple Macintosh ('Mac') compatibility. Software programmes should include a database for contacts, a word-processing programme for letters and publicity material, a spreadsheet on which to do your accounts and a graphics package to print out artwork or photo reproductions. Peripherals include a good black-and-white or colour printer (inkjet or laser), a scanner to incorporate photos and, if you prefer to send and receive faxes from the computer, a fax modem. Decide whether to buy a desktop or portable system and where you are most likely to use it. Portables are more expensive and have inferior monitors and keyboards, but are extremely practical. Musicians who already use a computer for music-making can use it for all the above, as long as there is no conflict of space or time between one use and the other.

BOOKS

The musician's bookshelf should include some basics such as *The British Music Yearbook*, *The White Book*, *The British Performing Arts Yearbook*, *The Music Week Directory* and the *Musicians' Union Directory*. These are an invaluable source of data on musicians, venues, agents, clubs, record companies, management, competitions, bursaries, festivals, publishers, journals and other societies and services.

MAGAZINES

Subscribe to whichever publications will keep you up to date with news, competitions, vacancies and musical equipment. Examples are *Melody Maker*, *The Stage*, *Music Week*, *Classical Music*, *The Strad*, *Studio Sound*, *Music Teacher*, *Jazz Journal*.

FILING SYSTEM

It helps to keep details on record of fellow musicians and contacts in the profession with a brief note of who they are and in what context they were met. This can be kept in a personal organiser, a computer database, filing cards in a box, or any convenient means. Computer records are probably best, since they can then be printed out in a variety of formats or transferred into personal organisers and back. A small filing cabinet is invaluable for storing correspondence, sheet music, accounts and all the things that usually clutter up bookcases, cardboard boxes and plastic bags.

UNION MEMBERSHIP

In Britain, it is not expensive to join the Musicians' Union (MU) at its basic level, and it serves two important purposes. First, it ensures that the union exists, and has the clout to defend the musician's livelihood in all respects – from negotiating rates to supporting medical services. Second, it offers you a large number of effective services – the *MU Directory*, regular information on lost instruments, reports of unreliable fixers, cheap instrument insurance and support for hardship or legal action. Given that we have a particularly good union in Britain, membership is strongly recommended. It can do a lot more for you than you may realise.

OTHER SOCIETIES

This is less important than membership of the MU, but for certain key issues many societies do invaluable work and offer worthwhile benefits to members. Prominent societies include the Royal Society of Musicians and the Incorporated Society of Musicians.

• Recorded Material

These days recorded material means both audio and audio-visual. Both include a bewildering array of formats, which tend to expand much quicker than they settle down into accepted standards. We are in a particularly volatile period of 'format wars', caused as much by cynical marketing and bloody-mindedness between the major manufacturers as by genuine technological progress or benefits to the consumer. The formats at the time of writing are:

Audio Formats

ANALOGUE

Analogue sound means 'analogous (similar) to reality'. Audio formats that use analogue sound include the following:

- LP records – good analogue sound but now discontinued.
- Audio cassettes – mediocre sound quality but widely available playback systems in cars, homes, personal stereos and studios, so good for cheap demos. They currently occupy a huge slice of the market, but lack the impact of CD, and like all tape formats are becoming obsolete as discs take over.
- Video cassettes – those who have tried recording in hi-fi stereo on video cassettes know they sound good, and better than most audio cassettes. The sound varies little over 8 mm, Hi–8, VHS and Super-VHS, and tape costs are cheap. The problems are long spooling times and awkward access for editing, but they make good masters which can be copied down to audio cassettes.

DIGITAL

Digital sound is similar to the format used in computers or fax machines for streams of data. Audio formats using digital sound include:

- CD (compact disc) – the accepted digital standard for modern audio recordings. Like all optical discs, CDs have the benefit of immediate access (no tape spooling) and no degradation of the surface due to contact in playing (no tape drop-out). CDs come in 'write once read many times' (WORM) or re-recordable format. They also have a variety of other uses, including recording films, interactive games, computer data and photos.
- CDr (recordable CD) – the best sound quality and impact for demos but costly to produce. At the time of writing recorders cost £2,000 or more. CDr should become the best format available when prices come down to sensible levels, because CD players are so widely available.
- Mini-Disc – similar to CD and uses the same technology on a

smaller disc. They are likely to become popular because they are produced on the same production lines as CDs and have a parallel market in recording computer data. Sound quality suffers at present from the compression system used to squeeze information onto a smaller disc but advanced technology should steadily optimise the format.

- DAT (Digital Audio Tape) – the standard professional two track digital recordable medium, used in broadcasting and studios. Great for making masters but impractical for demos because replay machines are not widely available outside studios. Like CD it does not use compression systems, but records the full signal.
- ADAT/multi channel DAT – currently available in two 8-track formats, using either S-VHS or Hi-8 video cassettes. Expensive and good for masters, but again useless for demos because replay machines are extremely rare.
- DCC (Digital Compact Cassette) – a compressed version of DAT technology using a digital tape format which is backward-compatible with ordinary audio cassettes. DCC recorders play back cassettes but only record in the DCC format. This makes them a poor bet for the future, since they neither sound as good as DAT nor use one of the current disc formats. Replay machines are likely to remain rare, and the format will probably die out.
- Computer formats – are being used more and more by musicians. Music is played through a MIDI (Musical Instrument Digital Interface) port into a computer and stored by the software in computer files, ready to be called back up by the same programmes for producing final masters in studios. The storage format can be any of the above, in addition to hard or floppy discs or some other typical computer format. Demos, however, are currently produced from masters rather than supplied in computer format.

Recording and Converting between Formats

Sound starts in an analogue format. It can then be recorded and played back totally in the 'analogue domain', or it can be encoded into a digital format, such as is used in computers or fax machines for streams of data. The converter used for this is called an ADC

(Analogue to Digital Converter). When digital sound needs to be converted back to ordinary analogue sound for reproduction through loudspeakers it then goes through a DAC (Digital to Analogue Converter).

The advantages of keeping sound in digital format is that, once it is encoded, the 'integrity' or accuracy of the data is maintained from copy to copy and from one stage to the next. In the analogue domain, sound quality is compromised with each step in the reproduction chain. The disadvantage is that some of the original signal is compromised in the encoding and decoding process. Most engineers now believe that the advantages of digital sound outweigh the disadvantages, while some golden-eared musicians continue to prefer the sound of analogue formats, such as LP records.

Audio-visual Formats

Since videos are so widely used for promoting pop music bands, they should be thoroughly understood by musicians. The current formats available are:

- VHS and Super VHS (S-VHS) – these are the normal 'large' cassettes, and consequently by far the best for demos. Their long spooling times and large size, however, makes them less user-friendly than 8-mm cassettes.
- 8 mm and Hi–8 – lead the camcorder market and are quicker to spool and much smaller for storage.
- Laser discs – the current digital standard, using large CD-type discs. Quality is excellent, but availability is scarce, so this is hopeless for demos.
- Compressed CD formats – these are set to come. Visuals use huge amounts of data, and advanced compression methods are needed to accommodate 120 minutes on a normal CD size. Like laser discs, the ability to re-record at home is still in the pipeline, and costs are equally high. CD players may steadily be adapted to play all newly developing formats, making playback machines more widely available.

Making Demos

First decide which of the above formats to use. Then the following steps are recommended:

1) Make sure you package the demo in an attractive way, preferably in a total package with your other promotional material. Put a clear label with your name, address and phone number on the tape or CD itself, not just the box – tapes get thrown around and mixed up. Address all material directly to the person you are targeting, not vaguely to the record company. Ring up in advance to get the name, spelling and title of the person concerned, and ring back to make sure he or she has received it.
2) Make sure any audio or video tapes are set to start in the right place and do not need to be spooled or turned over. This does not apply to discs.
3) For an audio demo include two to four songs, with the best first. The first seconds and minutes must be effective because the tape will be ejected the moment boredom sets in, particularly if the person playing it is going through a very large pile. The songs included should vary in tempo, mood and key (often overlooked). Lyrics and band details should be supplied in a printed format, not handwritten. For a video cassette one song is acceptable, though more are better. A video of a live event is permissible if the sound and camera work are good.
4) Make sure your video/audio recording is of professional quality. If it is not – and that applies to anything unprofessional – leave it out. Acceptable quality means clear and detailed pictures in good lighting, and hi-fi sound with a full frequency range and a dynamic noise-free response. Copies of cassettes are not acceptable: make a good master, e.g. on DAT or VHS hi-fi stereo, and then make all cassettes off that master. If SCMS (Serial Copy Management Systems) copy-inhibit circuits are present (e.g. on DAT machines), then buy a special box to disable them, available from studio-equipment suppliers. You have copyright of your own material, so you are not infringing copyright by making demo copies.
5) If you are doing your own promotion, get a press officer, 'plugger' or popular club DJ to push the demo consistently

for a short period in the hope of a quick kill, such as a first contract with a small independent label. When signing contracts, get them checked extremely carefully and sign only for as long as you want or need to, reserving the right to make future changes without financial obligation once the period of the contract has expired. The Musician's Union can help with this.

6) For more about demos, see the songwriting section in Chapter Ten.

• Forming and Running a Band

Forming a band is easier than running it successfully, but both require a number of distinct talents. When asked how he kept his band together, Duke Ellington replied 'easy, I pay them money'. This may be the humorous response, but it is also the first essential. Musicians have to live, so they need money as soon as possible to stop them from straying into other musical environments. Some of the other essential factors in keeping a band together are:

- Make sure all band members are committed. Commitment means turning up on time to rehearsals; being available; putting time and effort into a team project; and often some initial investment in equipment or pooling of resources, if necessary via a joint bank account where all investments are carefully itemised against future compensation.
- Find a regular rehearsal venue which is affordable and easy to get to. If possible, secure sole use of it, or use of it for prolonged periods, so you can set up and leave equipment and get used to doing sound-checks. All equipment should be under lock and key and insured for 'all risks' use. Check all clauses in the insurance contract – some policies exclude, for example, gear that is unattended in a vehicle for over 30 minutes.
- Decide on a group image. To make this easy to maintain, it should be fairly close to the members' personalities, e.g. intellectual, outrageous, ecologically-aware, socially radical, good-looking, sulky, humorous, sexy. Actively promote this image and design marketing material around it. In business this is known as your 'unique selling point', and should be reflected

in clothes, hair, logos, handouts, videos, demos, interviews and media appearances. Your image should suit your target market, age group, social group, language, country or continent.

Gigs and Publicity

Publicity and gigs go together – the more publicity, the more gigs and the more people at gigs. When pub gigs are paid on the door, this directly affects your income: the more effort you put in, the more you get back. The more beer the landlord sells, the more often he will have you back. When you have a regular circuit of gigs, preferably at least once a month, you start to get known and build up regular audiences who bring friends and relations. You then have the basis of a 'following', which means you can invite talent scouts from A&R (artists and repertoire) departments of record companies to live gigs. This is a much better way of getting a record deal than sending unsolicited mail through the post. Ways of getting a local following include:

- Hustle all possible friends and family to come to initial gigs so the evening goes well and you get return bookings.
- Do 'new songwriter' evenings and new band contests. They are often attended by A&R people.
- Get the band's name known through logos, stickers, T-shirts, badges, posters, leaflets, or anything that makes the name stick in the public memory.
- Draw up a mailing list of fans, and send them monthly or quarterly lists of gigs.
- Make good press contacts and send them regular press releases and any stories that might make news. There is a huge press industry and they swallow up copy, so you just need to say the right thing at the right time.
- Get on to television and radio as often as you can.
- Take important people out to lunch. This is the established way of getting a favour out of someone by giving them something first. You get time to talk and put your point across, the person gets well fed (or drunk) and you are all happy.
- Do not give up. Extreme persistence is a basic starting point, and fanatical devotion to becoming known is not unreasonable. Count on your 63rd mail-out getting a result, and if it

does not, send out another 100.

- Do things at once. Follow hunches immediately; pick up the phone on a whim. Actions, not thoughts, produce results in promotion. Be nice and witty on the phone, and phone when you are fresh (not 'tired and emotional'). Make as much contact as is tactful with people that matter. Do not go on and on. Make a clear point and ring off. A little often establishes you in people's memory.

Media Coverage

All media coverage is arguably a good thing, even scandal. Do not ignore children's television programmes or anything your band may be connected with (fast cars, helping the aged, gardening) which may give you a chance to appear on specialist programmes. Things to remember if you want maximum media coverage are:

- Get the articulate members of the band to talk most, and if anyone has a special charisma, coach him or her for more 'media personality' work. The appeal of the personality can be political, social, witty, off-beat or simply that he is intelligent and a good communicator. Many musicians have made the transition into media personalities, and in numerous cases the public is oblivious to the fact that they actually started off in the music business. So if you have got media talent, flaunt it. If you get on to media databases and guest lists you can be used again and again, either for your general appeal or for particular news issues you are known to support.
- When on screen be natural, humorous and relaxed – do not sound vague or apologetic, or bore everybody with clichés like 'we owe it all to our fans, they've been wonderful'. Take time, do not rush your words, and emphasise your points with body language and good eye contact.
- If you are a 'known commodity' you can cultivate lots of gossip material in chat magazines, women's and teen magazines, music magazines and national and local press.
- If you are a new or relatively unknown act, try to get coverage in the specialist music press as an 'emerging new act'. Journalists like to tip emerging acts, so that they can later claim to be the first to discover them.

- Try to be 'sexy', as media hounds put it. This ridiculous word is slang for 'everything the average public loves and goes for', and includes being seen with Royals, going out with a film star, being seen at society gatherings in striking clothing, and many other such activities that many musicians find totally alien.
- Try to be 'news'. This is probably a more palatable option than the previous one, but does require something original, like being the first all-female band to tour China; first recording of Tibetan Chants with a string quartet; starting 'post-punk minimalism'. Always useful is touring a war zone, giving aid to starving countries (especially if you really mean it), helping in spectacular Greenpeace picketing or parachuting into live events.
- Try to be remarkably anything in the first instance – you can always grow older and wiser. You can be remarkably rude, remarkably badly dressed, remarkably incomprehensible, remarkably underground cult, remarkably hairy or hairless, remarkably low or high voiced... in fact remarkably what you will. Style and image magazines love this sort of thing. All sorts of artists, from Elvis Costello to Gilbert O'Sullivan, and a number of classical musicians besides, became remarkably unremarkable once sensationalism grew into a solid reputation for original talent.

Employing Business Professionals

When asked what he would do again in his career, Chuck Berry replied that he 'would take a course in business studies, then become a musician'. It is the job of managers, agents, accountants and lawyers to be good at business skills. Since you pay them, you employ them, so in theory they should do what you tell them to. In practice, their management and negotiating skills can be quite intimidating, and you need to make sure they are directed at others who can further your career and not yourself. So any written agreements should be analysed in detail before commitment, preferably with advice from the Musicians' Union or another reliable independent source. Once you have protected yourself, a good team of professionals backing you up can do wonders in launching and managing your career.

The more of your accounts you can do yourself, the cheaper it is.

Consider the following steps:

- Taking a simple course in book-keeping and accounts, manual or computerised.
- Finding out about your tax and Social Security status.
- Subscribing to pension, insurance and sickness plans.

A clear business plan with costings and future projections is not only the best way to deal with a bank manager, it may also be the only way of getting results. The more you understand accounting the easier it is to launch your band.

9 Assertiveness and Negotiating Skills

Assertiveness and negotiating skills call on the management mental attitudes of the musician rather than the awareness skills that are so useful in performing. This is not to say that listening skills and awareness are not useful – they are. But positive behaviour designed to get the results you want or need is not a passive process, and requires a more practical, cynical and hard-headed approach than the musician would normally employ with friends and acquaintances. This may well be a learned process which goes against the grain, but it usefully protects the musician from being exploited by those in the profession who have such skills in abundance.

Assertiveness is the easier of the two skills for the musician to master. As music is a largely public business, which consists of projecting one's talent to others, musicians tend to have good communication skills and working knowledge of their emotional world. They can acquire fairly easily the ability to empathise fairly accurately with what others are thinking and feeling.

The major problem for musicians is their 'nice' bits – their generous, sincere and feeling nature, and their tendency to be naive and see the best in people and situations. When it comes to negotiating, this is the absolute opposite of what is required, and all these 'nice' bits must be resolutely put aside.

The musician does, however, have some potentially useful personality traits: above-average intelligence, creativity, spontaneous reactions, listening and learning skills. To this needs to be added a completely objective and shrewd factual approach to what is being negotiated, without a trace of sentimentality or generosity. Musicians are critical and can analyse situations, so with practice this can be done. In time, they may learn to take pleasure in negotiating for the variety and creativity it can involve, and for the protection it gives against being taken advantage of by others.

Questionnaire: How Assertive Are You?

1) In a situation with someone close to you where you are simply not getting what you want, is your voice typically:
   a) Raised or shouting?
   b) Calm and controlled?
   c) Pleading or whining?

2) You find yourself complaining about being unjustly treated. Thc person you are confronting seems uninvolved, and a little abrupt. Do you find yourself:
   a) Looking at the person aggressively to make him look away?
   b) Maintaining normal eye contact?
   c) Looking down a little as you speak?

3) You are with other people you feel are wasting time. Do you express your impatience by saying:
   a) 'Come on, let's stop wasting time and do something'?
   b 'What do you think about moving on to something else'?
   c) 'Would any of you mind very much if we sort of...'?

4) Someone you know enters the room muttering in an obvious state of anger. There is no obvious cause for it. Do you react by saying:
   a) 'Now look here; don't take that tone with me'?
   b) 'You look angry. Why?'
   c) Nothing, or moving to another room?

5) A fellow musician plays badly on a job you are doing, leaving you frustrated by the performance. Afterwards do you:
   a) Start criticising?
   b) Ask what went wrong?
   c) Feel embarrassed, pack up and leave?

Feedback

Work out if you answered mostly a, b or c to the above questions, then consult the feedback below. However your answers came out, do not expect to be 'perfect' at once or even at all. As with all cases of modifying behaviour, small gains can be reinforced with practice.

MOSTLY 'A'S

Your typical behaviour may be seen by others as a little forward or aggressive at times. You will find that the assertive alternative may be equally effective and may leave other people without any defensive or bad feelings.

MOSTLY 'B'S

You seem to have made a good start towards positive, assertive behaviour.

MOSTLY 'C'S

The person absorbing the bad feelings may be you. You may feel that with a little practice, and starting with small but positive gains, you can use words instead of silence and come away from situations more often with positive thoughts rather than a feeling of 'I wish I'd....'

• Defining Assertiveness

Assertiveness is not:

- Passive behaviour, such as when you want to say something but do not. This is the notorious 'Waiter, there's a fly in the soup' situation – you pull it out by the wings and somehow convince yourself that flies are clean, sweet-tasting little things, then drink up the soup because you do not like to make a fuss.
- Aggressive behaviour, demonstrated in confrontational statements such as 'Now just you look here, I've got shares in this company'. Aggressive behaviour tends to get negative results

because people do not like it. Assertive behaviour gets positive results because it is constructive and can be done pleasantly.

- Manipulative behaviour. This may produce short-term results, but it loses friends in the long term. It is usually characterised by indifference and insensitivity to other people's feelings and wants. Assertive behaviour recognises these, and so can get results without losing friends.
- Arrogant or 'superior' behaviour. A standpoint of 'I'm OK, you're not OK' is that of the cynic, complainer and general malcontent. The assertive standpoint is one of 'I'm OK, you're OK, but there are a few things that need pointing out'.

Assertive behaviour should leave a situation clearer and better. It may arouse emotions and bring matters into the open, but it need not offend.

When to Use Assertive Behaviour

If assertiveness could be used everywhere and at any time the world would be a clearer and less frustrating place. As it is, some of us can be assertive with people we know well but not with strangers, with partners but not parents. Or we may be assertive on stage but quite shy off it.

Assertiveness is most useful in situations where we need to put a point across to others. This should be done in a form which is clear, reasonable and true. The way we communicate should be open, direct and as pleasant as possible in the circumstances. Criticism should be fair, and compliments sincere. We should be able to receive as well as give in a positive way.

We can also use assertiveness when we want to convey our true feelings and our actual needs, wishes and desires. It promotes understanding with everyone the musician has to deal with – fellow professionals, agents, teachers, record companies, friends and partners.

Conveying Feelings

Common feelings can be divided into their basic origins:

- Happiness

- Sadness
- Anger
- Fear
- Desire

Other feelings are essentially subsets of these:

- Happiness: elation, enthusiasm, satisfaction, fun
- Sadness: nostalgia, depression, homesickness, melancholy
- Anger: frustration, irritability, fury, rage, seething
- Fear: anxiety, phobia, foreboding, unease
- Desire: greed, envy, lust, ambition, longing, yearning

We are conditioned by our parents and the atmosphere in which we grew up in to believe that some of these basic emotions are 'OK' to express, and others simply are not. Some families put on a happy face, and brush sadness, fear and anger under the carpet. Others express irritability and envy but rarely happiness. A father may show only happiness or anger, while the mother shows sadness and fear. The child may chose one or the other as a role model. The result of all this is that our vocabulary of emotional expression is frequently incomplete. We may need to learn to recognise the full extent of our own feelings, and then find ways of speaking them out loud.

Musicians play all the known emotions through music. As such they have the complete vocabulary of feelings within the sounds they create. But like painters or dancers this may not mean that they can express such feelings in words. A more profound implication is that unless there is a true empathy for the whole range of emotions, then they may be contained within the music but not actually realised in the interpretation of it. Musicians who find certain emotions verbally difficult may ignore or suppress them in performance. So gains made in expressing them verbally may allow more emotions to come through musically.

For someone who finds anger difficult, saying 'I'm angry' may be very embarrassing. Yet bringing it out into the open makes it possible to deal with. The anger gets expressed and can die away, rather than lingering on as unresolved bad feelings and bitterness.

If a band member is frequently late for rehearsals, this wastes valuable time and angers those who have to wait. Assertiveness is about learning to say 'I'm angry about this – it keeps happening. What do you suggest we do about it?'. If the answer is 'Go jump in a lake', the reply is 'I'm still angry about this – I'd like some kind of solution'. If there is no suggestion of a solution, the feeling is 'I'm still not satisfied with this. If we can't resolve it now, we will have to come back to it later'. In this instance the anger can be conveyed verbally, without necessarily raising your voice. The anger is used like a barometer to read out your emotional state and wait for a reaction. If there is no reaction, the barometer 'reading' remains the same.

Sadness is another emotion that some find difficult to express verbally. In music it is one of the most expressive emotions, whether in ballads, blues or in Tchaikovsky and Rachmaninov.

Here are some examples of feelings being expressed verbally:

- You played really well – it was a pleasure listening.
- That music is so sad it almost makes me cry.
- I get quite nervous of flying – I don't know why.
- I feel quite unhappy at the moment.
- I'm angry you fixed that up for yourself behind my back.

• When Assertiveness Fails

Even if you are able to communicate what you want clearly, you may be met by a negative response. What then?

- If you are met by a show of superior bargaining force, you will be unable to get what you want. Such power techniques may work, but in the long run they lose respect and friends.
- If you are in actual physical danger, the 'fight or flight' response will override the desire to negotiate verbally.
- If you are dealing with someone with highly developed manipulative techniques, you may find assertiveness and negotiating skills help you some of the way, but that ultimately you will end up playing sophisticated games for which you may or may not have a taste.
- You will find that some people in life simply do not give you the care and consideration you would like. This may be unfair and hurtful at times, but it is their problem, not yours. Difficult people may have problems of their own which show up as rigid or negative behaviour. You can change yourself and be more positive and adapting, but you cannot change the rest of the world, which will remain basically imperfect.

• Assertiveness as a Personal Statement

Musicians are accustomed to communicating and giving pleasure through their work, and this desire to please people works best when there is praise and positive feedback. Without that, musicians feel frustrated and at times depressed. There are ups and downs, and not every job is a perfect one – this much is understood. What is more difficult to learn is that, despite many efforts you may have put in, there is little point in trying to please those people who do not understand you. Other people have their own ideals, sensitivities and lifestyles. This may not change, but assertiveness makes your own standpoint clear to others and to yourself. It also makes it easier to live by your own values rather than those of others.

You may come to the awareness that your own happiness, fulfilment and dignity mean more to you than getting what you want all the time. You may win some and lose some, but if you stand by your words and actions you will be judged for what you are rather than what you get.

• Negotiating Skills

Musicians are usually self-employed, and as such find themselves in potential or actual negotiating situations a lot more often than they may realise. To start with, each gig offers chances to negotiate items such as the fee; method and time of payment; expenses for travel, food or overnight stay; equipment available. Then there is the manager, the agent, the record company, the bank and so forth – each representing a source of negotiation and sometimes a written contract. And then there are all the day-to-day situations, such as buying and selling instruments and bits of equipment, where a better deal on several items can add up to a lot of money.

Most musicians have no formal training in negotiating skills, and may not even be aware of them at all. As such they are notoriously easy to 'rip off', which is the commonest complaint in the popular music business. Since they may be attempting to negotiate with record company executives who have full legal backup, or with music stores, managers and agents who have better than average business skills, it is hardly surprising that the distribution of negotiating ability is somewhat one-sided. Here, then, are some basic principles.

Who Is Buying and Who Is Selling?

This sounds simple, but may be harder to assess accurately than it seems. Take, for instance, that experience we all go through in the most impressionable years of our lives – school. To the young child, it feels like going to a factory – you clock-in and clock-out at regular times; a record is kept of your work; you are given a periodical report; you have to work regularly with time off for meals; and in time you may get promoted by the 'manager' to the 'executive' position of prefect. It all feels as if the school is employing you to do work.

But who actually pays for education? Parents pay for state education through taxes, and for private education directly, and in time the student takes over through fees and loans. So 'being employed' is an illusion – you are buying your education, and employing the school to provide it. You are the purchaser, and this is reflected by the power of parents in Parent–Teacher Associations, particularly in the United States, who act with all the assertiveness they expect as the 'employers' of the school.

The same applies to banks, agents, managers, hospitals and all the bodies that we employ to give us services. We are the purchasers in each case, and the long-term effects of being constantly told what to do in school prepares us badly for seeing realistically who is employing whom in daily life, and for insisting on value-for-money service from the institutions we use.

When it comes to taking out a bank account, it is easy to see the bank manager as the 'manager' of our finances, and to obey his commands and terms. But it is the holder of the account who pays the bank and should be able to negotiate terms. Those who have successfully obtained a reduction in interest rates or bank charges will testify that this is achievable. In fact, it is quite normal negotiating practice.

Another familiar illusion is the agent. Many musicians are overawed by the apparent power agents have to make or break their careers via their contacts in the business. But again, it is the musician who employs the agent. In theory this means that the band should interview the agent and find out the best percentage terms that can be had, what he is going to do to earn his money and what advantage he has over the many others in the business. In reality it feels as if the agent is interviewing the band to determine whether he will take them on or not, and imposing his terms.

The first basic step in successful negotiation is, therefore, to work out who is buying and who is selling, and then assume the correct attitude when negotiating.

When Do You Use Negotiation?

There are many potential opportunities for negotiating – all the occasions when you do not want to give in to someone else's terms without modifying them to suit yourself. These include the following situations:

- Negotiating can be about making a deal. Whether you are buying or selling, you are after the best price and terms.
- Negotiating can also be about entering into a contract. You want to get the terms right, and make sure you will not be compromised later on. This can be a written contract, as with a recording company; it may also be a more 'explicit' explanation of something you are involved in, for example what your student rights are when you pay for a music-college education.
- Negotiating in its wider sense can be about getting terms that suit you for whatever you are doing. For example, if a fellow band-member regularly delays rehearsals by turning up late, you will want to negotiate a verbal 'contract' that gives you some assurance that your time will not continue to be wasted in this way.
- Negotiating is something you do all the time with parents and people you live with. Whenever you say 'If... then...' you are probably negotiating something. Children learn to negotiate more pocket money in return for doing homework or helping with the housework. Parents with newborn children negotiate constantly about who is going to look after the baby while the other sleeps or works.

In all these examples, you are seeking terms that suit both parties, and you are negotiating how much you are going to give away to get what you want. This tells us that negotiating is a process of exchange. In trading one thing for another the terms need not be equal or even entirely fair, but they should be perceived as acceptable by both parties. The reason for this is that negotiating is a voluntary activity, where either side can decline to participate or walk out. So the decision made will be a reflection of the wishes of both parties, either of whom can change the terms if they want to. Where there is no room for manoeuvre, then you are not negotiating.

Making a Deal

Let us take the example of buying a guitar from a music shop. You want it even though you think the price is a bit high. You ask the salesman for a reduction, but he says the price is fixed. You can challenge this, and if the salesman has no authority to lower the price you can ask to see the manager, who does. Or you can 'repackage' the deal, and ask for a case or some sets of strings to be included in the price. By doing this you are happier with the deal because you think the price is nearer what you wanted to pay. The shop manager should still be making a profit, so both negotiating sides have come to a voluntary decision, the terms of which are acceptable.

Here we see some of the essential components of negotiating:

- People like to haggle a bit so they feel the work they have put in has given them a better deal. Consequently they are happier with what they have bought or sold.
- It is only worth negotiating with the person who has the authority to make decisions.
- If you cannot change the price, change the package.

The first essential step in carrying out a successful negotiation is to ask a number of 'what if...' questions. This has distinct advantages over an immediate 'opening offer':

- It helps give you some background for the deal, including a feel of what the likely highest and lowest prices are or what could be included in the package, without revealing your expectations or committing yourself to an early offer.
- It gives you some idea of the authority of the person you are dealing with, and what they can and cannot do.

The next essential step is to come prepared with a list of good reasons for a discount. You will need solid arguments to beat down the price, since the seller usually (but not always) knows more about the goods than the buyer.

If you are selling, prepare a list of special features of the goods you are selling, including sound reasons why it is worth more than cheaper alternatives. Believe in the value of what you are selling and stick to it, discounting the competition. When you are selling you are practising the opposite of what you are doing when you are buying – standing your ground against the buyer and increasing the perceived value of the goods.

The overall strategy for negotiation is to find a route to completion. Wherever you see a way out of the negotiation, steer the opposite party towards it. This is particularly important, since the alternative is deadlock. Ask 'open' questions that keep the conversation going, such as 'how would you feel about...', rather than 'closed' ones that bring it to a possible stop with a yes/no answer, such as 'is that the best you can do?'. The longer you keep the negotiation going without suggesting an ultimatum, the more successful it is likely to be.

The success of the negotiation depends on your opposite partner voluntarily accepting your terms as a way of completing the negotiation, and this can be done effectively in a series of positive steps in which you go over each term and part of the package.

Entering into a Contract

The most important thing to remember is to get the terms right at the start. It is much harder to turn back and renegotiate later, and ground given away is unlikely to be regained for nothing.

VERBAL AGREEMENTS

Many agreements, such as between teacher and pupil, are predominantly verbal. Take the example of starting a year in music school. You will have more protection against possible events if you know:

- Whether you get a refund if you miss time through illness.
- If you can change your teacher should you not get on well, and whether you can change in mid-term or between terms.

- What solid guarantees you will be given about getting orchestral experience with the college orchestras.
- What the attitude is to performances or other work you may want to do during the year, and whether the college has any right or thinks they have any right to impose sanctions against you appearing in public without permission from them.
- If the college will pay for specialised medical treatment, counselling or careers advice if you need it.

There are many cases of students who do not get on with teachers, and it is particularly difficult to announce 'I want another teacher' in mid-term. Since the student is the one employing the teacher, this should in theory be an easy matter, but in reality the request is liable to be met with answers like 'you can't change mid-term', or 'we don't have the facilities to offer you an alternative'. For the student paying top money for a college education, such answers are unacceptable unless they have been pointed out and agreed to as part of the initial contract. If not, there is a clear case for negotiation.

The problem with teachers and colleges is the age-old law of supply and demand. Sometimes it is a buyer's market, and sometimes it is a seller's. If the service is very much in demand, then the seller can dictate terms. The owner of a well-stocked cabin in the middle of the North Pole could make the passengers from a crashed aeroplane do almost anything for warmth and food: the deal might not be equal, but the passengers would regard it as an 'acceptable' negotiation if it prevented them having to crawl through the ice and snow on a hungry stomach in search of civilisation.

Likewise, the teacher in demand can impose terms like 'you have to do this my way if you want to learn with me'. This may be the deal on offer, or a way of getting the particular tuition you are after, but it still needs to be considered in terms of the positive or negative effects that changes may have. Similarly the agent in demand can act in ways which seem disinterested or illogical when he is the one that has the top contacts and knows it. In all these cases, your best protection is to ask all the questions you can at the start. If you are not happy with the terms, change them or look elsewhere.

Once you take on the services of someone you are going to be paying, the next essential step is to state clearly what you want. There is an old saying that 'lawyers are only as good as the instructions they are given'. There are numerous variations on this, such as 'accountants charge less for auditing clear sets of figures than for shoeboxes full of bills and papers'. When it comes to paying for lessons, your teacher should be instructed as to:

- The styles of music you particularly like and want to add to your repertoire.
- Your career ambitions.
- The sort of technique that suits you, including factors such as your particular body build and size of hand. Also, the aspects of technique with which you are already satisfied, such as embouchure, and the aspects that could benefit from change.
- The auditions or competitions you want to enter, and how you want to prepare for them.
- Anything else you would like, such as a list of contacts in the business, periodic assessments of how your standards are improving and how you compare with others, or advice on buying and selling instruments and getting things repaired.

Your manager or agent should, likewise, be informed of your ambitions, your particular style, and all the ongoing changes in your situation or that of your band. He should be contacted regularly and asked for an update on his progress in getting you where you want to be in the business. As with teachers, any cause of dissatisfaction should be the signal to renegotiate terms in favour of a clearer understanding of what is expected for the money you are paying.

WRITTEN CONTRACTS

Written contracts with a number of clauses are a lot more serious than verbal ones. Be warned – they are usually drawn up by people who know an awful lot more about their effects than you do. In the United States, where lawyers are numerous and widely used in business, contracts are often skilfully drawn up to allow for a favourable outcome to all eventualities. This is what is usually contained in the small print. Such contracts are drawn up by lawyers familiar with typical legal loopholes and possibilities of litigation, and not only put you at a disadvantage but may cost you a good deal of money or bind you to terms you do not need or want. You are better off:

- Getting the Musicians' Union to read and give its opinion of any contract drawn up by another party.
- Getting your own specialised legal advice on what clauses may cause trouble, and insisting on changes. Here again, the MU should help you with a list of recommended lawyers.
- Suggesting a contract of your own. This could be based on a standard contract drawn up by the MU.
- Taking out legal services insurance (sometimes offered as part of a package deal with instrument insurance or the like), so you are insured against the possibility of having to use lawyers.

Threats, Complaints and Revenge Fantasies

Using any of these tactics when negotiating is a mistake. They put the opposite party on the defensive, and are more likely to lead to a counter-attack or a stand-off position where any prospect of agreement is aborted. If you have to make a threat as a last resort, be sure it is one that can be carried out, and not a 'sour grapes' one in which you are losing out yourself. For example, if you threaten to leave the band you are in, make sure you have an alternative in mind and can survive without the income. Otherwise carry on negotiating until total breakdown is unavoidable, while preparing 'plan B'.

Be careful about grievances, especially personal ones. Getting your own back is a common human emotion, and one way of releasing pent-up anger. But be careful that your grievance is not blown up out of realistic proportions by all sorts of psychological factors. You may be a person who rankles at the very thought of authority or being told what to do. You may hate businessmen, or cold, efficient people. If you are already prone to react to certain people or sets of circumstances, you may ruin a good deal simply because you cannot sit on your grievance and put your own interests first.

Be careful about complaints for the same reason. What you want out of a complaint is for the goods or service to be changed to your satisfaction. By being firm but pleasant and offering creative solutions you are likely to achieve this. By starting with 'Now look here...' tactics, you are more likely to be brushed off with 'There's nothing we can do. If you want to pursue the matter, that's up to you'. A solution is always better than a fit of temper and a series of sarcastic remarks. And your own proposal for a solution is likely to suit you better than someone else's.

The 'human factor' in negotiating is a whole study in itself. Unless you are particularly adept at reading other people's minds and emotions, it is better to make negotiating a neutral matter, and keep feelings out of it. Skilful negotiators are manipulative, and can act out a whole range of human emotions. The difference with this is that they do so to win, whereas fits of temper when you want something are almost always a way to lose.

The final word about bad feelings, stored-up frustrations and revenge fantasies is that they take up a lot of your mental time. The same amount of time could be much more productively spent planning positive things to make your situation better. It is much better to be independent and keep a clear head, so you can plan your future actions to suit yourself and not just to frustrate 'them'. Let bygones be bygones, and see each new day as a new opportunity.

Tips and Traps When Negotiating

- Do not accept your opposite party's first offer when buying or selling. This is not negotiating; it is just giving in.
- Be pleasant, treat your negotiating partner with respect, and avoid getting on his nerves. This allows you both to enjoy the negotiating process and feel happy with its outcome.
- One of the best negotiating tactics for buyers is 'I really want it, but I just don't have that much money'. This can be usefully accompanied by doleful accounts of hard times, many children, the recession etc. As long as 'I really want it' is convincing, the salesman continues to be interested. His response should be 'how much can you afford, then?', leading to a reasonable deal.
- Stick to the business in hand when negotiating. If you allow the other party to change the subject or waste time with unnecessary small talk you may become irritable and start losing ground mentally. If, however, you feel that small talk is creating a good feeling and enhancing the chance of a good deal, use it as long as it seems to lead to the main point.
- Negotiate on your territory if possible. Home games usually have better results than away ones.

- Come in strong with your first offer, but make it credible. Offer a low but defensible price if buying, or a high but defensible price when selling. Then move as little as possible from the price, or move in small increments.

- Use the old technique of a 'mandate'. When buying say 'My partner will allow me to go up to X price on this, but not beyond. If we cannot agree on that, I'll have to go back and talk it over'. Your mandate may or may not exist. Be prepared for the possibility that the same trick will be played on you. If it is, flatter the negotiating power of the opposite party by implying that he is not a mere stooge for his 'mandate'.
- Do not be pressurised by other people's time scales, whether they are too fast or too slow for you. Allow time for the negotiating process, and do not be afraid to slow down a speedy operator to a pace you feel comfortable with: he may simply be trying to lever you into an agreement with which you are

less than happy.

- Do not be afraid to say no.
- Do not be put off by all the props used to project power and wealth. Flashy clothes and offices, and 'I'm so busy' tactics such as keeping you waiting or taking telephone calls in front of you are all designed to imply that if you do not want the deal there are hundreds who do. Much of this may be total bluff. Salvador Dali was not the only one to say 'When I fell on hard times I doubled the waiters' tips'. Stick to your ground, and state your terms clearly.
- Do not assume that a salesman has to make a profit over and above cost price. If a business has debts which are costing a great deal in interest, it may need money in the bank more than goods on the shelves. A lot of firms go out of business simply because of cash-flow problems.
- When selling, do not try to create goodwill – by throwing in this or that, for example – with the idea that a little generosity promotes fellowship. The intended attraction of 'something for nothing' can just as easily be taken as a sign that there may be more easy concessions to be had, and your position may start crumbling.
- When advertising, do not use ONO (or near offer): it invites the other party to come in way below your price, making the price in itself useless.
- Do not use 'No Offers' in advertising either: it takes the fun out of making a deal, and sounds hostile.
- Some people are simply mean. They may prefer to walk away saying 'the price is too high' rather than accept a reasonable deal. Mean people can be spotted with a little practice – do not give them more time than you need to if a deal is unlikely.
- Do not put your foot in it by offering opinions and making idle comments that might offend. If you do not know your opposite party, do not make small talk like 'Elvis Presley was such a jerk, wasn't he?'. You may be dealing with a lifetime member of the Elvis fan-club.
- Do not get caught out by goods you do not really want because they are thrown in at a reduced price, or by items on special offer. You will end up with a cupboard full of stuff you never use. Go for quality and a minimum of good things you really need. Good quality items last longer and have better resale prices.

- Remember that all the skills you acquire in negotiating are just as likely to be used against you. With a little practice you will begin to see them coming, and when you have developed the ability to identify and resist them, this will add enormously to your confidence.

10 Creativity

• Exercise

Take a sheet of paper. Write at the top the words 'The first time I met Henry'. Look at it for a moment. Then continue with whatever thoughts or feelings come into your head until you are satisfied, or have filled in the page. Then stop. When you are finished (and please, not before!) read on for an analysis of what you have done.

Analysis

This simple exercise is about what could be called 'the window of choice' when you start to create. You may start with a narrow window of 'assumptions', or you may decide that you want a wide-open viewpoint with as few initial assumptions as possible. The fewer assumptions you make, the wider your choice will be. A simple joke illustrates this:

> *A man goes into a pub and stands at the bar. Next to him is another man with a large and restless dog. The first man says 'Does your dog bite?' The other replies 'No, not at all, she's very friendly.' The first man holds out his hand and says 'Nice dog.' The dog bites his hand. Crying out in pain and surprise, the man says 'You said your dog doesn't bite!' The other man replies 'She doesn't. This isn't my dog.'*

We can identify with this joke because most of us would 'automatically' have made the same assumption. So when you write 'The first time I met Henry', you have a similar set of 'automatic' responses, usually:

- 'I' refers to yourself.
- 'Henry' is a man.
- Since you have been given a title, what follows must be a story of some kind.
- Because the title contains the word 'met', this story is about an actual meeting.
- Henry is therefore a man whom you met for the first time, and the story describes the meeting, what happened, your feelings and reactions and his.

If you were to restrict yourself to these initial assumptions, you would be behaving in the same way as the man in the joke. By exploring alternatives we start to see the role played by originality in creativity. Among the possible alternatives could be:

- 'I' is a person of the opposite sex, a historic person (e.g. Henry VIII), an animal, an alien, etc.
- 'Henry' is a woman, an animal, an alien, a historic person (e.g. Henry VIII), an organisation called H.E.N.R.Y, etc.
- Instead of a story you could write a poem, make a sketch, add music or make a paper dart with it and throw it out of the window.

If you were to do this exercise again having seen the possible alternatives, you would probably be tempted to do something different. During the minute or so that you have been reading this, your assumptions would have embraced a much wider 'window of choice'.

You might, however, decide that you would prefer to write a story about a meeting with Henry because that is what you would do best. Originality does not replace talent, but ways of creating other than those you habitually use may eventually combine both.

The joke about the dog makes us react because it works against our expectations. In the same way, the innovators in music made us react because they did things that at the time were unexpected. This is true for everyone from Beethoven and Stravinsky to Charlie Parker and Frank Zappa. Even ABBA started out by winning the Eurovision song contest with a song called not 'Do dee dee bum

bum' but 'Waterloo', and how many names of famous historic battles have won a popular-song contest?

Musical Creativity

Creativity in the world of music is extremely important. Without it, in fact, there would be no music. Musicians whose main skill is in interpretation have to interpret something that someone has created, and their interpretation then contributes creatively to how it sounds. Creativity in music is commonly about:

- Writing music
- Writing lyrics that fit the music
- Improvising music
- Creating formats within which musicians function, such as bands, festivals etc.

The Creative Personality

Creative people have certain common character traits that predispose them towards creative activity. Foremost among these are:

- Intelligence. This is one of the factors that directly affects the quality of the creative process and the products it generates. It is not the same as creativity, but a certain level of reasoning ability makes a difference between the profound and the superficial. As Dante Gabriel Rossetti said: 'Conception, my boy, fundamental brainwork, is what makes the difference in all art'. Psychologists have suggested a sort of 'basic threshold' of about IQ 120 below which output suffers, but above which output varies not with intelligence but with personality.
- Sensitivity. This provides the subtle appreciation of incoming sensory information and the ability to pick up veiled levels of meaning and nuance.
- Imagination. This is the very essence of creativity. Imagination generates the huge quantity of ideas which are the food for the whole creative process and make the difference between richness and poverty of conception.
- Competitiveness. This is the motor or dynamo that initiates

creativity and keeps it in motion.

- Critical detachment. Psychologists often hold that introversion is an essential part of the creative process. Inner emotional energy, the creative search for meaning and beauty and the process of critical detachment are clearly factors that contribute to the process of creating, whether it be composing in private or improvising in public on the bandstand. It is a quality that may be present in otherwise sociable people.
- Radicalism. This makes the difference between accepting traditional solutions to problems and constantly seeking new or better ones.
- Non-conformity. This embodies freedom from obligations to the social norms, and allows for the creation of work that challenges existing ways and standards.
- Self-sufficiency. This is the ability to work alone. Self-sufficient people also have independence of judgement and action, which is part of the quality of originality.

INGREDIENT	PROVIDES
Intelligence	Power
Sensitivity	Refinement
Imagination	Scope
Competitiveness	Motivation
Critical detachment	Judgement
Radicalism, non-conformity, self-orientation	Originality

Figure 10.1. **The creative 'menu'.**

Of the above attributes, musicians show ample intelligence, sensitivity and imagination and high competitiveness. Although they are capable of applying critical detachment to their work, they tend to show much more warmth in social situations. While conceptually independent, popular musicians are more team-spirited than average and than their classical counterparts. While all musicians are radical in their approach to problem-solving, classical musicians tend to be more conscientious and less non-conformist than popular ones.

Factors in the Creative Process

Besides character traits, there are some factors which typify the creative process itself.

CONTINGENCIES

Creativity cannot come out of a void. It has to start with some stimulus or environment that provokes thoughts and feelings. Added to this must be some way of taking down the flow of the creative imagination, such as a tape recorder, an instrument or some manuscript paper.

SYMBOLISM

Imagination makes leaps into the unknown, linking all sorts of thoughts and feelings without apparent logic, just as the unconscious does in dreams. Freud described the unconscious as having no sense of time, linking apparently incongruous ideas not chronologically but by their hidden connections. Likewise the imagination creates symbols out of unusual links. The quality of 'sweetness' may link 'my love' to 'a red rose', giving the lyric 'My love is like a red red rose'. Music may similarly evoke strong unconscious links with familiar emotions and perceptions, symbolising feelings, moods, actions, landscapes, even people. What it symbolises is often shared by large numbers of listeners. This is shown in the popular titles that have been given to pieces of music, such as 'Appassionata', 'Winter Wind' and 'Moonlight'.

COMPLETION

It is important to distinguish between spontaneity and originality, and the ability to achieve a finished creative product. Free-flowing ideas are what improvised music is made of, and while such music has a once-only completeness, only a fraction of the ideas it produces may be written down and worked on. Composers have no choice but to complete works so that they can be transcribed and performed.

ORIGINAL CHOICES

If we got a computer to supply a random series of notes it would be original but not necessarily creative because no process of 'choosing' has taken place. Originality of choice is essential. Without it we would get the same sounds again and again; with it we get all the advances in harmony, melody, rhythm and sound quality that distinguish the pioneers in music. Originality is 'unusual but adaptive' – it is rebellious but has an inner logic to its choices. Thinking implies hypotheses, and if there are no consistent patterns or orderly links between input and output, the process is random 'unthinking'. This is what is usually separates the genius from the madman.

FLEXIBILITY AND FLUENCY

Flexibility is determined by the degree to which ideas are free to jump about and find new forms. Fluency is the strength of the flow of different ideas. Together with originality, flexibility and fluency are considered to be the vital elements in what psychologist J.P. Guilford calls 'Divergent' thinking.

COMPLEXITY

During the creative process many ideas jostle for place in the final product. Juggling all these parallel thoughts requires a capacity for complex thinking. Typically, while one idea is actually conscious and being dealt with in a 'step-by-step' way, several others are bubbling just under the surface, ready to emerge into consciousness at any moment in the process. These 'unthinking' ideas are often much faster than the conscious process, and can combine easily into the shape of the creative thought-pattern.

INTEGRATION

The first processes in creativity are often unstructured and chaotic. This 'need for disorder' is the primary process which deals with immature forms. The 'need for order' is the secondary process, and the third process is the integration of both, creating a new 'order out of chaos'.

HUMOUR, AMBIGUITY AND ABSURDITY

One part of creativity is closely linked to humour – that of making an apparently absurd association that contains some unusual or startling hidden link. This happens when you are set to react to one thing (A), and find yourself reacting to another (B) because A and B are both similar and different. A good example is the feminist saying 'A woman without a man is like a fish without a bicycle'. This is the opposite of the 'logical', which seeks the clearest link between like things, and represents the 'false logic' behind comedy. Another element of humour is ambiguity, in which the solution is left open to the imagination rather than logically stated. Often there are two or more possible interpretations. This common factor of new associations links humour with creativity, and we receive a jolt of surprise when we can combine different ideas with surprising quickness and on different levels of meaning. Because it is so obvious and predictable, logic alone lacks this novel or humorous effect.

Steps in the Creative Process

Many models have been proposed using different steps, but one of the most widely accepted is the four-step theory. During all four stages, unstable or unsatisfactory situations are continually being turned into situations that offer solutions. Gaps are filled, and more harmonious relationships are formed between ideas. This requires grouping, structuring, and dividing wholes into parts which are worked on and recombined into better wholes which better fit the overall concept.

PREPARATION

This includes choosing material and forms to work with, and 'orienting' oneself to the desired goal. It involves trial and error, re-evaluation of ideas, and it calls upon the total past creative experiences available.

INCUBATION

After the preliminary gathering of ideas, problems are turned over in the mind without trying to 'force' solutions. This can take anything from minutes to years, as material is elaborated and organised internally.

INSPIRATION

Material suddenly springs into an organised concept or form. Ideas come easily and spontaneously.

COMPLETION

Solutions are produced and ideas put into practice. These solutions can then be generalised and applied in other circumstances.

Types of Creativity

Not all of us may be creative in the same ways. Creativity may take different forms, such as:

- Expressive creativity, where the emphasis is on the quality of expression, not the 'product'.
- Productive creativity, where the emphasis is on the quality or quantity of the 'product'.
- Inventive creativity, where new uses are made of old elements, and common experiences are transformed into something quite different.
- Innovative creativity, where completely new ideas or principles are developed.

Creatives in the Education System

A study by Getzels and Jackson in 1962 compared highly creative students and students of high intelligence but low creativity. The results showed that the creative students:

- Showed a good sense of humour
- Chose more unusual vocations
- Went for satisfaction rather than success and goal-achievement
- Were less well-liked by teachers
- Could obtain lower grades because of tendencies to indepen-

dent ideas and stances rather than conformity and group-work

The study also found that the conventional school system can fail to identify creative people and use their potential – as creative people know from their own experiences. Creatives, as described by Piers in 1968, have a richness of positive traits that are largely accepted, such as flexibility, tolerance of ambiguity, sense of humour, intuition, ability to deal with complex ideas, self-acceptance, self-confidence, strong motivation and involvement in what is happening. They also have rebellious and stubborn traits that can result in conflict, such as independence of judgement, persistence, curiosity, dissatisfaction with things as they are, autonomy and self-sufficiency.

The poor record of some schools in developing creativity is witnessed in punishment for rule-breaking, pressures to eliminate fantasy and curiosity, and suppression of unconventional attitudes and novel attempts at problem-solving. More emphasis is placed on stereotyped role-play, conventional sex-roles and goal-achievement. If the environment of the creative individual is not flexible, stimulating and accepting, such rebelliousness can easily lead to a self-perceived alienation from the system, resulting in, at worst, confusion, fear and timidity.

Many of the most creative musicians of all time, such as Handel, Mozart, Chopin, Verdi and Schubert, grew up in stimulating and accepting environments. Music has historically been a popular, rather than elitist, interest, and many precocious talents – including children of relatively underprivileged homes – were not only encouraged but pushed hard to do well. Many benefited from family encouragement, good guidance, tuition and practice opportunities and a generally sympathetic milieu of fellow musicians. The typical musical education also gives many opportunities to show one's accomplishments, build on them and take on new challenges.

• Self-expression

Self-expression starts with knowledge of the self. This is instinctive in children who follow play patterns and interests that naturally motivate them, singing and making noises as they feel the desire and without caring what they mean. These noises are the most natural and real form of expression known to us.

In later life we make noises in the way we 'ought' to. It may be impossible to find again the spontaneous quality of the sounds we made in the first natural moments of life, but neither do we have to confine ourselves to learned or accepted forms of expression. As babies we had a strong and demanding individual voice, and that voice is still contained inside ourselves.

Since our most natural expression corresponds to our inner impulses and the noises we naturally make, singing teachers may start by getting pupils to speak words and then gradually turn that speech into notes. The result is not only nearer to natural expression but also shows the potential singer how to use the voice in its most unforced way, producing a better tone, breathing and range.

In creative writing classes the first instruction given to any potential writer is 'write about what comes naturally to you'. A postman writes about life as a postman; a soldier writes about war. It is possible for a postman to write about war and a soldier to write about life as a postman, but this is probably not the best way to find one's identity as a creative artist.

Our first stages of self-expression may be fairly clichéd, as when we imitate the style of middle-of-the-road chart material:

I don't like foursomes, they talk too loud,
I don't like threesomes, 'cos three's a crowd,
I don't like onesomes, or mirrors on the wall,
But there's one number that's got it all:
And that's two, ooh ooh ooh,
Just two, ooh ooh ooh,
It's two, ooh ooh ooh,
Just two, baby, me and you... me and you.

Even this type of writing, which is unashamedly 'popular' in style and intent, can become much more individual whilst retaining a catchy 'hook':

You wear the latest image from your head down to your toes,
You're turning all the heads around in every place you go,
You've tested all the pieces so you know they all will fit,
You're the ultimatest, up-to-datest identikit.
Image image image, image day and night,

Image image image, the image must be right.
Image image image, it's the only thing you know,
Image image image, you're the star of your own show.

© Andrew Evans 1983

It is nevertheless the 'personal' songs that have the most overall impact and are valued for their words as well as their music. Such songs reveal much more of the inner emotions and seek to identify particular human traits that resonate with the experiences and thoughts of many of us:

Don't think that I'm indifferent,
Don't think that I don't care,
Although we've never spoken,
I've always known you're there.
I see your face before me,
I hear each word you say,
It's only when you're near me,
I have to turn away.
And I love you so,
Though you're so far away,
And it's all so strange,
Not a word to say.

© Andrew Evans 1983

The Original and the Establishment

Few great artists were not ahead of their time. They were true to their own ways of expression rather than what they 'ought' to have done at the time, or what had gone before. The irony is that once this freshness of approach had got past its initial critics and an uncomprehending public, people gradually started to like and value its novelty. During the inevitable course of history the iconoclasts became the establishment, and their way of doing things became the accepted way.

Nothing was further from their minds at the moment of creation than how they *ought* to create what they did, and the same willingness to listen to the inner voice guarantees the same freshness. Even if talent and acceptance emerges gradually, the right path leads to the right goals.

To imitate is easier for a beginner who has as yet no original voice. This is not artistic freedom; it is freedom from care. It may also be freedom from poverty, since many people like what they know. To leave the cosiness of tradition is to 'leave home'. And to leave home means to accept the need to look after yourself in fair weather and foul until such time as you can stand on your own two feet. The sacrifice of the cosy is a price many creative artists have thought worth making. Others have not wanted to make it or, like Stravinsky, reverted to the traditional in later life when they had other insights and artistic priorities.

• Composing and Songwriting

Composers have a number of different styles of writing. Sometimes they stick mainly to one; sometimes they change according to taste or circumstance. Variations include:

- Recording music acoustically on tape through playing it on instruments.
- Hearing music in their head and writing it down straight to manuscript.
- Writing with a piano, guitar etc. to hear directly the notes as they write to manuscript.
- Writing at a polyphonic multi-timbral keyboard to 'hear' different instruments as they write.
- Playing into a keyboard connected to a computer and recording it as a MIDI file (*see page 166*).
- Recording music as above and printing it out on manuscript from computer software.

The advantages of recording into a computer are the same as writing text on a word-processor – one has complete control over it, and it easy to make changes or take the computer file directly into a studio and add further tracks.

Stages of Composition

Composers differ in how they approach a new work. The first question is what to start with:

- The overall structure?
- The exact instrumentation?
- A rough plan?
- Some actual fragments that need putting together?

Composing is a bit like building a house. Do you first make a complete architectural drawing, or do you find a suitable bit of land and stake out the foundations so you can see the overall effect? If you want to capture the overall effect of a piece of music you may want to sketch quickly, as an artist does prior to painting. If this is the case, what shorthand do you use for getting music down quickly? Do you try to record it from a keyboard, or write out top lines and chord symbols in pencil before filling in the full score?

All such methods should be considered before finding ways that suit your writing personality. Some of us are planners and some are spontaneous and intuitive. We may want to follow our personality style closely – plan if we are planners or see how it turns out if we tend to improvise. On the other hand we may want to explore deliberately the consequences of doing it 'the other way'. Improvisers may improve their work with more planning, planners may be able to explore more possibilities if they allow themselves to try things out rather than start with a complete structure or instrumentation.

Songwriting

Britain has a strong tradition of songwriting. Unlike other countries including the United States (particularly Los Angeles, the songwriting capital of the world), songwriters in Britain generally write for their own use in bands rather than on commission for other singers. This makes it harder for 'songwriters' to exist in their own right.

The reasons for this are partly creative – the British are historically a creative and inventive people and tend to 'have a go at writing'. But there are sound financial reasons for writing your own material. A member of a band who pens a song on the band's record stands to gain a considerable amount of money in royalties if the record sells well. In fact, the royalties from records can easily come to more than the band would ever get touring or doing gigs. So band members need considerable inducements or threats to let go of their chance to write the band material. Inducements include the opportunity to cover a hit and make quick money, while threats can come from the record company or producer to record a particular song or else. So the choice for songwriters is to be in some recording situation already, mostly in a band, or to make a living by a combination of associated activities open to musically literate writers. These include:

- Producing others' work.
- Acting as Musical Director for one or more artists.
- Writing commercials.
- Doing soundtracks for film and television.
- Doing 'library' material.
- Proofreading scores and writing out parts.

STAGES OF COMPLETION

Musicians frequently start composing in a rough and sketchy way, then progress to better and fuller ways of putting music together. There may be distinct moments of transition when confidence is felt to move on to another stage. Sometimes necessity forces the musician to attempt more than usual.

The musician may feel he can write music but not words. He will try to find others to write the lyrics, with more or less success. Then something happens to create the idea of writing lyrics himself. A friend may persuade him he can do it; there may not be a suitable lyric writer available; he may find some ideas on an old piece of paper and try them out. Whatever the stimulus, he finds himself with a complete song. If this looks fairly good, he may then try more. Creative people are creative by nature, and it is not so difficult to change from one medium to another. If you want help with rhymes, use a rhyming dictionary – the end justifies the means.

Expand your capabilities – you do not know what you can do until you do it. When you are writing songs, try singing them – many songwriters have ended up singing their own work, and usually better than other artists for whom they originally wrote. If you need a songwriting instrument and do not play one, learn the basics of keyboard or guitar. Guitar is easier to learn, but keyboard is much more practical for recording via MIDI. Use other musicians to help you when you need it. If you are having difficulty with a rhythmic feel, get a drummer to help you establish the basic rhythm. If you need more sophisticated chords but cannot find them yourself, get a keyboard player or musician with a good knowledge of chords to show you some alternatives until you locate what 'sounds' right. If you like to work directly with sounds, get someone familiar with MIDI to show you samples and get the ones you need down on tape or into your computer software.

There is a learning process involved in all these stages. In terms of songs – both music and words – you may have to write 10 to get one good one, or 30 to get a 'set' you can perform live. So do not attempt to judge the quality of your work until you have a broad selection of good, bad and indifferent efforts. Quantity not quality is the first essential. Do as much as you can, either finished or fragments, because:

- It gives you a good idea of your personal style and how it is developing.
- It helps you distinguish good from average from bad.
- It gives you a whole library of ideas you can later incorporate into other songs.
- It keeps you writing regularly and gets you used to 'being' a songwriter.

Above all, the transition to professionalism consists of turning out work that needs no excuses. If you find yourself saying 'I'm sorry about all the crossings-out; I hope you can read it', or 'I've got the song somewhere on this tape – it may be on the other side – just ignore the phone ringing in the middle and imagine the bass line which I haven't got round to doing yet...', then you are wasting other people's time and creating the distinct impression that you are not very serious.

Typical transition stages include the following:

- Writing chord symbols on a piece of paper
- Writing complete tune
- Writing parts for other musicians
- Writing arrangements for front line
- Writing songs with lyrics
- Singing own songs
- Leading own band
- Performing original material

Your work should be visually attractive and filed in an organised way. Lyrics should be typed or printed wherever possible – you may need to show your lyrics to people who could further your career. Keep your compositions in a loose-leaf file. If using a word-processor, store printouts in the same way.

Finished work is necessary for any proper musical use. This means:

- In a final form, i.e. proper length with all intros and instrumental breaks worked out.
- Neatly typed out or written on manuscript paper or recorded on demo-quality tape.
- With any individual parts necessary for performance (guitar, bass etc.) written out.

WHEN AND WHERE TO WRITE

Songs generally come in two sorts: inspirational ones and perspirational ones. The inspired ones can come in 5 minutes: they seem to be 'already worked out' and little effort is needed to get them together. This is because they have followed the classic creative

process – idea–incubation–realisation. Your mind has done the work for you while you were unaware of it. Sometimes this happens during sleep and, if it does, get some paper the moment you wake and write it down instantly. This also applies to inspiration in general – whether you are in traffic, with friends or shopping in a supermarket, make an instant note of any sudden inspiration. Beg or borrow something to write with and note down as much as you can: words, chords and melody line (e.g. CCDBCD).

These 'instant' songs are often very elegantly put together and have a natural flow and meaning – your own brain is capable of amazing feats of artistry if left to its own unconscious devices. If such songs are incomplete the problem is finishing them, because it is difficult to match this inspirational quality and the added bits can appear monotonously contrived. If this happens, come back to it and by then your inner processes may have moved forward to a better solution.

Worked-on songs come into being by perspiration, patience and a certain amount of 'craft' – familiarity with the writing process and how to make things happen. The ideas may come more slowly and may be less inherently artistic, but after knocking ideas into shape a good product can gradually emerge.

Writing at an instrument has the advantage that you can try out different alternatives directly, and quickly keep or discard ideas. This sort of 'fooling around', waiting for ideas to come can be quite useful, but does have the disadvantage that you may be skirting around the real 'essence' of a song, only changing the mechanics. A more natural spirit of creation can be achieved by allowing your imagination to do the visualising. Get away from your instruments, if possible, into a conducive environment. This varies with individuals. Some like an empty hotel room, some a park or the countryside, some a train, some a busy café. Others like some rhythmic stimulation, such as walking. The time of day is also helpful – some write best at night, some in the early morning, some in the afternoon.

Never underestimate your brain – it never sleeps. It carries on rearranging, modifying and restructuring material during both sleep and waking hours. It works on material when you are doing any number of other things. Rather than getting your conscious mind to labour on when no inspiration is coming, pass the whole thing over to your inner mental processes, and come back to it later. If the song being germinated hits a sympathetic chord somewhere inside you, it will grow and spark off other ideas quite naturally.

WRITING A POP SONG

The typical pop song is only three to four minutes long. Nevertheless, this particular form of songwriting is extremely common in the music world, and makes a lot of money when it gets into the popular music charts.

There are certain mechanics to writing a pop song which are not too difficult to master. As a starting point you should have a rough title, some lyrics and some music. Then:

1) Work out a verse, which should be narrative in quality.
2) Work out a bridge from the verse to the chorus. This could be a change in key.
3) Work out a chorus, which should be simple, memorable, and usually half-tempo in that the words go at half the speed they do in the verse.
4) Decide how long you want the song to be, e.g. 3 minutes.
5) Work out the tempo and give it a metronome marking in beats per minute, e.g. 120.
6) Calculate the number of beats in the song by multiplying the beats per minute by the number of minutes, e.g. 120 x 3 = 360.
7) Divide this by the beats in the bar. Four beats in the bar gives 90 bars total.
8) Divide the total number of bars into the average length of a stanza of verse or chorus, which is often 4 bars but usually 8 bars, verses or choruses being multiples of the stanza length. So 90 bars would give 11 eight-bar lengths plus one four-bar length.
9) Work out the running order, e.g.
   Intro: 8 bars
   Verse 1: 8 bars
   Verse 2: 8 bars
   Bridge: 8 bars
   Chorus: 16 bars
   Instrumental break: 8 bars
   Verse 3: 8 bars
   Bridge: 8 bars
   Chorus: 16 bars
   Fade-out: 4 bars
   Total: 90 bars

10) Write out the finished structure as a template, or record it into a sequencer with the basic rhythm.
11) Fill in the basic music (bass, chords), and change lyrics, bars and keys as necessary.
12) Fill in the rest of the musical arrangement, e.g. guitars, percussion, saxes, strings.
13) Add lead and backing vocals.

The above is a simple guide to the steps you would take either by writing everything out to score or recording it at home via a MIDI setup. The next steps are:

1) Record all tracks to a multi-track recorder, if this has not already been done. The recorder can be analogue reel-to-reel tape or digital, including the new 8-track format on ADAT (VHS tape) or Hi 8 video tape.
2) Adjust the levels to get the final 'mix'.
3) Record the final mix to a stereo (2-track) master ready for making copies. Note that by using a home computer set-up, all the instrumental tracks can be replayed simultaneously and mixed down in one operation to the final master, so that if vocals are added at that point no multi-track recorders are necessary. This is cheap but needs to be done carefully, and is only suitable for demos.

When you start using studios, there are a few more things to be aware of in order to get the best out of them and pay the least money:

- Haggle for the best price, e.g. in empty (unused) time which may be available at short notice.
- Rehearse three tunes completely before booking the studio and stick to the arrangements you have worked out.
- Work out what effects you want from the engineer and what formats you are using, and ring in advance to make sure everything is ready and all technical equipment is compatible.
- Get the best possible voice for your demos. If either yourself or the 'band' singer is not up to the task, book someone else.
- If you use a producer, be aware that he or she can make any amount or type of changes, including rearranging the music or altering the lyrics. In doing so, the producer may ask for a

share of the royalties. This is a clear negotiating situation – constructive changes that get the recording released and doing well are best accepted. Slight changes with a demand for royalties are probably 'trying it on'. The bottom line is not to lose your temper, but keep negotiating – your eventual percentage of royalties depends entirely on how well the recording does, and the record company is also investing time and money and wants a producer to make sure the risks they take are likely to pay off. A call to the Musician's Union is recommended in cases of deadlock.

- Do the final mixing session at a later date when you are fresher and have listened to the rough mixes.
- Above all, everything on a demo must be right – sound, effects, musical quality, mix.

COPYRIGHT

In Britain, copyright comes into being from the moment a song is written down or recorded. Protecting copyright can be done as follows:

- Mark demos, scores, song sheets etc. with the copyright sign © together with the year the song was written and the name(s) of the writer(s) of the lyrics and music.
- Deposit all such marked material in a bank or with a solicitor, or send them back to yourself by registered post, keeping them unopened with the posting slip.
- Get copyright signed to a publisher, who protects it and collects any money that becomes due to you.
- Join the Performing Rights Society (or the equivalent in another country) – they can supply details of eligibility.

The money you make out of copyright comes mainly from recordings and radio/television play. Sheet music is becoming steadily less lucrative, but a publishing deal can help generate new work if publishers promote songs. Smaller companies may be more dedicated than larger ones for promotional purposes, even if they have less overall influence and access to foreign markets – it depends how much interest the majors have in you. A larger company may also loan money for demos, recouping it later. But if little promotion results from a deal, the writer is 30–40 per cent better off owning his own publishing rights, and many start their own companies to do this. Pressure may be put on artists to sign to a record company's own publishers, but the artist is free to negotiate, and may prefer two separate deals giving two chances of promotion happening.

11 Developing Musical Abilities

• Identifying Your Musical Map

The term 'musical map' can be used to define the systems by which you can locate notes, rhythms, intervals and instrumental sounds within the total musical experience you hear in your head i.e. how you 'map' sounds. The first process that will help you identify the characteristics of your own musical map is to imagine a piece of music (either a familiar one or some music of your own) and try to establish the following:

- What do you hear? How much of the individual musical lines or harmony ? Melody and bass or inside parts as well? All instruments, or just a characteristic 'timbre' e.g. woodwind, brass, strings?
- How much do you hear? How good is your recognition of harmony and melody? Can you hear unusual melody lines with unusual intervals? Can you reproduce in your mind difficult harmonic shifts or only fairly straightforward ones?
- How strong and accurate is your sense of rhythm? Do you hear music without a precise beat, or do you hear a precise beat which tends to stay in time?
- What do you remember? How far 'into' a piece can you hear? Can you hear a whole song or short piece? Can you hear a whole movement of a classical piece? Do you hear just the 'main bits' and not the linking passages that may be much less distinctive, or can you hear everything?
- What do you dream? Do you often dream music or only

rarely? Can you remember any of it on waking? Are you able to write any down or play it? Do you recognise actual melodies and harmonies or is it just a general effect?

Between them, these questions cover auditory and rhythmic ability and the strength of musical imagery available to each person. Some of these capacities may be inherited, such as 'auditiveness' rather than predisposition to visual images, or the sort of 'note-perfect' memory that exceptional musicians such as Mozart possessed. Modern research shows that many musical abilities, however, can be learned and improved with practice and familiarity. This includes pitching notes either 'perfectly' or in relation to each other, and a variety of performing and compositional skills.

• Pitching Notes

Perfect Pitch

Perfect pitch is a way of locating notes on your musical map by hearing their 'absolute' pitch, which can easily be checked for accuracy against a tuning fork or piano. Classical musicians with perfect pitch are greatly envied by those without it, who can feel quite unjustifiably inferior. Though not the only way of pitching notes, it has distinct advantages. Experiments with pianists who were asked to learn pieces on a dummy silent keyboard showed that those who had perfect pitch were better able to 'hear' the notes and so memorised the pieces more easily.

There are also times when perfect pitch is a problem. In a playing situation where there is conflict about pitch, as when other players are sharp or flat, this can cause discomfort, anger and frustration. Once absolute pitch is identifiable it can become over-sensitive. This is particularly true of violinists and instruments where pitching notes is crucial. The pitch may even become more important than the music.

Relative Pitch

Improvising or jazz musicians are particularly good at hearing melody and harmony. They often know hundreds of different chord progressions from memory, and can imagine in their head or sing out loud innumerable improvisations over common 32-bar progressions. From a very early age – maybe the first time they try playing the piano and locating notes on the keyboard – they are used to hearing the relationship of one note to its surrounding ones. They quickly become good at identifying intervals, and so can follow quite complex melodic lines in their head by relating all the notes to each other by means of their pitch within the melodic context.

Using this system, the pitch heard in the head may be quite different from its 'actual' value – C may be G, for instance. But even in transposed form, the melody is just as accurate and the harmony just as correct. In the same dummy keyboard experiments with pianists, improvising musicians also did well through being able to hear and remember the moving harmonic and melodic context of the pieces.

• Musicality

The question of what musicality is has been discussed for centuries, and the answer is likely to remain more in the realms of taste and aesthetics than in that of scientific fact. For example, who is the more musical out of the following?

- An orchestral violinist with a good technique but mediocre aural ability, who cannot improvise or play without music.
- A master drummer from Africa who knows nothing of Western music.
- A well-known music critic who does not play an instrument.
- The world's best piano tuner.

Without agreeing what musicality is, it would be hard to chose between the above. All have elements of musicality, but these are different in each case. The violinist has performing ability, the drummer has creativity, the critic has taste and the tuner has aural ability. Between them, these elements cover most of what we loosely understand to be 'musicality'.

Some, like aural ability, are easy to test, while taste is virtually impossible. Creativity can be measured in some way, while performing ability is constantly disputed by critics. Different people give different weight to factors like technical ability, interpretation, originality and style. Such disagreement is notorious among the juries of international competitions, where technique and the ability to carry out all the concert dates that result from winning may predominate over charisma and the capacity to please an audience.

'Musical ability' may be easier to understand as a collection of different aptitudes, Some of these are:

- tonal memory – identifying and remembering notes
- pitch – identifying notes and intervals
- rhythm – identifying and playing different rhythms
- harmony – identifying and using chords
- melody – distinguishing and using phrases

These abilities are easily taught and tested, but are only the basic ingredients of musicality. The talent is in how they are used and combined with ideas. This extra quality contains many of the elements of creativity: originality, fluency of musical thought, heightened powers of imagination and the ability to create and resolve suspense within a musical structure. The imprisonment of classical performers in the actual notes of a score is the result of the invention of printing. Within the oral tradition of troubadours, and even in later musicians such as Bach and Liszt, the powers of improvising were still considerable. Any trend back to improvisation within modern scores and also within musical education would allow the modern musician a much greater expression of individuality and musical imagination. This would surely increase overall musicality and actual technique.

One good way of finding your own style is totally free improvisation, rather than variations on a structure. Allowing ideas to come freely into your head, then playing or singing them helps contrast your own style with external influences, and is a way of getting closer to your inner ideals. For the jazz musician it is a way of cleaning out the influences of favourite heroes, and establishing what sounds are really going round in the head. These may include impressionistic classical music, gamelan music, ethnic influences or a whole variety of different sound images put together. Doing this helps you go back to and start stylistically from first principles, mapping out the kind of music that comes spontaneously to mind when you are not trying to imitate or play any particular style or chord progression.

• Music and the Brain

Much has been said about the relationship between musical experience and the two sides of the brain. Some is stereotyping and guesswork, but much is proven within the inherent difficulty of mapping the functions of individual cells in a living brain. The first principle is that the 'dominant' side of your brain partly depends on whether you are right-handed or left-handed. The right hemisphere of the brain controls the left side of the body and vice versa. Right-handed individuals have 'typical' distributions of functions with the 'dominant' left brain controlling the 'dominant' right hand. In left-handed individuals, some of the 'dominant' left-hemisphere functions, like speech, can develop in the right hemisphere.

The left side of the brain is called the dominant one because it deals with language and calculations and so tends to be the analytical or problem-solving side. It is also called the major hemisphere as opposed to the minor one. The right side of the brain usually has only elementary language function but superior spatial and pattern sense. For this reason it is associated with non-verbal mental imagery like colour and design, and spatial visualisations like perspective and shapes. Research suggests that the right brain plays a particular part in artistic or musical expression as well as being more closely linked to emotions and dreams.

Experiments with musicians suggest that the right side of the brain tends to respond to the overall emotional and auditive effect of music and is used more by those with little understanding of theory and little professional music training. The left side of the brain tends to be used in a more advanced way to analyse music, and is correspondingly used more by professional musicians. This is quite interesting, since it suggests that professional musicians develop a critical left-brain activity which is progressively overlaid on their more primitive responses to sounds. Whilst this has the obvious function of monitoring the quality of music-making, it may sometimes be an advantage to disable such analysis and to let a more emotive way of listening to sounds take over.

It is likely that this happens in music therapy sessions or free improvisations, where participants are left free to explore sounds uncritically rather than being expected to make any musical sense. Musicians who try this experience a 'spatial' feeling which accesses all sorts of emotions and visualisations, and may recall childlike responses associated with a good deal of innocent pleasure.

Other effects of disabling the critical left brain function can be achieved by drugs which inhibit accurate judgement. Deprived of a critical analysis of its form, music will then tend to become a pleasant 'soundscape' where each element of the music has an enhanced emotional appeal: the reediness of a clarinet, the crash of a fortissimo, the hypnotic rhythm of the drums. This way of hearing music appears 'better' at the time because it is new and intense, but it is effectively a distorted reproduction in which particular elements are brought forward and others pushed back. In the long run, if music were heard without structure, no effort would be made to create the masterpieces we know today.

• Learning Musical Abilities

If you do not have perfect pitch, you can improve your musical map by practising other ways of locating notes in your memory. You can improve your ability to link notes and chords to each other by improvising either on your instrument, by humming or whistling, or silently in your head. Start with easy sequences, or 'changes' as they are called in jazz, and build up to more challenging ones. In jazz terms this would mean going from a blues to John Coltrane's 'Giant Steps'. Where you encounter difficulty in shifting from one chord to another, rehearse it until you can do it. Doing this away from instruments is a good way of filling in idle moments in queues or on journeys, and has the added virtue of rehearsing purely mental solutions to chord changes. This results in a fresher and more original approach without the clichés that come from well-practised phrases, and imagined solutions can later be practised on the instrument.

Classical musicians can rehearse awkward leaps and intervals in the same way. Away from the keyboard, notes can also be usefully memorised by visualising them on a keyboard, on the frets of fretted instruments, or in relation to fingering. They can be visually stored by reading or imagining a score. By establishing both sound and location you are increasing your understanding of the notes and consequently your ability to learn them.

Body learning is also important, since it stores habitual movements in our automatic memories. When well rehearsed they take place automatically – like reaching for your keys when approaching the front door. Such movements include scales, arpeggios, chord shapes and fingering patterns. While learning actual notes, awareness should be given to the movement of playing them, so this gets naturally stored in the memory like a snooker player's action or a golf player's swing. Like mental imaging, such body movements can then be rehearsed away from the instrument.

Learning with Love

It needs to be said again and again that the root of musical pleasure is actually loving music. Musicians who deeply love music are rewarded by the permanent satisfaction of being part of a constantly changing and evolving world of sound. They love practising both technique and actual sound production. Musicians who approach practice as a burdensome and boring necessity are rehearsing a lack of love, and the more they do so, the more they become 'conditioned' to associate musical activity with boredom and tedium. If it is not possible to enjoy every minute of practice then, at the very least, include something enjoyable in each session. This can be a piece of music you particularly enjoy playing, a new improvisation on a tune in your head at the time, a piece you have heard and liked and got the sheet music for, or some music that is close to your emotions. It is a little like the old saying 'something old, something new, something borrowed, something blue'.

Remember that practice is what you make it – you make the rules. It can include anything in any order. If you are not happy with practising, vary it in any way you like in order to get more pleasure and love of music out of it. Practise like an 'amateur' who does things out of enthusiasm without anyone telling him where or when or how to do his favourite activity. And when you decide on practice schedules, include technique, pleasure and time off in every session.

Practice is not 'different from' music-making; it is a form of music-making. When it is positive and pleasurable it does not become repetitive. This is becoming increasingly recognised in the diagnosis and treatment of Repetitive Strain Injury (RSI). If practice is regarded as detached, inhuman and purely mechanical, essential signs of discomfort may be ignored and practice may continue past the threshold of pain. Compulsive repetition and mental stresses progressively overload the body and problems start to occur. Music-making carried out with love is unlikely to be misused, and when continued pleasure ceases, a natural break will prevent overuse.

Verbal and Non-verbal Learning

Learning from instructions alone, rather than from actually playing alternatives, has distinct disadvantages. As a result, modern learning theory has swung heavily towards 'show and tell' and interactive learning. The principles of this are as follows:

1) Words are a 'reductionist' version of the whole experience – they focus only on parts of it. A verbal account of a non-verbal experience may be inadequate or confusing. Words also convey the critical or left-brain instruction, but not the structural/spatial right-brain content or the bodily movement.
2) Instructions are given from the teacher's point of view and may not be fully felt or understood by the student. The student may disagree with either the instructions or the view of the teacher, or may be incapable of carrying out what is suggested.
3) After a certain point, instructions overload the student and are not taken in, so the best that can be achieved is a little often. Instructions in themselves are not very memorable – it is the process of understanding that becomes memorable as it is absorbed and carried out.
4) Instructions that proceed in a random and arbitrary order without reference to an understandable overall framework may confuse the student more than no instructions at all – research shows that grouping elements into understandable chunks ('chunking') improves memorising. Random letters like PKX, FLV, HYQ are confusing. Understandable arrangements like ABC, IBM, KGB are instantly absorbed.
5) Instructions without examples are boring when you have long periods of idle listening. This is why orchestras like con-

ductors to give instructions while they are playing continuously in rehearsal, rather than stopping the orchestra every time a point needs to be made.

If the 'telling' part of instruction suffers from the above difficulties, the 'showing' part has the virtues of allowing the student to take in selectively what he sees or wants to know, ignoring parts which are either obvious or as yet beyond him. The student also learns at his own pace, and can repeat what is shown. The process of repeating is one of the student's own discovery, and is therefore much more easily absorbed into memory. Showing points out not only the sound and notes but also the body movements necessary to produce them.

The only problem with showing is again that it should be a little often. There is no point in showing a passage which is too long, complex or off the precise point to be either memorable or of use.

State-induced Learning

A known way of enhancing learning is to carry out the process of learning in the same state you will be in when you want to retrieve the information. This could refer to your surroundings or to your mental or physical state. The idea is that a memory stored in a particular circumstance may come to mind more easily if that circumstance is reproduced in performance. In practical terms this may mean doing some learning on stage, or at least learning at the same volume.

In a more theoretical way it raises the question of whether we should 'learn' as we would 'play', or whether the two processes are better done in different ways. Should we consciously analyse to learn, then forget the analysis when on stage? Both systems have their proponents. Classical soloists often recommend that practice be conscious, and playing be 'unconscious', in that once all the elements are mastered they take place automatically. The Inner Game technique (*see Chapter Five*) proposes that as much learning as possible should be 'experiential', and based on feelings and insight into the 'whole experience' of playing the music rather than a constant analysis of detail. It says that 'to play in Self 2 you need to practise in Self 2', which accentuates feeling, body learning, intuition and self-directed pleasurable activity. It is possible that optimum learning may do both. This may mean getting the 'overall feel' first, correcting details, then playing through in a performing state of mind.

Mastering the Elements

The individual elements of music are the nuts and bolts of performance – the melody, chords, fingering, shifts, dynamics, tempos, body movements and the whole process of memorising. Mastering the elements is made easier by a number of methods that are generally well known to teachers:

1) Find the optimum way of expressing a passage – the right speed, loudness and rhythm – then play it either side of the optimum to give you the flexibility of response you need in the moment of performance. Practise 20 per cent faster, to allow you to feel comfortable at the right tempo. Play it fortissimo to gauge where mezzo forte is. Feel secure that you have options you have practised.
2) Do not practise mistakes. On first acquaintance with the music, start slowly and surely, then gradually build up tempo. With jazz tunes, work out the chord progression and the melodic scales that fit the chords. Work out the fingerings you need and the choices of chords that sound best. Then play and enjoy. The alternative of playing a piece through first to get a general feel for it may help, but only if you can do it without mistakes that later need to be unlearned.
3) If you are nervous of forgetting the end of the music, start memorising it from the end, so that it becomes progressively more familiar. Such 'backwards' learning is favoured by some soloists, though is not a general recommendation.
4) Make a point of resolving problems rather than ignoring them. Practice is designed to eliminate problems, so cowardice in learning results in mistakes on the platform. Nothing is to be gained by massaging your ego into thinking that it will be 'alright on the night'. What cannot be played in practice cannot be played with certainty in public. Play around the problem areas – practise approaching them and leaving them as well as actually getting through them. Speed them up, then slow them down.

5) Feel the rhythm of the music, and if possible the dance element behind it. This applies to more classical music than many players imagine. The lively, dance-like interpretations of composers from Bach to Stravinsky, or the Chopin playing of Rubinstein, is on another interpretive level from the 'heartfelt' meanderings which reduce a lot of music to nonsense.
6) Work out the logic of the music. Music is non-verbal but contains clearly understandable logical progressions in terms of sound, harmony and musical 'argument'. It may also be possible to establish what is the climactic point or essence of the piece, and to play towards this and then away from it.
7) Practise effectively by using time-management to prioritise essential learning goals, then moderate and lesser goals. Use 'prime time', when you are fresh and in a good state to memorise, to deal with the most important aspects of learning such as new challenges, problems and passages that need to be learned perfectly.

Much of this can be summed up as the psychological attitude of eliminating mistakes. It is quite plausible and may feel superficially pleasant to dwell on your strengths in practising. It gives a euphoric seductive fantasy of the attainments you wish for in a perfect world. Those that have progressed beyond this illusion know that reality is the most seductive thing of all. The pleasure of confronting and mastering difficulties is that much more real because it is effective and takes you forward into better and richer realms of music-making, rather than leaving you in an impoverished world of daydreams.

Musicians that want to plan their goals in detail may want to give more emphasis to calculating how close each step brings them to that goal. They may then plan practice routines systematically to make sure all steps are done on time, even using calendars and written schedules. This may not be to the taste of everyone, but is one way of meeting deadlines like recitals in a balanced way that allows for leisure activity to be fitted in regularly.

Creative people are by disposition natural 'bingers'. They take life as it comes and when on the crest of an enthusiasm are capable of immense effort, followed by slack periods of inactivity and contemplation. Such binges – while they should not exhaust or overtire the body – may result in great things, and have meaning and worth up to the point when the mind or body naturally tires.

Practice

When to practise? The easiest answer is 'when you most feel like it'. This has to take into account sociable hours and neighbours, but can vary according to your natural rhythm or your typical schedule. Examples are:

- Early morning, for early risers.
- Midday or early afternoon, for late risers.
- An hour or two before going on stage, for soloists or touring musicians who want to be 100-per-cent effective on the night.
- Late at night, for impulsive creatives without neighbours, or with silent keyboards.

The main point is comfort and motivation. Both show that the mind is at its most receptive, and that memorising will be effective. The mind should be fresh and alert, the body relaxed. If it feels stiff, start with some light body exercises or go for a short 'wake-up' walk or jog.

For how long to practise? How long is essentially 'as long as a piece of string', with the following exceptions. Many classical musicians have been taught a practice schedule that takes them through all the keys and includes set scales, arpeggios and common movements. There may even be different variations of this for different circumstances, such as a short 20-minute version, a one-hour one and a full two-hour one with breaks in-between. Such a schedule gives security, because it practises the essential rudiments present in all music and maintains technique at a constant level.

Such schedules should be used at the discretion of the musician rather than out of a compulsive sense of duty, and can be varied to suit other commitments such as learning new pieces and touring. Duty breeds boredom and contempt, while personal motivation allows for positive learning. Motivation is often a question of mood – in a good mood two hours may be too little; in a bad mood 20 minutes may be too much.

Client-centred Teaching

The student should have as much say as possible in the learning process. The teacher has the benefit of objectivity and experience of past students, but may also be subjective and unable to recognise useful ideas suggested by the student. The student starts with the huge disadvantage of having little experience of what methods work, but still has gut reactions and a common-sense idea of the direction in which he wants to go. With these provisions in mind the student should have a say in directing:

- Content – the student should learn what he wants to, because the music to be played should be loved and give pleasure.
- Teacher – what is right or wonderful for one person may be wrong or boring for another. So it is wise to choose a teacher who is sympathetic and likes what you do.
- Style – in the interests of playing comfort and individuality the student should maintain any useful elements of his own style or technique as long as they work well. Changes should lead to progress, not be done solely for the benefit of the teacher's method. Where a teacher insists on a method, the student needs to look at its results in other musicians before embarking on it, and monitor whether it is making useful changes. Changes to embouchure, in particular, can give mixed results – with one player they work, with another they cause confusion and are later discarded. Realistically speaking, a teacher may know his own method inside out and be less effective outside it.
- Instrument – some children are manipulated into playing a second or third choice of instrument, or are given an instrument for 'logical' or economic reasons rather than because they like it (tall people are often given double basses, for example, and children are given recorders). Motivation is clearly strongest when there is the strongest possible bond between musician and instrument, and neither logic nor economics come into what is a bond of love.

A client-centred attitude is also about asking as much as telling. Common questions include:

- How do you think that sounded – was it how you wanted it ?
- Which alternative sounds better to you?
- Where exactly are you experiencing problems?
- What exactly don't you understand?
- What are your goals – playing as a soloist, orchestral, session,

or small-group musician? What do you need to learn to realise them?
- How much do you think you have learned at this point – is it more or less than you expected?

The client-centred attitude is, as much as possible, non-judgmental. Common transactions can be rephrased so that they turn the attention away from the person and on to the music:

- 'That wasn't very good' can become 'You seemed unhappy about that'.
- 'Can't you do better than that?' can become 'How do you want to play this?'

The client-centred attitude also makes a point of rewarding positive change and growth:

- 'That was a lot better – it sounded excellent.'
- 'I'm pleased with the progress you are making.'
- 'You really have worked on this, well done!'

The Learning Environment

Music-making should be pleasant at all times wherever possible, because good associations with music reinforce a positive attitude towards it. The learning environment should be:

- Pleasant to be in, with natural light from windows and space in which to teach.
- As quiet as possible, using soundproofing to stop sound going out or coming in. This means the student can play at proper volumes and not feel guilty for making a noise. Where this is impossible, learning aids like practice pads or electronic keyboards with volume controls or headphones may be used as a second-best solution.
- Firmly sealed off from others – some students are very put off by being watched or listened to by other students, family or passers by.
- Uninterrupted – phones should be put on automatic answering and others told to respect your privacy.

All learning theory shows that learning is faster when positively goal-directed rather than enforced through fear of unpleasant consequences, so a good attitude to teaching is vital. Teachers enhance the learning process by showing humour and pleasant personal contact, and by not being sadistic. Uncontrolled critical comments are very debilitating: the student acquires unpleasant associations with music and the learning process, feels belittled and useless, loses interest in learning and experiences unnecessary personal discomfort or distress. This is one of the single most destructive things in the whole of professional music, and damage done by sadistically over-critical teachers may have to be undone in therapy many years later.

Assessing Skill and Talent

Assessment of skills and aptitudes is a process that psychologists, scientists and statisticians learn to do systematically and objectively. Everyone else tends to do the same thing subjectively, using intuition and personal experience. While assessment of musicians by other musicians has the benefits of inside knowledge, it runs the risk of being biased, inaccurate or of favouring certain elements over the whole picture.

Many great figures of history, such as Einstein and Churchill, were written off as mediocre in school. Their assessors saw them doing one thing in one context and made a subjective reaction. The results were grossly wrong. In the same way musicians have been ignored or written off by teachers because they could not do things the teacher wanted, but could do many things the teacher did not value or sympathise with. Consequently, teachers should:

1) Make a global evaluation of skill, capacity for learning, motivation, personal characteristics like leadership and persistence, and potential for creativity. An evaluation based on playing ability is not a total picture of useful aptitudes.
2) Allow for negative side-effects of positive qualities. Creative people, for instance, are typically admired for being competitive, imaginative and sensitive, but thought of as a tiresome nuisance for being radical, individualistic and unconventional. There is a well-documented history of creative students being underestimated because of their unorthodox ways of

approaching theories and problems.

3) Recommend another teacher if they think they are negatively biased. Counsellors and therapists do this as a matter of course – if there is not sufficient mutual sympathy they may decline to take a client and refer them on. An assessment based on lack of sympathy is starting out badly.
4) Consider objective assessment tools, such as tests of aural skills, to get a fuller view of a student's potential. Many teachers do this as a matter of course.

Peer Learning

Experience is an essential part of learning. Besides lessons, practice and individual creativity there is the invaluable process of working with others. This is called 'paying your dues' in the business, and should be done as soon and as much as possible. Without it the musician is like a child with a personal tutor who never goes to school. Such a child has no idea of how to interact socially, how to find a level of activity to which others respond, how to be part of a team or how to deal with problems involving others.

With the advent of home recording many musicians are turning into socially isolated technocrats who labour for hours making demos on computers then attempting to convert them into recording contracts. This is undeniably a creative way of working and one with many rewards, but it may sacrifice the wide range of musical skills that can be learned from interacting with other musicians' approaches. It also ignores the whole process of putting a band together and keeping it together, and the experience of playing to audiences and handling stage equipment. Live music is the 'lifestyle' of the musician, and the language that musicians understand and communicate with.

• Improving Music-making

Staying Fresh

However experienced you are, it pays to keep your music fresh. Those who have been in the business for several years may develop predictable playing habits which leave them slack or restricted. Desirable habits at all stages of a musical career include:

- Practising regularly.
- Listening to other musicians.
- Including new pieces in practice periods.
- Taking on a variety of work.
- Going back over favourite pieces from time to time to rediscover their qualities.
- Talking to colleagues about music, not just about money, cars or mutual friends.

Sharing

Many desirable qualities in the musician's life come from sharing. Examples of sharing include:

- Talking honestly about difficulties and fears. This is only considered 'forbidden' because it is assumed that musicians will put about the idea that you are unusable. Musicians who do talk freely can find that it has surprisingly little effect on the quantity of their work or their reputation, provided that their actual music-making is of a reliably high standard.
- Asking others if what you are doing is appropriate and how they would like it played, and explaining what or how you want them to play. Be suggestive rather than judgmental, and leave solutions open.
- Amateur music-making. This is a particularly 'sharing' and voluntary activity, and musicians say that something special happens when money is not involved, even if there will always be some cynic who says 'what's the tax on nothing?'.

Playing in Time with Others

Conductors have a number of unprintable opinions of violin sections in which the members play 'follow my leader'. The effect is like a wave of entries through the section rather than a razor-sharp entry by everyone. By trusting your judgement you can become part of the ensemble, not an accessory to it. Bass players need to play the beat, not rely on the drums. Pianists and guitarists need to have their own swing as well as 'commenting' on the soloists. Where all the musicians are equally confident and playing the same rhythm, music moves on to an altogether higher level and seems to flow automatically. If this cannot be achieved by collective rehearsal, conductors should get musicians to play in pairs, twos and threes until the rhythm is correct, then build up the ensemble.

Avoiding Intimidation

Humiliation, intimidation and other aspects of sadism are 'last resort' methods. They should be used either not at all, or with caution and a good idea that the result will justify the means. Many conductors and bandleaders have worked in aggressive, autocratic ways, and achieved good results, despite being generally disliked. Where they succeed it is because of their musicianship, not their intimidating aggressiveness. Where they fail, they cause untold mental damage in musicians, all of which can severely inhibit playing confidence. Directors who 'allow' musicians to work in their own ways within the basic framework of the ensemble are much loved and become legends with in their professions.

Relating Your Part to the Musical Context

Although it seems obvious to say that any player should be aware of the function his playing has on the overall context, a number of orchestral players are at any given moment more aware of their own part in relation to themselves than in relation to what is going on around them. Their awareness may, for example, be focused on technical problems, bowing, fingering or notes. It is both musically better and personally more satisfying to listen to the musical context rather than get caught up in excessive ego-involvement. Asking yourself questions such as the following will help:

- How does the part fit with the music? Is it required to be melody, bass, rhythm, harmony, inner voice, special effect or something else?
- How does the part fit into the overall dynamics? How loud/soft should it be?
- How long/short should notes be to fit the context?
- How percussive/legato should your part be?
- Is there any part of the music that is relying on you at any point?

Relating instructions to the musical context rather than the musician is more pleasant and also clearer. Examples of instructions that emphasise this include:

- 'Play slightly louder than the violins', not 'play louder'.
- 'Come in with the trombones', not 'come in earlier'.
- 'Place your beat with the hi-hat', not 'don't drag behind the drums'.

The secret of all collective music-making is in relating each part to the music. As we have consistently seen, the music itself holds the key to its own understanding.

12 Couselling and Therapy

The preceding chapters in this book are about all the practical and psychological measures that musicians can use as a source of self-help. This last chapter is about using other health professionals to help with certain areas of the musician's life.

The need for help mostly comes about when there is a specific cause of anxiety, but this is by no means the whole story. Performers in the world of sport now regularly use sports psychologists, as well as physiotherapists and other specialists. You do not need personal problems to do this – you may simply be taking all the steps available to maximise your performing potential. The same applies to musicians. Good posture and manageable performance nerves are now seen as an achievable goal rather than a miracle. Neither are the bogeys they once were.

• What Help is Available?

The whole range of help available may be a little bewildering at first sight, so here are some basic definitions of who is who.

The Psychologist

Psychology is the study of human behaviour in all its forms, and its theory is made up of a large number of accurate and reliable 'studies' of varied aspects of human life. All psychologists do a three-year degree course followed by further study in their speciality. Occupational psychologists deal with careers, psychometric tests and people at work; 'clinical' psychologists deal with mental health and brain function; and 'counselling' psychologists use various therapy methods including cognitive or behavioural approaches.

The Counsellor

Counselling describes individual or group work which aims to create a good working environment for solving problems and increasing the positive self-worth of 'clients'. Sessions usually last for 50 minutes and take place weekly, but counselling does not have to be long-term. As well as general counsellors, there are specialised ones. They might concentrate on counselling students, for example, or on people who need specific help with their careers or in dealing with stress.

The Psychotherapist and Psychoanalyst

Psychotherapy covers longer-term work done in greater depth, working with childhood memories, dreams, the unconscious, and the 'patient's' subjective perception of the therapist, called 'transference'. Sessions take place at least once a week, sometimes twice or more, and therapists expect a long-term commitment. General psychotherapists draw on the whole available theory from Freud to the present day, while those that train and specialise in the classical methods, such as those of Freud and Jung, call themselves psychoanalysts or 'analysts' for short.

The Psychiatrist

The psychiatrist is a doctor who goes on to specialise in mental health. As a doctor he is authorised to prescribe drugs, and typically is attached to a hospital unit where he looks after patients with more serious mental problems, some needing ongoing medication.

The Postural Specialist and Physiotherapist

Posture work is typically done by teachers of the Alexander and Feldenkreis methods. Both are excellent for musicians and have a long history of positive results. Physiotherapy also deals with posture and ergonomics and has an important role in correcting misuse of the body.

The Medical Specialist

Certain medical specialists are particularly important to musicians. Ear, nose and throat (ENT) specialists cover hearing and the use of the voice; orthopaedic specialists deal with problems with bones and joints and the treatment of injuries; and occupational-health specialists are concerned with health issues related to people's jobs.

The Complementary Medicine Practitioner

Complementary medicine is a developing field to which the musician is often attracted for its relaxed and informal treatment methods and its 'spiritual' belief system. Some methods, such as acupuncture and homoeopathy, have a long tradition, while others are part of a rapidly expanding culture of alternative methodologies. The effectiveness of such methods may include wider issues than absolute scientific proof.

The Creative Therapist

Music therapy, art therapy, dance and movement therapy, drama therapy and psychodrama are often called the 'creative therapies', and sometimes referred to as the 'expressive therapies'. They use the conventional art forms to elicit creative and expressive results in their subjects, and can be remarkably effective for musicians. Some methods use the art form alone; others combine it with a therapeutic 'talking through' of issues and problems. Since they access non-verbal feelings and emotions they can be both subtle and powerful in their effect. Therapists in this field are arts professionals with an intensive training in their particular therapy form.

Common Therapy Methods

Several different types of counselling can be of help to musicians. No single one is 'ideal' since much depends on the particular problem being presented. Career counselling helps with career choices and changes; personal counselling with personal problems; and specialist counselling addresses particular issues such as marital problems, bereavement or substance abuse. Therapy methods that have established their usefulness include:

- Transactional Analysis: ego-states, contracts, permissions and injunctions, life scripts (*see Chapters Two and Three*).
- Psychoanalysis: repressions, sublimations, projections and the unconscious.
- Rogerian counselling: client-based work and positive self-regard.
- Cognitive counselling: challenging and restructuring personal beliefs.
- Behavioural counselling: using psychological techniques to change behaviour patterns.
- The creative therapies: evoking creative-expressive responses, working non-verbally.

Whatever the method, it helps to make the counsellor aware of all the issues that you want to deal with, and if possible to suggest the sort of outcome you want, such as a reduction in performance nerves.

Specialised Counselling

When we talk of counselling for the musician we are not referring only to 'general' counselling, which is available to everyone. Loneliness, loss of confidence, general depression and difficulties with family and relationships are all issues that affect the musician as well as everybody else. Counselling for the musician refers particularly to therapy techniques that approach and treat the musician as a 'musician'. This means taking into account a number of extra factors such as ability to perform, relationship with one's instrument, stage fright, career-management and all the factors that promote happiness and satisfaction in the musician's work. For the counsellor, it also means acquiring some insight into the language, lifestyle, technical problems and work habits of the typical musician.

Dealing with Musical Problems

The musician seeking counselling may want to deal, among other things, with a particular musical problem. If specialised musical knowledge is not easily available to the counsellor, there may be a risk that he will 'see' the problem in the light of his normal counselling experience. When there are a number of simultaneous problems such as depression, relationship difficulties and bad performance nerves, the counsellor may start with the area that is most familiar – possibly depression or relationships – and relegate more unfamiliar issues until later in the treatment.

Although this is the right way to proceed in some cases, in others a general approach may not solve the musical problem. Musicians who feel that music problems are being sidelined may stop mentioning them. Others may not mention the music problem at all unless they feel they have been given 'extra' permission to talk specifically about problems at work. Encouragement to do this is often a way of breaking through the musician's habitual reluctance to discuss career problems with others.

If the problem is a performing one, then the right steps should be taken to deal with it regardless of how closely it may be related to personal issues. This is because making music is an essential source of personal confidence and financial security. There is a belief among some 'whole person' therapists and indeed some doctors that 'once the person feels generally better, the musical problems will solve themselves'. As one experienced doctor put it, 'Once the patient is in a better general mental and physical shape, the problems affecting his work will spontaneously improve.'

Analysing the long-term history of a number of musicians shows, however, that in many cases a particular problem has continued to be unresolved over successive periods of good, bad and indifferent general health. If, in addition, the problem lies out of consciousness, it is quite reasonable to assume that it will not be dealt with until it is accessed directly by appropriate therapeutic methods.

Another fallacy is the idea that 'being a musician is itself the problem', and that the musician would be better advised to avoid some aspects of the musical life for his own good. Without knowing how widespread this view is, it has certainly occurred in the therapeutic history of some musicians. Alcoholics have been advised to avoid the stress of surviving in an insecure profession where there can be a lot of competition and social drinking. Creative people with rich fantasy lives have been advised that their 'art' is the problem and that the therapeutic solution is to give it up. The idea that art is essentially a type of 'sublimation' of real life emotions is put forward by Ernest Jones: 'When one considers the material used in the five arts – paint, clay, stone, words and sounds – any psychologist must conclude that the passionate interest in bringing an orderliness out of chaos must signify at the same time an extraordinary sublimation of the most primitive infantile enjoyments and the most extreme denial of them.' This is a view that a large number of specialist counsellors would strongly disagree with, seeing music – both melody and rhythm – as an essential expression and extension of primitive enjoyments.

The Musician's Typical Working Life

Musicians' professional working habits are clearly outside the normal life experience of the non-musician counsellor. This is the area where the specialised counsellor can play an important role. To illustrate this, here are some actual cases and treatments:

'Why do I get really nervous in concerts?'

A detailed analysis of previous anxiety situations led to identifying and dealing with 'trigger' factors. Working through some more adaptive responses to audiences and audition panels led to a general increase in confidence.

'I don't know whether I can satisfy my need for independence in classical music – what are my chances of satisfaction as a rank and file player?'

A detailed career analysis of this talented student showed high independence and below average capacity for working under instruction. Talking this through led to a successful career in chamber music.

'Why do I get depressed about my violin – I can't take it out of its case?'

Counselling gradually revealed ambiguous and tense feelings for the parent that had bought it. The problem was solved quite simply by selling it and buying another.

Such responses may seem obvious to a musician trained in counselling, but how would a non-musician deal with some of the specifically musical issues involved? A good counsellor will trace any problem back to its roots and break it down into its essential parts, whatever these may be. Such a counsellor may also learn a lot from the musician in therapy, and use this accumulated knowledge to get a good idea of what is really happening. But there is a great benefit in already having covered some of the basic essentials of the musician's life.

The Musician's Language

At its most alien, the language of musicians can be full of jargon and technical terms.

This means not only familiar terms such as 'gig' (job), 'dep' (substitute) and 'band' (orchestra) but more specialised terms like 'toys' (percussion), 'kit' (drumkit) and 'axe' (guitar). In addition, there is all the rich slang like 'cat' (person) 'out to lunch' (weird), or 'cooking' (playing well), and a variety of sardonic understatements like 'he doesn't care, does he?' (he's just done something totally outrageous) or 'this is what we will find... we will find this...' (resignation at having to suffer another totally outrageous incident).

A musician talking freely to a colleague may say 'I'm a bit untogether because I mainly do toys, and at the moment I'm depping for this guy on kit and my snare technique is getting really slack.' A violinist may say 'I'm happy in the seconds but I was put in the firsts the other night and I freaked out on second desk.' A horn player may say 'As you know, horns play 1–3 2–4 and I knew that on second horn my chances of a trial were pretty limited when they were auditioning for a new number one.'

It may be difficult for any counsellor to know the full range of 'music-speak', partly because it varies within jazz, rock and the classical world. The more the musician can talk freely, however, the easier it may be to access particular problems. A therapist can talk for a whole session, for instance, about a drummer's way of dealing with practice routines, including whether to use a practice pad at home or book a studio and use the full kit. To avoid frequent interventions, it is an advantage to know not only what such technical talk is about but also the actual performing difficulties it is based on, such as posture, embouchure or voice production.

The therapist who specialises in musicians may be an amateur musician or even a professional who has had training in therapy. He may have acquired a good knowledge of the typical problems and 'language' of the musician from seeing a number of musician clients or through living alongside professional musicians. Such specialised therapists are taking forward the research and practice of dealing with musicians, making us increasingly aware of the stresses suffered by musicians and how best to deal with them. They frequently attend conferences on the performing arts, know others working in the field, and build up referral lists to deal with special needs.

• The Musician as Counselling Client

The musician in therapy starts with one important advantage – he is likely to be creative by nature and a good problem solver. This means that he is likely to play an active part in getting better and gaining insight into problems. Many musicians are almost 'ideal' clients in counselling, and can make substantial progress quickly.

In terms of profession, the musician may be mainly a 'performer' or mainly a 'creator'. The 'performers' are typically orchestral musicians who are bound to the notes of a score and need confidence in performing them accurately and predictably. The 'creative performers' are typically rock and jazz musicians whose improvisations are 'the sound of surprise', as music critic Whitney Balliett put it. The 'creators' are the composers and songwriters who need continued creativity and a free flow of ideas.

All share the need to eliminate conflicting inner motivations and to neutralise feelings that people are hostile to their work or expect too much of them. Since most people in the music business are self-employed, self-dependent and self-absorbed in terms of the work they do, they are also liable to be very sensitive to any loss of their capacity to function properly. They may blame themselves and become depressed when they feel their capacities are being threatened or taken away.

Counselling Students

In the life of the student there may be particular anxieties over teachers, exams and auditions, money and career choices. The figures below give some idea of a typical term's counselling in a music college:

- Three-quarters of students seen had problems that concerned music-making.
- The typical student seen was either just starting a course or facing final exams.
- More than expected were postgraduates, mature or overseas students, or had families living abroad.
- There was no difference in numbers of either sex.

A recurring profile was of a foreign student who had just arrived at the college and was older than the typical college student, often doing an advanced course. Counselling work dealt with performance problems, motivation, adjustment to course and tutor, stage fright and career counselling. Medical referrals were made in specific cases, particularly for singers needing to see voice specialists.

• How to Get Counselling

Firstly, it is important to have an idea of the length of treatment you want or can pay for, such as:

- Up to 10 sessions – brief therapy.
- 10 to 15 sessions – intensive short-term therapy.
- Over 15 sessions – longer-term therapy.

You do not have to have an accurate idea of how many sessions are needed – in fact it is highly unlikely that you would know this. But have a general idea of what sort of outlay you can justify or afford. This includes considering how seriously the problem affects your livelihood, and the difference between typically shorter methods like cognitive counselling and a more lengthy psychoanalysis.

Be prepared for change. Counselling is about positive changes, but can include all manner of changes, both to the individual and to the wider social, career and relationship context. Professional counsellors are trained to manage change so that any unpredictable effects should be put into context and interpreted in a way you understand. Counselling is a safe process in the sense that it is designed to proceed at the speed with which the individual can cope. Any anxieties that are not yet conscious may take whatever time is needed to come to the surface, emerging when your general confidence level is sufficient to accept them. Again, professional counsellors are trained to manage this.

Know Your Rights

You are purchasing the counselling process, so you have a number of rights. Among these are the right to break off, to try a different counsellor, and to arrange sessions as much as possible to accommodate your work schedule. It is helpful to discuss each of these aspects with the counsellor, who may point out alternative views, but at the end of the day the decisions are yours.

The first session is sometimes called an 'assessment interview', and this initial talking-through of problems and desired solutions establishes the general 'contract' for the work you intend to do, and also whether or not the client and counsellor get on well and feel positive about working together. The initial contract should also establish the level of fee you are capable of paying – with or without any support from relevant charities – and how often such counselling should take place. Normally this would be once a week, but to deal with problems quickly or in cases where immediate support is beneficial, it is possible to meet more frequently.

You should have some knowledge of the qualifications and experience of the therapist you choose, and issues such as this can be brought up at this initial session. Details of the various types of qualification can be obtained from one of the therapy bodies specialising in the arts. In Britain these include Arts Psychology Consultants and The British Performing Arts Medicine Trust (*see Useful Addresses, page 253*). Be aware, however, that qualifications are many and varied, and that the overall quality of the therapist may depend on a number of equally important factors: experience, ability, suitability to your own personality and gender. You may feel more comfortable talking to a man, a woman or have no particular preference.

• The Physical Therapies

Our body and our mind, including emotions and thoughts, work together to create the states and moods we go through:

- When we feel depressed we slouch.
- When we feel angry we shout.
- When we feel anxious we tense up.
- When we feel happy we relax.

Dealing with the interaction of physical and emotional states helps us regulate them, since one can influence the other. Body therapists emphasise harmonious body states as the basis of harmonious mental states. Since we cannot be both tense and relaxed at the same time, it is difficult to feel mental tension when the body is very relaxed and comfortable. Other good reasons for physical therapies are:

- Good posture means good ergonomics. A relaxed way of holding instruments creates a relaxed way of playing.
- Physical exercise is healthy in itself and creates natural emotional wellbeing.
- Physical exercise creates respect for the body as a part of the musician, not just a vehicle for carrying around the intellect and emotions.
- Physical movements have an elegance and meaning in themselves.

Such are the general goals of bio-energetics, yoga, t'ai-chi, Alexander and Feldenkreis techniques, aerobics and a whole host of other disciplines. Certain techniques have a particular application for musicians, and have been specifically developed by musicians for use with fellow musicians; foremost among these are Alexander and Feldenkreis. The Alexander technique was created and developed to facilitate proper use of the voice and body in performance, and many musicians have benefited from the informed help that teachers of this method can offer. The same is true of the Feldenkreis technique. Further details of such techniques can be found in the appropriate textbooks.

Drawbacks to physical therapies are largely to do with the typical mental make-up and attitudes of musicians:

- Musicians list 'physical effort' as the second-most disliked job value, showing a dispositional tendency to avoid it. In contrast, they list 'learning new things' as a very high job value, and may appreciate the effort once it has been made.
- Physical methods are more disruptive of lifestyle, and may be indulged in occasionally or irregularly. They cannot be rehearsed in the car or bus or easily fitted into a hectic touring schedule.
- Physical remedies for stage fright or motivational problems may do little to explain the root of the problem, even though they create a state of wellbeing.

Benefits of these techniques include reduction of stress and misuse of the body and, in some cases, a substantial ergonomic improvement. Protecting the whole muscular-skeletal apparatus which sustains the musician's playing career is essential, and here the physiotherapist or osteopath can play a vital role. Also essential is keeping muscles relaxed so that they work well within their natural range and tolerances and do not become stiff and inflexible, something that massage can help to maintain.

• The Future of 'Arts and Health'

One of the exciting things that typifies the new research into health aspects of the arts is the team approach that is being used. At the forefront of this are the specialists in arts medicine. These professionals already have the status, influence and often use of clinical premises to make a substantial contribution.

There is a traditional link between doctors and a love of music, and a number are keen amateur players. In both Britain and the United States they have started important multi-disciplinary networks for medicine and the performing arts. Conferences bring together specialists of all kinds, and information is exchanged between doctors, teachers, psychologists, counsellors, posture specialists and musicians themselves. When a team of health-care practitioners is used, the musician benefits by having the highest level of expertise and familiarity with the particular problem. Examples are:

- Medical issues that need to be referred to a voice clinic or orthopaedic specialist. These include problems of the voice, muscular-skeletal problems, tendonitis and Repetitive Strain Injury (RSI).
- Posture problems needing Alexander or Feldenkreis technique.
- Psychiatric problems that require liaison with a psychiatrist and monitoring of the effects of medication on arousal and performing.
- Academic problems that require liaising with teachers or academic staff.
- Specialised counselling needs, such as for eating disorders or drugs and addictions.
- Rehabilitation for loss of function.

Clinics are being set up in Britain that use such a team approach, and close cooperation between practitioners is rapidly increasing the pool of available knowledge and the ability to refer musicians within the arts and health networks. Prominent bodies currently involved in this include Arts Psychology Consultants, the International Society for the Study of Tensions in Performance (ISSTIP) and the British Performing Arts Medicine Trust, which organises performing-arts clinics at the Middlesex Hospital Voice Clinic, the Royal Free Hospital and the Royal Edinburgh Infirmary, and has an Association of Medical Advisers to British Orchestras (AMABO). (For details of these organisations, *see page 253–4.*)

With charitable aid, some very ambitious programmes are being set up: These include:

- Regular clinics in various parts of the country, staffed by a team of specialist health-care professionals.
- A national network of health-care professionals with a referral directory listing experienced practitioners.
- A 24-hour helpline which can refer performing artists to the appropriate sources of help.
- A central office coordinating national services, and linking up with international ones.
- Funding for low-income clients from a range of charities
- Free access to specialist doctors under the National Health Service.
- Funding of specialist treatment by health-insurance companies.
- Research into new areas of treatment, and the compiling of essential data on existing treatment methods.
- Diploma courses for training health specialists in the problems of artists.
- Permanent funding of a national arts and health service by the major arts charities.

Major funding for these schemes in Britain has come from the Musicians' Union, the Musicians' Benevolent Fund, the Equity Trust Fund and the Royal Society of Musicians of Great Britain, all of whom are particularly committed to the health of the musician.

The United States has a larger network, with clinics on both the East and West coasts, some attached to institutes of the performing arts. Both countries have enormously important music industries, so an adequate health network to deal with musicians is entirely appropriate.

• A Healthier Future for Musicians

Although the music business has seen a number of wounding financial cutbacks in recent years which have left classical musicians in particular with less work, musicians themselves are showing some changes in attitude that are entirely positive. There was a period in jazz and rock history where it was not only acceptable to drink and take drugs to the point of being a physical wreck, it was considered to be 'paying one's dues' and living up to the image of hard-living dead heroes. This has changed considerably for the better, not only with a saner younger generation but with a healthier generation of older stars who have put earlier excesses behind them. The 'tired and emotional' jazzer and rocker has become the mineral water-sipping friendly and alert career musician.

Musicians are not only paying more attention to their health, they are also talking more frankly about issues that concern them and reading more self-help books. They are finding stage fright unacceptable in an age when it can be successfully dealt with, and are taking active steps to reduce stress. The increased social relaxation in musicians is being supported by a widespread public acceptance and enthusiasm for 'minority music' such as jazz and rock. Musicians are no longer required to become teenage misfits as they were in the pioneering 1950s and '60s. Nowadays jazz is something you can learn in music college, and the stars of yesterday are the professors of today.

The musician's life may never be as widely accepted as that of the establishment professions, such as medicine and law, but within it musicians have hopefully become a happier breed. It would be good to imagine that the richness music has brought into the lives of so many people may one day be reflected in the respect and affection given to those who have made a lifetime commitment to creating and performing it.

Further Reading

Chapter 1

Hopson, Brian and Scally, Mike. *Build Your Own Rainbow – a workbook for career and life management*, Lifeskills Associates, Clarendon Chambers, 51 Clarendon Road, Leeds LS2 9NZ (1984)

Myers, I.B. and P.B. *Gifts Differing*, Consulting Psychologists' Press, Palo Alto CA (1980)

Chapter 2

Berne, Eric. *What Do You Say After You Say Hello*, Corgi (1983)

James, Muriel and Jongeward, Dorothy. *Born to Win*, Signet (1978)

Lloyd-Elliott, Martin. 'Witches, demons and devils. The enemies of auditions and how performing artists make friends with these saboteurs' in *Psychology and the Performing Arts*, ed. Glenn Wilson, Swets and Zeitlinger (1991)

Stewart, Ian and Joines, Vann. *TA Today*, Lifespace (1987)

Chapter 4

Wills and Cooper. *Pressure Sensitive*, Sage Books (1988)

Chapter 5

Blackstone, Judith and Josipovic, Zoran. *Zen for Beginners*, Writers and Readers NY (1986)

Bullock, Alan; Stallybrass Oliver and Trombley, Stephen. *The Fontana Dictionary of Modern Thought*, Fontana (1988)

Capra, Fritjof. *The Tao of Physics*, Fontana (1976)

Green, Barry and Gallwey, W. Timothy. *The Inner Game of Music*, Pan (1986)

Chapter 6

Atkinson and Atkinson. *Introduction to Psychology*, (11th edition), Harcourt Brace Jovanovich (1992). (A comprehensive guide to the principles of psychology. This marvel of concise and readable information has been the inspiration of countless psychologists and medical students. It is not a book to read at a sitting, but every page holds some fascinating insight into human behaviour, and the origins of almost all the principles in this book can be found in it in some form.)

Havas, Kato. *Stage Fright – its causes and cures, with special reference to violin playing*, Bosworth (1986)

Reubart, Dale. *Anxiety and Musical Performance – on playing the piano from memory*, Da Capo NY (1985)

Salmon, Paul G. and Myer, Robert G. *Notes from the Green Room*, Lexington Books NY, Macmillan (1992)

Chapter 7

Wills, Geoff and Cooper, Cary. *Pressure Sensitive*, Sage Books (1988)

Chapter 8

Barbour, Sheena (Ed.). *The Performing Arts Yearbook*, Rhinegold Publishing (published annually)

Ludman, Kim. *Making a Living as a Rock Musician*, Kogan Page (1987)

The Music Week Directory, Spotlight Productions, Greater London House, Hampstead Rd, London NW1 7QZ

Pearcey, Leonard. *The Musician's Survival Kit*, Barrie and Jenkins (1979)

Stewart, Andrew (Ed.). *The British Music Yearbook*, Rhinegold Publishing (published annually)

The White Book, Birdhurst Ltd, PO Box 55, Staines Middx. TW18 4UG (published annually)

Wilson, Mary. *How to Make it in the Rock Business*, Columbus (1987)

York, Norton (ed.). *The Rock File*, Oxford (1991)

Chapter 9

Kennedy, Gavin. *Everything is Negotiable*, Business Books (1990)

Lindenfield, Gail. *Assert Yourself*, Thorsons (1986)

Chapter 10

Arieti, Silvano. *Creativity, the Magic Synthesis*, Basic Books N.Y. (1976)

Ghiselin, Brewster. *The Creative Process*, Mentor (1958)

Storr, Anthony. *The Dynamics of Creation*, Penguin (1983)

Storr, Anthony. *Solitude*, Fontana (1989)

Chapter 11

Storr, Anthony. *Music and the Mind*, Flamingo (1993)

Useful Addresses

Please note that with all the listed organisations it is essential to make an appointment first by writing or telephoning.

Arts Psychology Consultants

29 Argyll Mansions, Hammersmith Road, London W14 8QQ
(071) 602–2707
Provides both specialised councelling for musicians and the tests used in Chapter One.

ASE, NFER Nelson

Darville House, 2 Oxford Road East, Windsor, Berkshire SL4 1DF
Provides information and literature on the Cattell 16PF and John Holland's occupational preferences (*The Self-Directed Search*).

British Performing Arts Medicine Trust (BPAMT)

18 Ogle Street, London W1P 7LG
(071) 636–6860, Helpline (071) 636–6960, Fax (071) 636–6880

Equity Trust Fund

112–114 Africa House, 64–78 Kingsway, London WC2B 6AH
(071) 629–6137

Incorporated Society of Musicians

10 Stratford Place, London W1N 9AE
(071) 629–4413

International Society for the Study of Tensions in Performance (ISSTIP)

28 Emperor's Gate, London SW7 4HS
(071) 373–7307

Jazz Services

5 Dryden Street, London WC2E 9NB
(071) 829–8353

Musicians' Benevolent Fund
16 Ogle Street, London W1P 7LG
(071) 646–4481

Musicians' Union
60 Clapham Road, London SW9 0JJ
(071) 582–5566
The MU publishes a directory of members and numerous useful fact sheets.

Oxford Psychologists Press
Lambourne House, 311–321 Banbury Road, Oxford OX2 7JH
Supplies information and literature on the MBTI (including *Gifts Differing* and *Type Talk*).

International Organisations

International Society for Music and Musicians (ISMM)
c/o Dr Ralph Spintage (Exec. Sec.), Paulmannshoherstr. 17, D–5880 Ludensheid, Germany

Performing Arts Medicine Association (PAMA)
c/o Dr Richard Ledderman (President), Dept. of Neurology 5–91, Cleveland Clinic Foundation, 9500 Euclid Avenue, Cleveland, Ohio 44195, USA
Publishes the journal *Medical Problems of Performing Artists.*

International Arts Medicine Association (IAMA)
Richard Lippin (President), 3600 Market Street, Philadelphia, PA 19104, USA

Index